2nd Australian (
New Zealand Edition

Fishing

FOR

DUMMIES®

**2nd Australian &
New Zealand Edition**

Fishing
FOR
DUMMIES®

by Steve Starling

WILEY

Wiley Publishing Australia Pty Ltd

Fishing For Dummies®

2nd Australian & New Zealand Edition published by
Wiley Publishing Australia Pty Ltd
42 McDougall Street
Milton, Qld 4064
www.dummies.com

Copyright © 2010 Wiley Publishing Australia Pty Ltd

The moral rights of the author have been asserted.

National Library of Australia

Cataloguing-in-Publication data:

Author:	Starling, Stephen
Title:	Fishing For Dummies/Steve Starling
Edition:	2nd Australian & New Zealand ed.
ISBN:	978 1 74216 984 2 (pbk.)
Series:	For dummies
Notes:	Includes index.
	Previous ed.: 2002.
Dewey Number:	799.1

Cover image: © 2009 Steve Starling

Typeset by diacriTech, Chennai, India

Printed in the United States of America

10 9 8 7 6 5 4 3 2 1

About the Author

Steve Starling is one of Australia's best known and most respected fishing writers and television/DVD presenters. At the age of seven, he pulled his first fish from the Lachlan River in central western New South Wales, and Steve claims he was just as firmly hooked as that little redfin perch. Thus began a passionate commitment to recreational angling that has only strengthened over the intervening decades.

A teenage Steve had his first magazine article on fishing published in his final year of high school and five years later went on to become editor of the title that had accepted his story. Four years later, he turned freelance and has since written 20 books, thousands of magazine features and numerous video and television scripts. His work has been published in a dozen countries and several languages, and Steve has travelled and fished across the globe, catching several world record fish in the process.

Through the 1990s, Steve became known to a much wider audience at home and abroad as a regular co-presenter on the long-running *Rex Hunt Fishing Adventures* television series. As well, he has performed stints in front of the camera as a presenter on *The Great Outdoors*, *The Australian Fishing Show* and *AFC Outdoors*. Steve and his close angling mate, Kaj 'Bushy' Busch, also completed three series of an outdoor adventure, fishing and cooking television series called *Hooked On Adventure*, which was set initially in Western Australia, before moving east to the rest of the nation. Today, Steve is a major contributor to the quarterly magazine-on-DVD known simply as *The Fishing DVD*.

Steve Starling — better known to many of his fans these days simply as 'Starlo' — is a graduate of the University of NSW, where he majored in Modern History and English Literature, briefly teaching these subjects at high school before embarking on his full-time fishing career. He has two grown up children, Tom and Amy, and now resides in Darwin with his partner, Jo, and her daughter, Charlotte, with plans to eventually return to his beloved far south coast of New South Wales.

Dedication

This book is dedicated to my fishing partner, business mentor and soul mate, Jo, who never ceases to inspire me, and whose intuitive, left-field/right brain take on angling has taught me to not only give better answers, but also to ask more meaningful questions!

Author's Acknowledgements

I need to thank plenty of people for their help with this book, and I'm sure to miss a few. First and foremost I'd like to acknowledge all those fellow anglers I've met over the years who've so willingly shared their knowledge and enthusiasm with me. Whatever I know about fishing today is the sum of their wisdom, not mine.

I'd also like to give a big thanks to Wayne Wells, who created the clear, concise illustrations you see on these pages. Having a friend and a fellow fisher as my illustrator made life so much easier.

Writing the original version and now this updated Australasian edition of *Fishing For Dummies* has been an interesting exercise. I've penned lots of how-to material in the past, but before my *Dummies* experience, I had never been called upon to write in a manner that's so accessible and transparent, even to people with zero knowledge of the subject matter. This feat is harder than it looks, and I owe a considerable debt of gratitude to the editors of the original version, Carolyn Beaumont and Karen Earnshaw, and to the always affable and good-humoured Robi van Nooten, my editor on this new version. All three pulled me into line every time I strayed towards jargon and insider-speak, and they constantly posed the simple, incisive questions a newcomer to the sport might be expected to ask. Carolyn, Karen and Robi have made this a much better and more useful book than it would otherwise have been.

Finally, my sincere thanks to Bronwyn Duhigg, the Acquisitions Editor who first suggested and then made possible this timely update of the original book, and its expansion to include our friends across the Tasman in New Zealand. Bronwyn was always a joy to deal with and never got cross with me, even when I bunked off to go fishing instead of finishing my allotted chapters on time! Thank you.

Publisher's Acknowledgments

We're proud of this book; please send us your comments through our online registration form located at http://dummies.custhelp.com.

Some of the people who helped bring this book to market include the following:

Acquisitions, Editorial and Media Development

Project Editor: Robi van Nooten, On-Track Editorial Services

Acquisitions Editor: Bronwyn Duhigg

Editorial Manager: Gabrielle Packman

Production

Graphics: Wayne Wells and the Wiley Art Studio

Cartoons: Glenn Lumsden

Proofreader: Justin Coughlan

Indexer: Karen Gillen

Contents at a Glance

Table of Contents

Part III: Using Your Equipment the Right Way .... _147_

Introduction

· ·

Surveys of the leisure activities of Australians and New Zealanders constantly place recreational fishing among our top three most popular outdoor pursuits, along with swimming and the various court sports (tennis, squash, bowls and so on).

As many as one in four of us over the age of ten casts a line each year, representing an army of some five million hopefuls, each one captivated by the promise of catching a dream and hauling home a whopper. Yet the vast majority of foot soldiers in this angling army are occasional danglers and casual anglers, and the sad reality is that most of them rarely hook anything more exciting than a lump of weed or an old boot.

My aim in writing this book is to redress the imbalance and empower these rod-wielding dreamers to a stage where they actually begin catching fish on a regular basis. A big call? Yes. But I believe this challenge is achievable.

About This Book

Back in the 1970s, I remember there being a great deal of talk about the coming social revolution. Computers and robotics, it was said, would free modern man and woman from the drudgery of work, making the closing decades of the 20th century a golden age of unprecedented leisure. People would be required to invent stimulating new ways to entertain themselves in this brave new world of unbridled recreation...Huh! Sure thing!

As with so many predictions about the future, this one missed the mark by a country mile. In reality, Aussies and Kiwis are toiling longer and harder today than at any time since the introduction (in Australia in 1856) of the 40-hour working week. Like most of the Western world in this new millennium, Australia and New Zealand are nations of workaholics; rich in material goods but increasingly starved for time to enjoy the fruits of this hard labour.

One symptom of time poverty has been a dramatic shift in the way anglers acquire new skills such as the ability to rig a rod, tie a knot, hook a fish and clean the catch. In my youth, budding junior anglers typically spent a long and unstructured fishing apprenticeship at the elbow of a wise parent, grandparent, sibling, aunt, uncle or mate. For better or worse, those days are largely a memory. Today, people's lives are part of an era of out-sourcing, re-training and power seminars, where everything from cooking a meringue to changing an oil filter is taught in high energy bursts of instruction, employing multi-media presentations, spreadsheets and interactive computer displays. Today, people want to know how, and they want to know *now*! So, this book is for anyone who wets a line in Australian or New Zealand waters or plans to do so, regardless of age (assuming they're old enough to read!) and initial skill level.

While much of this book is pitched squarely at the new chum (especially those time-poor individuals I mentioned earlier), these pages contain plenty of information that benefits more experienced anglers. The truth is: You're never too old to learn. I pick up new tidbits of fishing know-how every time I cast a line, read a magazine article or visit an angling website. I doubt you're any different.

Conventions Used in This Book

Important bits of information are formatted in special ways to make sure you notice them right away:

- **In This Chapter lists:** Chapters begin with a list of the topics I cover in that chapter. This list represents a table of contents in miniature.

- **Numbered lists:** When you see a numbered list, follow the steps in the specific order to accomplish a given task such as learning the art of tying knots.

- **Bulleted lists:** Bulleted lists (like this one) indicate things that you can do in any order or list related bits of information such as what to pack into your everyday fishing kit.

- **New terms:** Recreational fishing terms appear in italics and are closely preceded or followed by an easy-to-understand definition.

- **Web addresses:** When I describe activities or websites of interest, I include the address in a special typeface like this: `www.fishnet.com.au`. Although the website is current at the time of writing, web addresses can be pretty fickle. So, if you can't find the site, try looking for it by using an internet search engine.

- ✔ **Currency:** When I give you an idea of costs, for example, the price of fishing tackle, all figures are in Australian dollars unless otherwise stated.

- ✔ **Sidebars:** Text enclosed in a shaded grey box consists of information that's interesting to know but not necessarily critical to your understanding of the topic.

Foolish Assumptions

Forgive me for making assumptions about my readers, but as part of the large and ever-growing *For Dummies* library, *Fishing For Dummies,* 2nd Australian & New Zealand Edition, is a how-to book that assumes absolutely no prior knowledge of the subject on the part of the reader. At times, my definitions and explanations may seem overly simplistic. I apologise in advance for times when you may feel I'm spelling out in painstaking detail what our English friends so aptly call the bleedin' obvious. But for every reader who rolls his or her eyes skywards and mutters 'I knew *that*', at least another three faces are going to light up with understanding of a concept or a process for the very first time. This book is especially for those people...and also for the rest of us!

How This Book Is Organised

This book is divided into six parts.

Part I: Getting to Know Fish

This part does what it should do: it introduces you to a fish. You may think fish are just waiting to be caught, but to achieve a catch you have to know how these little critters operate. Part I fills you in on the basics of understanding fish.

Part II: Tackling the Right Gear

Without the right gear, you can't catch the right fish. By the time you complete Part II, you're likely to know enough to want to walk into a tackle store anywhere in Australia or New Zealand without feeling out of your depth and begin shopping for the bits and pieces you now know you need to go fishing.

Part III: Using Your Equipment the Right Way

This part teaches you how to put together all the bits and pieces you may need to go fishing. You can find out how to mount reels on rods, learn new twists on tying knots and discover how to construct effective rigs for different target species and styles of fishing.

Part IV: The New Age of Fishing

Knowing why you're going fishing is very important these days because more and more fisher-folk decide to return some or most of their catch to the water. This part examines both catch-and-release and kill-and-eat philosophies and explains their relative merits, as well as espousing the benefits of a sustainable approach to the sport. And when you do decide to take your catch home for dinner, you can also read about the most humane and efficient way to prepare your fish for the seafood feast you're planning.

Part V: What Kind of Angler Are You?

You're definitely not a deep-sea angler if you can't stand to sit up straight in a bath tub without getting nauseous. Anglers fall into many different categories and you may change from one category to another over your fishing life. Knowing which kind of angling best suits you is important, so take a trip through the chapters in Part V to find out who you really are.

Part VI: The Part of Tens

Here's where you get lists of helpful hints from my ten favourite websites to the best fishing destinations in Australia and New Zealand and all those little trivial bits that are usually left out of fishing books.

Icons Used in This Book

Throughout *Fishing For Dummies,* 2nd Australian & New Zealand Edition, you encounter little icons in the left margin of the pages that alert you to specific types of information in the text. Here's what the icons mean:

Catch Words are terms unique to recreational angling (and often specific to Australian or New Zealand fishing). The expressions are angling lingo or jargon. Sometimes these words mean very different things to their standard dictionary definitions when used in a fishing context. As well as being flagged with this icon and italicised the first time they're used in the book, all Catch Words are explained in layman's terms at their first occurrence.

Tips are little nuggets of know-how I've accumulated over a lifetime of angling. Often, the tips describe short cuts or sneaky tricks that make the fishing process easier and more efficient. Think of the paragraphs marked as tips as the piscatorial equivalent of insider trading on the stockmarket, but without the associated risks of prosecution and imprisonment!

Every now and then I mark a point to remember. These are the rules that can get you into catching fish and keep you out of trouble. Look for this icon every time you need to refresh your fishing fact file.

Warnings are exactly that — a heads-up to potential dangers facing you or your fishing tackle. Be sure to read and take heed of all passages of text flagged with the Warning icon!

Where to Go from Here

Fishing For Dummies, 2nd Australian & New Zealand Edition, is a teaching tool aimed at the time poor. I've squeezed four decades of personal experience into these pages, along with all the things I've learnt from a phalanx of grandparents, parents, sibling, aunts, uncles and fishing mates from Darwin Harbour to the Derwent River, and the Bay of Islands to the Buller River. If you can make the time to read this book, you'll understand at least the basics of the recreational angling process as it's practised in Australia and New Zealand today...and that's a promise!

For Dummies titles are reference books and if you don't want to read from Chapter 1 right through (maybe because you're a seasoned angler and way past the need to define what a hook or sinker is or be taken step-by-step through spooling up a reel), the beauty of this book is found in the way that you can browse here and there — rather like dropping a line at one snag, then moving to another, as the urge takes you. You can take on board those topics you know little about or want to brush up on and just skip over the others. All in a day's fishing really...um, reading, I mean!

Part I
Getting to Know Fish

Glenn Lumsden

'Apparently 1 have firm, white, fine-grained flesh and I'm high in Omega-3 fatty acids. No wonder I'm such a catch!'

In this part ...

*T*he most important ingredient in the fishing equation is the fish themselves. Chapter 1 gives you a vital overview of the anatomy of fish and how fish live — and survive — and the chapter offers a range of important insights into the recreational angling process. Chapter 2 and Chapter 3 describe, in detail, Australia and New Zealand's most popular saltwater and freshwater fish, where to find these fish, how to catch the critters and whether or not the fish listed make tasty treats.

Chapter 1

Fishing Fundamentals

. . . .

. . . .

*T*he delightful recreation we call fishing has many facets and in this book I'm taking on the challenge of attempting to explain all of them. First up, is the subject I regard as the single most important ingredient — the fish!

'How-to' texts on angling often bury the chapters that actually talk about fish way back in the book or they place information about this vital ingredient at the end. I can state this with authority because I've buried the poor old fish at the deep end of books myself, when in truth the act of fishing is a pointless exercise without these wonderful creatures. Fish deserve prominence and respect and that's why I'm dealing with fish up front.

Every other subject in this book is guided, shaped and dictated by fish and their behaviour, so it makes perfect sense to deal with these champions of evolution before any other subject. On the off-chance that you disagree with this approach and are eager to dive straight into the chapters covering fishing gear and techniques, by all means skip this section for now, but please do come back for a visit later.

Defining Fish

According to *The Macquarie Dictionary*, a fish is '... any of various cold-blooded, completely aquatic vertebrates, having gills, fins and typically an elongated body, usually covered with scales ...' While numerous exceptions to this simple definition exist — including a few fish with warm blood and others without scales or obvious fins — this definition is just fine for understanding the basics of the type of fish you're likely to catch for the pan.

In fact, I believe recognising a true fish from one of the many critters that are commonly but incorrectly called fish (see Figure 1-1) is more important. Dolphins, porpoises, whales, dugongs and many other aquatic mammals are definitely not fish. Neither are sharks, stingrays and skate, which have a type of skeleton made from cartilage (tough, fibrous tissue) rather than bone.

For this reason, these types of marine life are sometimes referred to as cartilaginous fish, as different from bony or 'true' fish ... Whoops! I'm becoming a little bogged down in the scientific stuff — sorry. How about I promise not to tell you off if you call a shark a fish, if you promise to put up with my occasional bits of technical ranting?

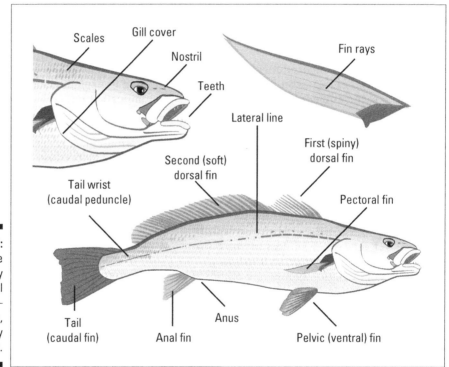

Figure 1-1: The anatomy of a typical bony fish — in this case, a mulloway or jewfish.

Doing swimmingly

Fish have been around for a long, long time — well over 300 million years, in fact. Fish were swimming in the Earth's oceans and rivers eons before the rise of the dinosaurs and have outlived those huge reptiles by around 65 million years. Clearly, the evolutionary process was onto a winner when fish began populating the world's waters. These wonders of the water have changed remarkably little in millions of years — living proof of the adage 'if it ain't broke, don't fix it'.

With such a long-term success rate in the highly competitive field of survival, fish are clearly well adapted to their watery environment. You need to bear this in mind when you hunt for fish because, while the fishy little fellows aren't intelligent in human terms and have only a limited capacity to learn, these critters are masters of the art of staying alive. And that includes avoiding being captured by the likes of you and me!

Fish galore

More than 2,000 different kinds of fish swim in the salty ocean waters around Australia and New Zealand, and a couple of hundred more in our rivers and lakes, but only a small percentage of these are of real interest to anglers. The majority of fish are either too small or live in unreachable depths. Fortunately, that leaves plenty of fascinating targets to pursue — more than enough to fill a long and interesting lifetime of angling. (I look at favourite saltwater fish in Chapter 2 and favourite freshwater fish in Chapter 3.)

In Chapters 2 and 3, I examine 16 of the most popular and sought-after Australian and New Zealand fish — ten from salt water and six from fresh. While you may well end up pursuing and catching fish not included in these chapters, a basic knowledge of these 16 common, widely distributed species provides an excellent basis to work from.

Fish wishes

Fish have simple needs and their lives appear to be dominated by three driving forces: the quest for food, the desire not to be eaten and the urge to reproduce. Eat, run away and have sex. What's simpler than that?

As an angler, the more you know about these three primary motivating forces, the better your chances of finding and catching fish.

A fish-eat-fish world

The vast majority of fish species eat other fish — at least some of the time. Even the so-called vegetarian types (such as mullet, carp and luderick) aren't above snacking on hapless small fry from time to time.

In addition to eating smaller fish (sometimes not that much smaller!), most fish dine regularly on other aquatic critters such as shrimps, prawns, crabs, marine worms, shellfish, squid, octopus and various forms of plankton. Freshwater fish and a number of saltwater fish also regularly snack on land-dwelling organisms such as insects, spiders, grubs, earthworms and even small birds and mammals unlucky enough to drop in for dinner. Several types of fish are also partial to feeding on the amphibians and reptiles — particularly frogs, lizards, snakes and baby turtles — that share their watery habitat.

Add to this a penchant for munching on dead and decaying animal or vegetable matter and scavenging for human detritus — including everything from discarded lunch scraps to the nastier items that pour out of stormwater drains and sewage pipes — and you come up with an extremely diverse diet! In fact, I'm constantly amazed at what fish eat, or at least take into their mouths. (And often I'm equally amazed that I'm still so keen to eat those same fish!)

Fish are an 'armless bunch

A handy item to remember is that fish don't have hands. And before you think I'm totally stating the obvious, this 'armless aspect is a key element in the hunt for fish.

Humans spend a large part of their waking lives picking up items or touching objects with their hands to find out more about the particular object. I call this the wet paint syndrome. Hang a Wet Paint sign on an item and watch how many people walk up to touch the surface of the object and then look at their fingers just to confirm that — surprise, surprise — the paint really is wet!

By contrast, when a fish (or a human toddler, for that matter) wants to explore an interesting object, the fish (just like the toddler) takes the object into its mouth and does a taste test. Nine times out of ten, the fish (or child) then spits out the object, having discovered the item is definitely not edible and is in fact a cigarette butt, a pebble, a scrap of aluminium foil or a fallen leaf. If that interesting object has a hook attached, which in turn has a line attached and you, the angler, are lucky enough to feel the fish bite and react to the nibble in time, you may well catch the fish. (I don't recommend fishing for toddlers. Their mothers are rarely impressed.)

The fact that fish explore the world with their mouths and that not everything fish take into their mouths is intended to be swallowed is an important lesson for you, the angler, as you can make wonderful use of this behaviour.

Fish fears

Hunting for food is pretty high on the priority list for fish, but even higher is the desire to avoid becoming a meal for another fish. Most fish are fair game for other fish or animals from the moment of hatching or birth.

Before man came on the scene, fish already had plenty of predators to worry about, including other fish, sharks, squid, seals, dolphins, birds, bears, foxes, cats, crocodiles, snakes, turtles and lizards. Death can strike a fish from above or below at any moment. Imagine the stress levels this must produce! (In fact, Valium for fish is bound to be a big seller if someone solves the obvious marketing problems.)

Even after fish grow large enough to have few likely enemies, a strongly imprinted, instinctive fear of being eaten remains, which is why big tuna, marlin and even sharks occasionally shy from the shadow of a passing seagull. Somewhere in the tiny brain of the fish is the memory of being hunted by seabirds when just a few days or months old and just centimetres long. And, after all, that kind of traumatic childhood experience is hard to forget!

Fish have three main ways of avoiding predation (a fancy word for getting eaten):

- Fleeing
- Hiding
- Fighting

In open water, escape is often the best policy, which is one reason why so many open-water fish are built for speed. When alarmed, these fish light the afterburner and vacate the scene — fast!

Closer to shore, fish tend to hide from potential threats using the cover of caves, weed, submerged timber, darkness, shadows, discoloured or highly aerated water and depth.

If none of these ploys work, a fish may be forced to attempt to fight off or trick and confuse the attacker. Another option is for the fish to make itself look unattractive as a meal. Many fish do this by puffing themselves up, erecting their spikes and fins and opening their mouths as wide as possible. These ploys do work — but not all the time.

Birds and bees ... and fish

The vast majority of fish reproduce or *spawn* (deposit eggs) just once or twice each year and the process is relatively impersonal. Mature females and males of most species gather to release eggs and *milt* (sperm), which mix together in the water or on the riverbed. Only in a few specific cases is any sort of ongoing parental care offered to the numerous offspring. More often, the small fry are left to their own devices and are at serious risk of becoming a meal for other fish, including mum or dad!

Pre-spawning, spawning and post-spawning behaviour is of enormous interest to anglers because this behaviour can affect how easy the fish is to catch.

As a form of protection, a number of fish species gather together in specific areas at spawning time, which can be a bonus for knowledgeable anglers. Other species become aggressive and fearless — making the fish easier to catch — or the fish may go off the bite completely. In a few instances, Australian and New Zealand authorities have introduced periods during which fishing is banned (these are called *closed seasons*) or have put other regulations in place to protect spawning fish (two examples are trout and Murray cod). As an angler, you need to be aware of these habits and rules because understanding the system helps to make you a better angler.

Fishing is for Everyone

Some people are about as attracted to fishing as I am to fixing a clogged kitchen drain. These types may see angling as a smelly, uncomfortable and frustrating pursuit, often undertaken in cold, wet and windy conditions in the company of big, boofy blokes with poor dress sense and a loose respect for the truth.

However, I'm sure that by reading this far, you don't necessarily agree with those jaundiced sentiments.

The fact is that fishing can be whatever you want — a casual pastime or a consuming passion. You can fish alone, with friends, with your family or with a club (see Figure 1-2). You can fish competitively, philosophically, intensely, half-heartedly or in whatever other way takes your fancy. Because of this flexibility, fishing is a remarkably individualistic sport or hobby and tends to attract followers who have an individualistic streak (organising anglers into any sort of meaningful group is nigh on impossible).

Figure 1-2:
Recre-
ational
fishing is a
wonderful
family
or group
pastime,
but one that
can also
be enjoyed
alone.

Like surfing or mountain climbing, fishing appeals most strongly to those people who prefer to test themselves against the challenges of the natural world rather than against other men and women. Check out Chapters 18 to 23 for information about the different kinds of angling — surf, jetty, estuary and more.

Hunting for your pound of flesh

Fishing is a form of hunting and no amount of glossing over this fact changes the reality. The chase for flesh strikes a deep chord in the human psyche and the act of catching food satisfies a primal need. However, recreational angling is unique in the field of hunting as when a shooter squeezes the trigger or a bow hunter releases an arrow, assuming his or her aim is true, the fate of the prey is sealed. This is not the case in fishing.

Anglers are in the fortunate position of being able to enjoy the entire hunting experience without actually making a kill. At any stage in the process you have the choice of keeping your catch or returning the fish to the water alive (despite popular belief, recent scientific studies show that the survival rates of most angler-caught fish are typically well in excess of 90 per cent).

Having said that, you still need to accept that fishing is a form of hunting. No matter how careful you are, or how committed you are to the principles of conservation, if you go fishing you're bound to ultimately kill a number of fish — intentionally or otherwise — and therefore have an impact on the environment. (Check out Chapter 17 for lots of information about sustainable fishing and the environment.)

Fishing for a top feed

While catching a fish and then releasing the critter (called *catch and release*, see Chapter 15) is becoming an increasingly popular part of modern recreational angling, the motivation to go fishing is still often the promise of a delicious and healthy seafood meal at the end of the day. However, don't fall into the trap of thinking that you can save money by fishing for your supper. Even the best anglers invest more money and effort into fishing than they can realistically hope to recoup in the form of fish, especially if measured at prevailing market prices. Happily, though, fishing is a lot more than just a matter of taste sensations or economics! (For more on cleaning, preparing and cooking your catch, see Chapter 16.)

All the same, fish you catch yourself always taste better and are more satisfying to eat than those you buy. Why? In practical terms, the fish you bring home are often fresher than fish bought at the market. Equally, your careful handling and preparation of the fish is likely to be of a higher standard than that used by commercial outlets. More importantly, the fish you work so hard to catch reflect an emotional investment that simply can't be found in the local fish shop or supermarket. Just like vegetables that you lovingly grow at home or eggs from the backyard chicken coop, self-caught fish are the sweetest seafood you can eat ... and that's a promise!

Choosing How to Catch Your Fish

At a commercial and subsistence level, fish are harvested using spears, nets, traps or even by crushing toxic leaves in the water. This book is about angling, which means using a line and a hook to catch fish, but even within this narrower definition of fishing, you have a multitude of possibilities, permutations and personal preferences to explore.

Quality versus quantity

Beginners often ask the obvious question: 'What's the best way to catch a bream/flathead/trout/snapper?', while more experienced anglers are likely to come at the same problem from a different tack and ask: 'What's the most exciting, interesting or challenging way I can catch this or that fish?'

When you first take up fishing, chances are you simply want to catch fish — and the more fish, the better. As time goes by, and you become more adept at landing fish, chances are you're going to start looking for different and more stimulating ways to catch the same fish. In a number of cases, these different methods may not be as efficient and you may actually end up catching less fish by using these techniques. Even so, if you value each catch more as a result of using these methods, you may obtain a greater personal return from the sport. In other words, quality becomes more important than quantity. (Chapters 9 to 13 cover all you need to know about getting your fishing kit together and how to use your equipment the right way.)

Easy versus hard

Often, more experienced anglers increase their personal enjoyment of angling by deliberately making the sport harder for themselves. For example, the following are various ways to catch bream and each way has a different level of difficulty. Our Kiwi friends can think in terms of snapper or trout, rather than bream, for the sake of this exercise.

The easy way

Apart from using a net (which is illegal for recreational anglers in most places), the best way to catch a bream is to use a live or very fresh natural bait such as a prawn, worm or saltwater yabby (nipper) on a small, sharp hook attached to a fine line weighted with a tiny sinker. All you have to do then is sit back and wait for the bream to bite. This method is the way most anglers catch bream and is the way I fished for these tasty targets for many, many years.

The hard way

Bream (or snapper or trout) can also be hunted using *lures* (artificial baits) made from wood, plastic, rubber or metal and cunningly manipulated by the angler to look like a live prawn, worm, yabby or small fish. Lure fishing for bream or trout or snapper involves constant activity — casting and retrieving the lure and moving from place to place in search of fish. This style of fishing is extremely active and engrossing.

Often, when fishing with lures for bream (or snapper or trout), you see the fish swimming by or aggressively following and attacking your little lure before you manage to snare the fish onto your hook. This element of using a lure makes the quest exciting and adds an extra dimension to the whole hunting process.

Because of the light, sensitive nature of the tackle that you need to use to cast small lures for bream, any large fish you hook is bound to put up a spectacular struggle. At least a percentage of the fish are bound to win their freedom by breaking your light line or shaking free of the hook. Again, the fight increases the challenge, and therefore enjoyment, of the sport.

Finally, because fish caught on lures are usually hooked in the lips or mouth, you can generally release those you don't wish to kill without doing terminal damage to the fish. While you're likely to catch fewer fish using lures than by using bait, the whole exercise can be a more active, exciting, challenging and environmentally friendly way of targeting bream (or snapper or trout). For that reason, increasing numbers of experienced anglers choose to fish for bream (and snapper and trout) using lures.

The even harder way

Fishing for bream (or snapper or trout) can be made even harder by using *fly-fishing* tackle. In fly-fishing (check out Chapter 8), the bait is an artificial fly made from fur, feathers or other materials bound to a hook with thread. Fly-fishing for these species is even more difficult and challenging than casting a lure for the same fish as the technique demands more specialised equipment and higher skill levels and is less efficient than using either bait or lures (see more about baits and lures in Chapter 8). Despite this fact, many people choose to pursue bream, snapper and especially trout with fly tackle simply because the technique is more satisfying.

And that's the whole point — fishing is primarily about having fun!

Chapter 2

Our Favourite Saltwater Fish

More than 2,000 different kinds of fish are found in the salt, brackish and fresh waters of Australia and New Zealand. The majority of these fish are of little interest to anglers because the critters are either too small or because of the fish's habit of cruising in water too deep for an angler to reach. That process of elimination leaves a couple of hundred species that anglers can, and do, target on a regular basis.

From this extensive list, in this chapter and the next, I describe 16 types of fish that have a wide distribution and account for the bulk of recreational fishing effort in Australia and New Zealand. Later, you're bound to graduate to target other species of fish not described here but, chances are, these 16 can keep you happy, challenged and busy for many, many years to come!

The ten fish I discuss in this chapter are listed in alphabetical order — from bream to whiting — and live primarily in salt water. Some are found only in Australia while others occur both there and in New Zealand. In Chapter 3, I look at another six fish — again arranged alphabetically from barramundi to trout — that are usually thought of as freshwater fish, although a number of these fish (especially bass, barramundi and chinook salmon) regularly venture into brackish and even salt waters. Fish are like that — the critters just don't stick to the rules!

Bountiful Bream

The term bream (pronounced *brim* in Australia, rather than the English *breem*) actually describes not so much a single species as a small family of fish. The bream clan is so widespread that this family accounts for more angling efforts in Australia than any other group.

The commonest and most widely distributed members of the clan are the eastern yellowfin bream (see Figure 2-1), the southern black bream and the pikey bream of Australia's northern waters. (None of these fish occur in New Zealand waters.) All three fish look very much alike and can be caught in exactly the same ways.

Bream are deep-bodied fish with reasonably large scales, a forked tail and a fairly small mouth full of strong, peg-like teeth. The colour of bream varies depending on where the fish live, but most bream are silvery on the sides with a darker back of bronze or green. The lower fins (especially the anal fin) often exhibit a flush of canary yellow. You can check out the placement of these fins in Chapter 1.

The bream most often caught are of a modest size and if you land one longer than 40 centimetres and heavier than 1 kilogram, you're doing very well indeed.

Bream live in coastal rivers, estuaries, bays and harbours and along beaches and ocean rocks. The fish feed mostly on small crustaceans including prawns, shrimps, crabs and saltwater yabbies (nippers), as well as marine worms, molluscs and little fish. But bream are opportunistic feeders with cosmopolitan tastes and these fish eat some weird and wonderful stuff at times! (I talk about fish foods as bait in Chapter 8.)

Figure 2-1:
The eastern
yellowfin
bream.
Several
other
species in
the bream
family look
virtually
identical to
this fish.

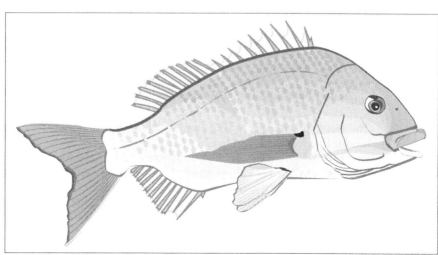

Fishing with finesse

Bream can be rather cunning and finicky, so catching a member of this family requires finesse. One of the best ways to catch a bream is to use a fine line (2–5 kilos breaking strain nylon), light, sensitive rods, small sharp hooks (Nos 4–1/0), the smallest sinker you can use in the circumstances and live or very fresh bait. I explain these different line strengths and unravel the mysteries of the rather convoluted hook-sizing system in Chapter 4.

The most productive bream baits are

- Bloodworms
- Prawns
- Sandworms
- Shellfish flesh
- Small estuary crabs
- Squirt worms
- Yabbies (nippers)

The types of shellfish you can use include mussels, pipis, clams and even oysters (assuming you can work out how to keep the slippery little blighters on a hook!).

Fish flesh, octopus and squid baits are productive for catching bream at times, as are unusual offerings such as cheese, bread, steak, chicken, tripe and various dough or pudding mixtures made with flour, water and a variety of so-called secret ingredients including anchovies, parmesan cheese and aniseed oil. (See Chapter 8 for all sorts of fish-tempting delicacies.)

Try a variety of baits until you work out what the bream in your area fancy the most. Whatever you use, cast your hook close to the shelter and shade provided by fallen trees, rock bars, oyster racks, bridge pylons or jetties, then sit very quietly and wait for a bite.

Luring 'em onto your line

As more Australian anglers discover every year, bream can also be caught on lures and flies, although effectively using these artificial baits is a little trickier than fooling bream with natural baits. Most people who crack the bream-on-lures puzzle also reckon the technique is more satisfying, so if you're looking for a real challenge in fishing, luring bream may be just the ticket.

 Because most of the items that bream eat are small, you need to use little lures and flies to catch these fish on a regular basis. The most versatile lures are floating/diving minnows and plugs from 4 to 6 centimetres in length (for more information on lures, check out Chapter 8). Light, sensitive threadline or spinning tackle is used to cast these lures accurately into the places where bream live (check out Part II for details about this type of gear).

Passing the taste test

Bream are highly regarded as table fish, although a number of people (me included!) argue that bream are actually overrated in this department.

Bream from the lower reaches of estuaries, harbours and the open ocean usually have moist, white flesh with a clean, sweet flavour, but bream from the brackish waters of upper estuaries or land-locked lagoons have softer meat and can taste a bit weedy or muddy at times. While I love catching bream (especially on lures), I'd rather eat flathead, whiting or leatherjacket, so most of the bream I catch are very lucky fish indeed — I quickly release them back into the water! (If you're keen to know more about returning your catch, skip to Chapter 15.)

First-Class Flathead

The large group of fish known as flathead are not likely to win any beauty contests but, looks aside, flathead are without doubt one of Australia's favourite fish. Why? Because flathead are abundant, widespread, fairly easy to catch (usually!) and are generally delicious. What more can you ask for from any fish?

The flathead's popularity is reflected by the number of regional nicknames the fish has picked up over the years. These handles include lizard, frog, yank and flattie.

Taking in the extended family

The flathead family includes more than 30 species, about one-half of which are taken by Australian anglers. (These fish don't commonly occur in New Zealand.) By far the biggest is the dusky flathead of Australia's east coast, which has been known to reach at least 1.2 metres in length and as much as 9 kilos in weight (see Figure 2-2). At that size, a dusky flathead looks more like a small crocodile than a lizard or a frog and is big enough to pose a real threat to your paddling Jack Russell terrier!

The other flatties — variously known as sand, tiger, bar-tail, rock, king and spotted flathead — are smaller fish, rarely topping 1.5–2 kilos, and, to be honest, most of the duskies you catch are likely to be well under this weight, too (but you can dream!). (For more information about what is the correct fish weight and size for legal keeping, have a look at Chapter 26.)

As the family name implies, flathead have compressed bodies and broad, spade-like heads. The fish have very large mouths filled with lots of fine, sharp teeth. As if that mouthful isn't enough armoury, flathead also possess several sets of razor-edged spines on their gill covers, covered in mildly venomous mucus, and these can inflict nasty injuries on unwary anglers. In other words, always handle flathead with extreme care.

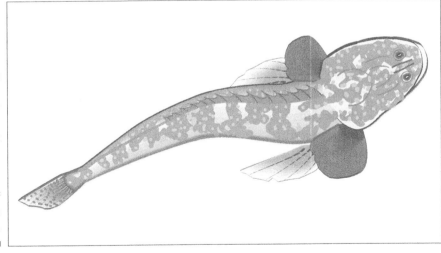

Figure 2-2:
The dusky flathead has the greatest growth potential of all the members of this large family.

Colouring to kill

The flathead's camouflaged colouration is extremely variable, ranging from a light sandy white or fawn with darker bars and blue, red and black spots to brick red, brown, grey and even jet black. By contrast, the flathead's soft underbelly is usually a creamy yellow or off-white.

Flathead are superb ambush hunters and lie concealed on the seabed, hidden by their camouflaged colouring and flat body, but always ready to pounce on an unwary prey. In attack mode, flathead are one of the fastest fish in the sea over a distance of one or two metres. This speed, combined with a cavernous mouth full of small, sharp teeth, must make flathead a living nightmare for the little fish, prawns, crabs, squid and octopus that constitute the flathead's diet.

Moving makes for success

You can fish for flathead in a variety of ways. Most are caught on natural baits presented on the sea, river or lake bed and the number of catches definitely improves when the bait is moved or slowly dragged across the bottom, either behind a drifting boat or by reeling the bait in slowly from the river bank.

The best baits to use to catch flatties include the following:

- Anchovies
- Bluebait
- Herrings
- Pilchards
- Small live or dead fish, for example, baby mullet (otherwise known as poddies)
- Sprats
- Whitebait

Almost as effective for catching flathead are cut strips of mullet, tailor, yellowtail, tuna or garfish flesh. Lots of flathead are also taken on saltwater yabbies (nippers), marine worms, shellfish, prawns, octopus and squid baits, so you can hardly call these fish fussy.

Flathead are also wonderful lure and fly-fishing targets. The fish respond particularly well to small- and medium-sized metal spoons, rubber-tailed jigs, diving or sinking minnows and plugs and *streamer flies* (I describe this type of equipment in greater detail in Chapter 8). When fishing with artificial baits, the best bet is to present the lure close to the bottom and move the spoon, jig or plug around in an erratic fashion.

Frying the best fish 'n' tips

Flathead are one of Australia's favourite table fish. The fish has firm, white and flaky flesh that tends towards dryness in larger specimens. As a result, flathead are best suited to recipes designed to maintain moisture content while cooking.

Although a number of people regard the process as a bit fiddly, I believe the finest way to enjoy the full flavour of flathead is to use the following recipe:

1. **Fillet and skin the fish.**

2. **Carefully cut the bones from the fillets.**

3. **Lightly dust the flesh in flour.**

4. **Toss the pieces into a hot frying pan containing a splash of high-quality oil.**

5. **Serve with a bowl of fresh salad and a handful of potato chips.**

The result is a seafood meal fit for a king or queen!

Glorious Garfish

The large family of fish species found around the world and known in Australia as garfish or gar is well represented in local marine and estuary waters. A couple of species also occur in New Zealand, where they're commonly known as piper. The more common types found in Australian waters include the virtually identical eastern and southern sea garfish, the river garfish, the robust garfish (also known as the three-by-two garfish) and the snub-nosed garfish, which lives in both brackish and fresh waters.

As mentioned, these fish are commonly called gars, gardies and beakies in Australia; while, across the Tasman in New Zealand the regional name for the same group of fish is piper. In other parts of the world, garfish or piper are variously known as needlefish, halfbeaks and balao (or ballyhoo).

What's in a name?

Naming fish can be an extremely confusing business. Most popular species have at least a couple of common names and the usage of these titles varies from place to place. For example, the big fish correctly known in Australia as a mulloway is hardly ever called by that name in New South Wales and Queensland, where the fish is generally referred to as a jewfish. Meanwhile, in Western Australia, a different kind of fish altogether is called a jewfish and the mulloway is sometimes called a river kingfish.

One way to remove this confusion is to use the fish's scientific title, but by the time you yell out 'Quick, bring the landing net! I have a big *Platycephalus fuscus* on my line!', that dusky flathead of a lifetime may well have escaped.

Recognising exactly what fish different anglers in various parts of the country, or across the ditch in New Zealand, are referring to when the words bream, snapper or perch are mentioned is something only learned with time and even then misunderstandings and confusion still occur. With fish, the name game is far from simple or clear cut.

Garfish or piper are small, slender fish, and most types have a bottom jaw that extends into a bill or beak, often with a red tip (see Figure 2-3). The body colour of garfish varies between species from bright, metallic silver to silvery-green or silvery-blue. A few varieties have dark blotches, bands or bars on their sides and the belly of a garfish is typically silvery-white or creamy coloured and semi-transparent, so you can see what the fish has had for lunch (usually yucky green stuff!).

The southern sea garfish and the robust (or 'three-by-two') gar of tropical waters are Australasia's largest members of the family, but even these only rarely reach lengths of about 45 centimetres and weights of 400 grams. Most garfish are under 35 centimetres and weigh less than 200 grams.

Figure 2-3:
Garfish are small, slender creatures characterised by an extended bottom jaw.

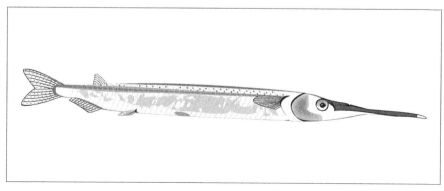

Working the surface

Garfish or piper usually swim and feed in the surface layers of the water and are present in most Australian and New Zealand estuaries, harbours, bays and inshore areas, as well as a number of freshwater lakes in tropical and sub-tropical latitudes in Australia (mostly north from about the Sunshine Coast region).

Garfish or piper are best pursued using the following float-suspended baits:

- Bread
- Dough
- Maggots (seriously!)
- Marine worms
- Prawn pieces
- Squid strips
- Tiny fish strips

The best hooks are small (Nos 14–6) and long-shanked (I discuss various hook patterns and sizes in Chapter 4).

Garfish or piper also respond well to a mixture of _pollard_ (a wheat by-product), crushed wheat or breadcrumbs, especially if the mixture contains a little fish oil. This mixture is a type of _berley_, which is simply material distributed in the water where you're fishing in order to attract and excite fish. (I discuss how to make and use berley in Chapter 8.)

Boning up on your skills

Garfish or piper — particularly the larger varieties — are delectable table fish with sweet, moist flesh. Unfortunately, the fish has many fine, greenish-coloured bones. You can overcome this drawback, however, by using a variety of techniques, most of which involve using a sharp knife and lots of patience, to perform the piscatorial equivalent of microsurgery.

After capture, squeeze the garfish or piper from the head towards the tail to expel the semi-digested vegetable matter and berley (that yucky green stuff) in its stomach. As with any fish, the garfish is best kept in a cool, shaded place, preferably on ice, until cleaned. The scales of a garfish are readily dislodged and, those not rubbed off by handling at the time of capture (and left stuck all over your fishing gear, clothes and hands), are easily removed during the cleaning process. (I describe cleaning fish in Chapter 16).

Luverly Leatherjackets

The leatherjacket story is another family affair, with at least 60 varieties of leathery or jacket living in Australasian waters. Of these different types, around 20 varieties are sought after by anglers.

The most frequently captured species include the rough, six-spined, yellow-finned, Chinaman, mosaic, horseshoe and fan-bellied leatherjackets.

Leatherjackets vary in colour, size, shape and distribution, but all are without scales, are rough-skinned and have tiny mouths with sharp, beak-like teeth. Leatherjackets also have a stout, serrated dorsal spine on the back, behind the head (see Figure 2-4).

Be very careful when handling leatherjackets, because both their dorsal spines and teeth can inflict nasty injuries on the unwary angler.

Leatherjacket colouration varies enormously from the bright and attractive six-spined leatherjacket to the drab and well-camouflaged rough and fan-bellied varieties. Correctly identifying the different species can be a tricky task, but fortunately this aspect is not overly important to the average angler.

Most leatherjackets are small. For example, the estuarine fan-bellied leatherjacket rarely tops 400 grams in weight. At the other end of the scale, the six-spined and horseshoe varieties occasionally reach 2 kilos, while the giants of the family are the mosaic and the Chinaman types, both of which occasionally exceed 3 kilos.

Figure 2-4: Leather-jackets have tough, leathery skins, small mouths, sharp teeth and a prominent dorsal spine on the back of their head.

Collecting a right hook

Leatherjackets can be taken on most types of tackle and many are caught on light handlines or the same rod and reel outfits used to catch bream, flathead, whiting, trout and the like.

When present in high numbers, leatherjackets are quite easy to catch, especially if a relatively small hook (Nos 12–4) is used in conjunction with the following soft baits:

- Abalone and scallop gut
- Cunjevoi (sea squirts)
- Marine worms
- Mussels
- Peeled prawn tails
- Squid or octopus pieces
- Strips of fish flesh
- Yabbies

The best way to catch leatherjackets is to use small, sharp, *long-shanked* hooks (the shank is the straight arm of the hook), because these types of hooks prevent the leatherjacket from biting through the line with all those sharp teeth. (I discuss hooks and their shanks in Chapter 4.)

Dressing for dinner

Both Aussie and Kiwi leatherjackets have white, sweet and slightly moist flesh, making the jacket an excellent food fish. As an added bonus, leatherjackets are also dead easy to clean and prepare for the table, as the following step-by-step guide describes:

1. **Slice down through the fish's back, immediately behind the dorsal spine.**

    This cut is the only one required to clean a leatherjacket!

2. **Pull the head and intestines away in one lump.**

3. **Peel the leathery skin from the body.**

4. **Trim the fins and tail (optional).**

5. **Pan-fry the leatherjackets in a little butter or poach the fish slowly in white wine.**

Mmmm!

Over the years, occasional reports of mild poisoning from eating leatherjackets — particularly the larger Chinaman variety — appear in newspapers or can be heard in fishing circles. Poisoning is most likely a result of a specific item in the fish's diet affecting the flesh. Fishermen in doubt have been known to try a small portion of the fish first and, if no symptoms of illness are detected after 6 to 12 hours, they consume the rest of the catch. I leave that decision up to you!

Super Salmon

Question: When is a salmon not a salmon? Answer: When it's an Australian salmon. The fact is, this wonderful fish is totally unrelated to the various true salmon of the Northern Hemisphere and is more suited to the Maori name of kahawai (*car*-why). That said, convincing Australians to call their much-loved salmon a kahawai is about as likely as talking Aussies into barracking for the All Blacks rugby team!

A number of Aussie anglers call the Australian salmon sambo, while other anglers, especially in Victoria and South Australia, know the juvenile fish as salmon trout or bay trout. In Tasmania, a small salmon is often called a cocky salmon, while around the country extremely large specimens are frequently referred to as black backs. In New Zealand, they are and have always been kahawai.

Strong swimmers

The salmon or kahawai is a medium-sized, elongated sea fish with a cylindrical body and a large, forked tail (see Figure 2-5). Adult salmon are bluish-green to black on the upper back, silver to greenish-silver or even purplish on the flanks and silvery-white on the belly. The back is patterned with darker green spots that extend well down the flanks. The fish's small eyes are yellowish around the dark pupil and the salmon's fins are light-coloured, except for the dusky tail, which often has a darker trailing edge and a narrow white or cream band along the leading edge of the lower lobe. The pectoral or side fins may be strongly tinged with yellow. You can see all these fins in Chapter 1.

Most salmon taken by Aussie and Kiwi anglers weigh between 200 grams and 3.5 kilos. Exceptional specimens occasionally top 6 kilos. Salmon over 1 kilo are extremely powerful and are sure to provide a memorable battle when hooked. Their Maori name — kahawai — is said to translate literally as 'strong in the water' — an excellent description of this terrific fish.

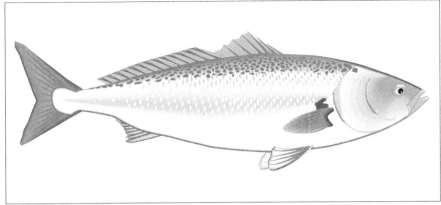

Wolves of the white water

Salmon or kahawai are a migratory, *pelagic* (free swimming) species found mainly in cool and temperate southern waters, though occasionally ranging up the eastern seaboard as far as Queensland's Gold Coast and north along the west coast to about Geraldton. This species is prolific in most New Zealand waters, but less common towards the very southern end of the South Island.

Salmon or kahawai prefer to live near the shore and are found in larger estuaries, bays and harbours, along beaches and rocky shorelines and also out on deeper reefs. The fish frequently hunt smaller fish in areas of strong wave or current action with a covering of well-aerated white water.

Salmon or kahawai are commonly taken using the following baits:

- ✔ Beach worms
- ✔ Cut fish flesh
- ✔ Garfish rigged on *ganged hooks* (see Chapter 4)
- ✔ Pipis
- ✔ Prawns
- ✔ Squid or squid pieces
- ✔ Whole pilchards rigged on ganged hooks

Salmon or kahawai also occasionally take crabs, cunjevoi or even bread, particularly when these are also provided in a *berley trail* (this clever tool is a trail of a mixture of fish food dribbled into the water). Larger salmon also take live yellowtail or live mullet baits.

Kahawai or Australian salmon usually prefer lightly-weighted, moving baits rather than those anchored to the seabed. The fish are also keen lure and fly takers, succumbing to cast-and-retrieved or *trolled* metal slices — the term troll means to trail a baited line or lure behind a slowly moving boat — as well as lead slugs, spoons, spinners, jigs, minnows, plugs, poppers and streamer flies. I discuss lures and how to use each type in Chapter 8.

Because salmon or kahawai have a habit of jumping and shaking their heads when on a line, many that are hooked on lures are lost before they can be landed. This scenario simply adds to the challenge and uncertainty of a successful capture.

Strong on a plate, too!

Australian salmon or kahawai make reasonable table fare, but aren't especially popular in this regard, at least not in Australia. Salmon are a dark-fleshed, blood-rich and strongly flavoured fish best suited to smoking, baking or being made into fish cakes.

If you find you're one of those people who don't particularly enjoy eating salmon, I recommend you adopt the habit of carefully releasing these wonderful sport fish to swim and fight again (check out Chapter 15 for how to release a fish with care).

Savoury Snapper

The snapper is one of Australasia's most important recreational and commercial fish species, so the fact that the fish has picked up an array of alternate names over the years is hardly surprising. Red, big red, reddie and pinkie are among the most common nicknames and — surprise, surprise — are based on the colour of the fish.

Throughout Western Australia, this species is called a pink snapper, to distinguish the fish from several unrelated types. In a number of regions, snapper also have different names depending on the size of the fish. For example, in years gone by, east coast anglers called the smallest fish cockney bream, cockneys or cockies, slightly larger specimens were called red bream, even larger ones were known as squire and the largest were called old man snapper (even though many were female!). Thankfully, this archaic system is now largely a thing of the past, although the term squire remains in common usage in southern Queensland.

In Victoria and parts of New South Wales, smaller snapper — from less than legal length up to 1 kilo or so — are often still called pinkies, while the same fish in South Australia are known as ruggers. For reasons hidden in the mists of time, snapper is often incorrectly spelt 'schnapper' by fish-shop owners and restaurateurs.

The Kiwis seem to have escaped most of this Aussie confusion. In New Zealand, a snapper is a snapper is a snapper! Well, almost. The Maori name of tamure is still used in parts of the Northland, and a few Kiwi anglers call small snapper bream, but generally speaking, snapper is the preferred handle in The Land of the Long White Cloud.

Making snappy headlines

The snapper is a deep-bodied fish with powerful jaws and strong, peg-like teeth. Larger adults often exhibit a distinct hump or bump on the head (see Figure 2-6) and occasionally have an enlarged nose area, but this is by no means universal. In New Zealand waters, snapper rarely develop these humps and lumps and in Victoria and South Australia, most large specimens have practically no discernible hump.

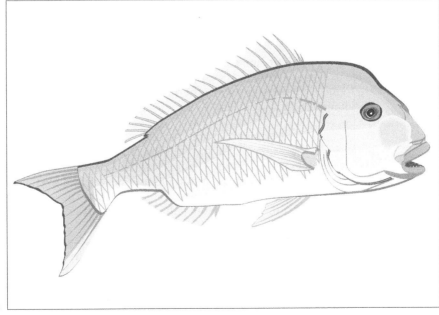

Figure 2-6: Snapper don't develop the charac- teristic steep forehead and hump until the fish reach a large size.

The colour of snapper varies with the location, but fish caught in deep water over reef tend to be a much brighter red than those taken on sand or mud bottoms. The typical snapper colouration is red to pinkish-silver or coppery on the head and back, rosy-silver with blue reflections on the flanks and silver or silvery-white on the belly. The flanks are also heavily peppered with small, iridescent blue spots. The fish's fins are usually dusky red, the anal fin is edged with blue, while the bottom lobe of the tail may be white along the leading edge. A big snapper is a handsome fish indeed and always a prize catch!

Outside of South Australia, parts of Western Australia and New Zealand, a 7–9 kilo big red is the catch of a lifetime. The majority of snapper taken from the east and south-east coasts of Australia today weigh from 300 grams to 5 kilos. Even in Melbourne's Port Phillip Bay — once renowned for big snapper — fish over 9 kilos cause large crowds to gather at the cleaning tables.

Being such a highly prized fish, snapper are protected by legal lengths and bag limits in every Australian state and in New Zealand, so be sure to check the state of play before slipping that pinkie into your bag! (Chapter 26 provides information about where to check up on the fishing rules.)

Tracking snapper from Tassie to the tropics

A relative of the bream and a member of a worldwide family with close allies in Japan, South Africa, North America and the Mediterranean, snapper are found right around the southern half of the Australian mainland from Rockhampton in Queensland to Carnarvon in Western Australia.

Once considered rare in Tasmania, snapper now turn up in reasonable numbers in the Tamar River and other north coast estuaries during summer and autumn. In New Zealand, snapper can be found at least as far south as Christchurch on the east coast of the South Island, and even further south on the west coast, while the same fish also inhabits the waters around Norfolk Island and, more sporadically, Lord Howe Island.

The ideal habitat for snapper is open ocean areas with hard reef or a gravel or sandy bottom. The fish prefer to swim in depths from 20 to 150 metres. In southern latitudes (and particularly in Victoria and South Australia), large spawning-related migrations of snapper occur seasonally (from late-spring to autumn) in relatively featureless sand and mud-bottomed bays or big estuaries.

Trapping your snapper

Thanks to the diversity of snapper habitats and the size range of the fish, the techniques and tackle used for snapper fishing vary immensely from place to place. However, certain basics apply wherever snapper are found.

- **In water less than 40 metres deep:** For the best fishing results, use an unweighted or very lightly-weighted line baited with one of the following fresh cuts of fish flesh:

  - Bonito

  - Garfish or piper

  - Herring

  - Mullet

  - Pilchards (whole or cut)

  - Tuna

  Offerings of squid, octopus, prawns and crabs are also effective, as is the use of berley. (I explain bait in Chapter 8.)

- **In water deeper than 40 metres:** For the best fishing results, sinkers weighing between 100 grams and 1 kilo may be needed to take the line and baited hook to the fish. The favoured bait options are

  - Cut fish

  - Prawns

  - Squid

Shore fishers mainly use 60–120 gram sinkers and baits of octopus, squid, pilchards or cut fish flesh, but at dawn, dusk and after heavy seas, excellent fish can be taken close to the rocks on unweighted or lightly-weighted baits called *floaters*. Big snapper also succumb to live baits and occasionally strike lures and particularly jigs.

Supping on snapper

While anglers in various regions may call snapper by a range of names and use different methods to catch these fish, everyone agrees on one subject and that's the rating of this fish in the culinary department!

Snapper are highly regarded as food fish. These fish have white, moist and slightly flaky flesh, occasionally tending towards dryness in larger specimens. Snapper also freeze well and lose little of their flavour or texture if frozen soon after being caught and eaten within a month or two.

Tasty Tailor

The fish called tailor in Australia is found in many parts of the world and has different names in various places. In the United States, tailor are called bluefish, while in South Africa the same fish is known as elf or shad. Locally, anglers occasionally incorrectly spell the fish as tailer or even taylor and the species also has a number of nicknames including chopper and green back. Just to confuse the issue even further, in Victoria, tailor are sometimes called skipjack or skippies, while in Western Australia, a skippy is a silver trevally. (I told you the fish name game is confusing!)

The tailor is a mid-sized, highly predatory schooling fish with a relatively elongated body, a forked tail and a large mouth lined with fairly small, but very sharp, teeth (see Figure 2-7). Typical tailor are green to greenish-blue through to slate grey or gunmetal grey on the back, silver on the flanks and silvery-white on the belly. The fins vary in colour, but the tail is usually darker, often with a black trailing edge.

The majority of tailor caught in Australia weigh from around 200 grams to 2 kilos. Small schools of much bigger fish, in the 2–5 kilo range, are encountered in a few areas, while outsize tailor, which are often caught further offshore than their smaller brethren, may weigh as much as 6–9 kilos on rare occasions.

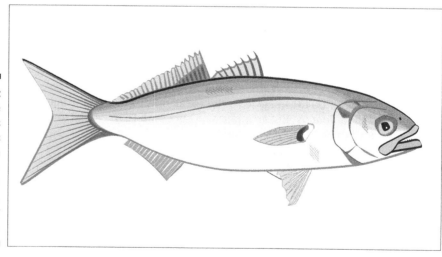

Figure 2-7: Tailor are voracious predators often encountered in large, hungry schools.

Sew simple if you know how!

In Australia, tailor are found in temperate and sub-tropical waters. The fish are most prolific on the east coast between Wilsons Promontory and Fraser Island and in the west from Albany to Exmouth. Tailor also occur sporadically along the southern seaboard, including parts of South Australia and western Victoria, but are uncommon in Tasmania. Rather surprisingly, considering their international distribution, tailor do not occur in New Zealand waters.

Tailor make use of a wide range of habitats from the upper, almost fresh reaches of estuaries, through bays, harbours and inlets to inshore waters, shallow reefs, islands and even out to the edge of the continental shelf.

A good indication of the location of schools of feeding tailor is the presence of wheeling, diving, squawking seagulls, terns, mutton-birds and gannets. These sea birds gather to feed on the scraps left when tailor rip into small fry with their razor sharp teeth, leaving plenty of floating scraps for the birds. Cast your line near the birds and success is almost sure to be yours.

Tailor are caught in a variety of ways, but one of the most productive techniques is to cast and slowly retrieve unweighted or very lightly-weighted pilchards and garfish rigged on ganged or linked hooks (I explain these hooks in Chapter 4). These rigs can also be used under *bobby cork* floats (described in Chapter 7) or with heavier sinkers when casting distance is required, particularly from the beach.

Other types of bait that are sure to lure in the tailor are fish flesh strips and small live baits.

Tailor are one of the most common lure-caught fish in Australian waters. The fish strike at a wide range of cast-and-retrieved or trolled lures and flies. A light *wire trace* (a piece of wire set between the hook and the line) is helpful to resist the tailor's razor sharp teeth (I explain traces and how to use these bits of wire in Chapter 7).

Fresh is best

Freshly caught tailor are quite tasty, although their soft, slightly grey meat bruises easily and doesn't freeze well. Tailor flesh is mildly flavoured, flaky and somewhat oily and is ideally suited to smoking.

All tailor destined for the table must be killed and bled as soon as the fish are landed (I describe how to do this in Chapter 16), and cleaned within an hour or two of capture. If you're unable to do this, simply unhook the fish (being careful of those razor sharp teeth!) and give the critter his or her freedom.

Trevally Treats

Trevally are yet another large family of fish rather than a single species and the representatives of this fishy tribe range from big brutes such as the aptly-named giant trevally of Australia's tropical waters to the more manageable silver trevally of the southern latitudes (see Figure 2-8).

Rather than cover each type of trevally found in Australasian waters, I'm going to concentrate on the silver trevally because this fish is found close to Australia's large population centres and is a popular angling species. It is also the only trevally species common in New Zealand. Having said that, most of the information given here about silver trevally is applicable to the fish's northern cousins.

The silver trevally is also known as white trevally, skipjack or skippy — the last being most used in Western Australia. One of the silver trevally's popular nicknames is blurter, which refers to the grunting noise made by freshly caught specimens. Trevally are also incorrectly referred to as silver bream in a number of areas. Trevally also have a number of regional Maori names in New Zealand, including arara.

Silver trevally are deep-bodied, laterally compressed fish with a relatively small, toothless mouth and rubbery lips. The fish are typically dark grey to blue-green on the back, silvery with a blue or purple sheen on the flanks and silvery-white on the belly. A yellow, longitudinal stripe running along the flanks is often seen on freshly caught trevally.

Figure 2-8: The silver trevally is a popular, hard-fighting fish, being common in many parts of Australia and New Zealand.

Prize fighters

Silver trevally caught by anglers typically run at 200 grams to 2.5 kilos, although bigger fish are occasionally encountered. Silver trevally over 6 kilos are exceptional, but specimens in excess of 10 kilos have been reported in offshore locations such as Lord Howe Island.

These hard-fighting, attractive fish live mostly in Australia's temperate and cool southern waters, ranging from around Gladstone in southern Queensland to about Geraldton or Shark Bay in Western Australia. The fish can also be found in Tasmania and New Zealand, being more common in the north of that country. The trevally's chosen habitat ranges from estuaries and bays to beaches, rocky shorelines, inshore reefs and offshore sand, mud and gravel patches.

You can catch silver trevally mainly with

- ✔ Cut fish flesh strips

- ✔ Small whole fish such as anchovies, whitebait and pilchards

- ✔ Whole or cut squid, prawns, yabbies (nippers), crabs and cunjevoi baits

These baits are best presented on unweighted or very lightly-weighted rigs (I describe these types of rigs in Chapter 12). You can also occasionally catch silver trevally on lures and flies.

Like so many other fish, trevally respond well to a berley trail of soaked bread or special berley pellets mixed with minced fish, bait scraps and tuna oil and then dispersed in the area where you plan to fish (I explain how to do this in Chapter 8).

Raw deal

The flavour of cooked silver trevally is fair to good with the tastiest being small, fresh specimens. The bigger trevally have a rather strong flavour and a dry flesh, occasionally infested with parasitic worms. The flesh sometimes has unusual air spaces or 'bubbles', especially along the backbone.

Silver trevally meat is fine cooked, but is also delicious eaten raw as *sashimi* (thin, bite-sized slices of raw fish often served with a spicy wasabi and soy sauce) or in *sushi* (small pieces of raw fish wrapped in sticky rice and sheets of prepared seaweed, and cut into small, bite-size lengths).

Terrific Tuna

If you're preparing those Japanese delicacies sushi and sashimi (see previous section), the acknowledged champions definitely belong to the tuna family. This large tribe of open ocean fish is well represented in Australasian waters, with the most common and sought-after types being the southern bluefin, yellowfin (see Figure 2-9), longtail, striped (skipjack), albacore and mackerel tunas. The closely allied bonito are not really tuna at all, but are similar enough in fishing terms to be looked at under the same heading.

The larger tuna species — especially the yellowfin and southern bluefin — are genuine heavyweights and both grow to well over 100 kilos and around 2 metres in length. That's right — longer than you are tall! The Central Pacific bluefin encountered off the west coast of New Zealand's South Island grows even larger and can top 300 kilos.

These bigger tuna are man-sized (or woman-sized) fish in every sense, and tackling these brutes on a rod and reel isn't for the faint-hearted or unprepared. Tuna are genuine game fish and demand heavy, expensive tackle. However, smaller tuna and bonito are definitely within the reach of less experienced anglers using the sort of fishing gear that can be found in most garages and back sheds around the country. (Chapters 4 through 8 answer your needs to do with fishing tackle.)

Figure 2-9:
The yellowfin is one of the biggest tuna found in Australasia's waters and can top 100 kilos.

Fast food

While the different species of tuna vary quite a bit in appearance, the fish share thickset, cylindrical bodies and short fins.

The canary-coloured second dorsal and anal fins of the yellowfin tuna become long and sickle-shaped in large adults. (You can check out the basic placement of tuna fins in Chapter 1.)

Many of the tuna's fins fold flat against the beast's body or even disappear completely into recesses to streamline the fish for swimming at top speed — a habit of all tuna. In fact, these fish are the dragsters of the fish world.

Most tuna are dark blue to gunmetal black on the upper back, metallic silver on the flanks and silvery-white below. A number of varieties such as the mackerel tuna and skipjack (striped tuna) have distinct wavy lines, bars, spots or longitudinal stripes on the backs or bellies.

Deep and meaningful

You can usually find tuna in deeper, ocean waters, but the fish occasionally venture close to shore and even enter bays, harbours and large estuary mouths. While most are caught from boats, a number of specific locations around the Australian and New Zealand coastline that have deep water close to the shore allow land-based anglers to hook tuna from rock ledges, wharves and breakwaters.

The usual method to catch tuna is trolling — dragging a bait or lure behind a moving boat — although the fish can also be cast and retrieved or fished from a drifting or anchored boat or from the shore.

Tuna have pink to dark red meat with a relatively high content of oil. All tuna destined for the table must be killed with a solid blow to the head immediately after being brought aboard and bled by severing one or more arteries (I explain how to do this in Chapter 16). The carcass needs to be cooled as quickly as possible using ice or an iced *brine slurry* (a mixture of ice and saltwater, which I explain in Chapter 16), before being eaten fresh or quickly frozen for future consumption.

Wonderful Whiting

As a group or family of fish, whiting are right up there alongside bream and flathead as Australia's favourite 'bread and butter' fish. Whiting are fun to catch, abundant, widely distributed and delicious to eat. No wonder these little fish are so popular!

The dozen or so species of whiting in Australia can be divided into two distinct camps — the King George or spotted whiting of Australia's southern waters and all the rest. The rest actually consist of several types of sand, yellowfin (see Figure 2-10), silver, diver, trumpeter and school whiting. The King George, however, is the unchallenged monarch of the whiting realm in every way.

The King George (which is also known as KG) whiting grow much larger than the fish's cousins and have been recorded at weights in excess of 2 kilos and lengths over 60 centimetres. This size is significant when you consider that 500 grams and 40 centimetres is very big for most of the other whiting breeds.

All the common whiting varieties have a long, cylindrical body and a conical snout with a fairly small, underslung mouth. The sand, school, silver and yellowfin whiting are mostly greenish or yellowish on the back with very silvery flanks, white bellies and yellow lower fins. By contrast, the King George whiting is golden-yellow to light brown to green on the back, silvery-gold on the flanks and silvery-white on the belly with numerous distinct spots of darker brown, ochre or brick red all over the fish's upper body.

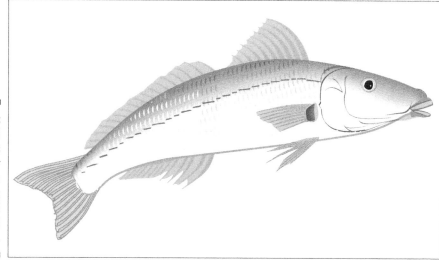

Figure 2-10: Several varieties of sand or yellowfin whiting are found around Australia.

Shallow-minded

While sand, school and yellowfin whiting are found in coastal waters, along beaches and in estuaries right around Australia, King George whiting are confined to Australia's cooler southern seas from the far south coast of New South Wales to about Geraldton in Western Australia. You can also occasionally find King George whiting in parts of northern Tasmania and around the islands of Bass Strait. These major whiting species are not found in New Zealand waters.

Whiting are most prolific in estuaries, bays, harbours and shallower coastal areas with sand, mud or fine gravel bottom strata, often adjacent to weed or sea-grass beds in waters less than 10–15 metres deep (and often much shallower than that). The larger King George whiting are sometimes caught from considerably deeper water near reefs.

Both King George whiting and the various sand, school and yellowfin whiting respond best to the following fresh, natural baits:

- Clams
- Cockles
- Marine worms
- Mussels
- Pink nippers (yabbies)
- Pipis
- Prawns

Larger fish are often taken on squid pieces and occasionally succumb to strips of fish flesh or even pilchards and pilchard pieces. More rarely, a whiting is willing to grab a small lure or fly worked near the seabed.

To catch whiting, choose light and sensitive tackles, much the same as that used for bream. In general, sinkers need to be as light as possible. The fish often respond well to a slow-moving bait.

Right royal repast

The King George whiting is a superb food fish and is regularly listed as being the best table fish to be found in Australian waters.

Smaller sand, school, yellowfin and trumpeter varieties of whiting also have delicate, sweet flesh and are held in high esteem by many seafood fanciers. However, fine bones can be a problem when eating smaller whiting and care must be taken to remove as many of the bones as possible during the cleaning process (I explain the best ways to do this in Chapter 16).

Chapter 3
Our Favourite Freshwater Fish

A ustralia and New Zealand have an abundance of rivers and lakes where anglers can fish for a large variety of freshwater fish from the shore or a boat. The 2,000 or so fish species that can be caught in Australasian waters include hundreds of freshwater species. In this chapter, I describe six of the most popular and readily caught freshwater fish and how to lure these fish onto your hook and then prepare the catch for your plate.

The techniques and gear used to catch these fish can easily be transferred to other species that have a similar size range and behaviour pattern.

Bagging a Barramundi

Barramundi may be first on my Australian freshwater fish list but, in fact, the species is actually only a part-time inhabitant of freshwater. The mighty barramundi needs access to both fresh and saline water to complete the fish's complex life cycle because barramundi are spawned in brackish or salt water and then go on to spend a significant part of their lives upstream in freshwater.

The barramundi — or barra as the fish are more widely known — is a handsome fish with big scales, a large mouth, humped shoulders, a deeply-scooped or concave forehead profile and close-set eyes that shine ruby-red in artificial light or with certain angles of sunlight (see Figure 3-1).

Figure 3-1:
Barramundi
are one of
Australia's
most
famous
and keenly
sought after
sport and
table fish.

The colouration of individual barramundi varies considerably depending on the environment. Freshwater-dwelling barra — particularly those from land-locked billabongs — are usually dark bronze or gold to chocolate brown on the back, with brassy flanks and very dark fins and black tails. At the opposite extreme, saltwater barra from tidal waters appear to wear suits of chrome-plated armour. Each scale is a metallic mirror and the fish has very little pigmentation apart from a mauve or purple sheen along the upper back. The fins of these saltwater-dwelling barra are light in colour and the tail is often tinged with yellow.

Barra backyards

Exceptionally large barramundi in excess of 100 kilos have reputedly been taken in nets in India's Bay of Bengal and chances are that Australian waters once held a few monsters of 60 kilos and more but, today, finding specimens over 30 kilos is rare. Fortunately, this situation may change due to the stocking of an increasing amount of barramundi in man-made lakes, such as Tinaroo, on the Atherton Tablelands above Cairns and Awoonga, near Gladstone. In most places, however, the barra encountered by anglers weigh between 1 kilo and 15 kilos and measure up to 1 metre in length.

In Australia, barramundi range from the Mary River system in southern central Queensland to the Exmouth Gulf in Western Australia, although the fish aren't common at the extremities of these areas. Barramundi are found in their biggest numbers on Cape York Peninsula, through the Gulf of Carpentaria, across the top of the Northern Territory and in the Kimberley. Sadly, the waters of New Zealand are too cool to sustain barra, so Kiwis with a penchant for catching a barra need to cross the ditch.

Barra occupy a wide range of aquatic environments from the inshore waters around rocky headlands and shore-fringing reefs or islands upstream through tidal estuaries and into freshwater creeks and rivers, billabongs and waterholes. The fish frequently inhabit isolated bodies of water that remain cut off from main river systems or estuaries for years or even decades at a time.

Best baits

One of the most exciting and popular ways to fish for barramundi is by casting and retrieving artificial lures or flies around snags, mangrove roots, rock bars, fallen trees and other cover or structures, as well as in creek junctions and gutter inflows. This method accounts for a large percentage of the fish taken each year, however, at certain times, slow- to medium-paced trolling with lures behind a moving boat or fishing with live and dead baits produces more and larger fish than casting.

Natural baits work well on barramundi, and the best baits to use to catch a barra include:

- Live cherabin (a giant freshwater shrimp)
- Live prawns
- Small live mullet

These baits may be cast or drifted on unweighted or lightly-weighted lines rigged with a small sinker, or suspended beneath a cork or float, depending on the terrain, water depth and strength of current. Barra are occasionally also taken using fresh dead baits. (I talk more about baits and lures in Chapter 8.)

The barramundi has a reputation as one of Australia's finest eating fish — and a market price to match. Many people argue that this reputation is overrated, but a fillet of saltwater barra or tidal river barramundi cooked with style (see Chapter 16 for more on cooking your catch) is certainly hard to beat. The saltwater barra's meat is white, firm, fine-grained and delicious. Barramundi that have spent weeks, months or even years in turbid, muddy billabongs are another story, however, and the flesh of these freshwater barra can range from tasty to inedible. For this reason, many sport anglers choose to release the majority of their barra catch.

Male-order brides

Many common fish species are capable of changing sex. For example, barramundi are born as males and only those that live long enough and grow to a certain size undergo the transformation into females.

A number of species do the gender swap the other way around. For example, blue groper, baldchin groper and a number of the members of the wrasse clan are born female. Most schools of these gregarious reef-dwelling fish have just a single large and brightly coloured male lording it over a harem of smaller and less brightly-coloured females.

In the case that the dominant male dies or is caught, the largest female in the school changes colour and develops fully functioning male sex organs within a surprisingly short span of time — often just days or weeks!

These unusual sexual strategies are important survival mechanisms for fish populations, allowing the fish to cope surprisingly well with depleted food supplies, increased predation and other natural or unnatural phenomena in their watery worlds.

Banking on Bass

The Australian bass is another fish that's equally at home in both fresh and saltwater and needs access to saline areas to reproduce, but most of the fish's life is spent in the freshwater reaches of coastal rivers.

Once better known by the generic name of perch and often confused with other fish sharing that label, bass are now treated with enormous respect by serious anglers and given the recognition as a distinctive species the fish clearly deserve.

This relatively small native fish occurs naturally in the fresh and brackish reaches of coastal rivers from south-eastern Queensland to the Gippsland region of Victoria, but has also been introduced into many man-made lakes, where the bass lives and thrives, but can't reproduce.

Bass are deep-bodied fish with moderately large scales, big dark eyes, a scooped forehead profile and a generous mouth (see Figure 3-2). Their colouring varies depending on the environment these fish inhabit. A number of the critters may be almost black on the back, with dark bronze or gold flanks and a creamy belly tinged with yellow, while others are bright coppery-gold on the back with silvery bellies. Still others are completely silvery with a green upper back.

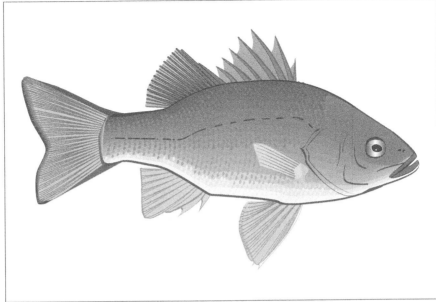

Figure 3-2: The Australian bass is a wonderful sport fish keenly targeted by many anglers in the south-eastern part of Australia.

Little Aussie battlers

Most bass caught in rivers weigh in at 200 grams to 1 kilo. While stocked lakes are nowadays producing the occasional larger specimens — up to 3 kilos and even 4 kilos — these huge bass remain rare. Despite this, what most bass lack in size, the fish more than make up for in sheer fighting spirit when hooked.

Traditionally, bass or perch were taken on baits of live black crickets, grasshoppers, cicadas or shrimps, which were often dangled or *dapped* onto the surface of the water close to the bank. Practitioners of this style of fishing often used a long cane pole with the line fixed directly to the end, rather than a rod and reel. This crude but effective set-up was known as a *Ned Kelly rig*.

Bass respond enthusiastically to the following live baits:

- ✔ Cicadas
- ✔ Crickets
- ✔ Earthworms
- ✔ Shrimps

However, most sport anglers prefer to cast and retrieve lures off a light, single-handed spin or baitcaster (plug) outfit or to throw artificial flies on Nos 5–9 weight fly outfits (I detail this gear in Chapter 5 and Chapter 6).

Lure and fly casting is generally considered to be more exciting and challenging than bait fishing for bass and, as a bonus, most fish caught with a lure or fly are hooked cleanly in the mouth, meaning the fish can be released without undue injury. (For more on releasing fish with care, see Chapter 15.)

Bass class

Bass from clean, flowing water make good to excellent table fish, rating among the tastiest of Australia's freshwater species. Specimens from muddy lake waters may be slightly less palatable, but are certainly still edible.

Despite the favourable eating qualities of Australian bass, modern sport fishers increasingly choose to release bass in recognition of the fact that the species has been reduced in numbers and the fish's habitat has been degraded over recent years. As a result, strict bag and size limits for bass are in force in most areas and you need to check these limits carefully before killing and keeping any bass (see Chapter 26).

Searching for Golden Perch

The golden perch is better known in outback New South Wales and Queensland as a yellowbelly and in South Australia and parts of Victoria as a callop. The fish is also sold in a number of fish shops under the name Murray perch.

The golden perch or yellowbelly is a real inland favourite for anglers (see Figure 3-3). The fish is a relatively large freshwater perch with a convex or outward-curving tail and a strongly scooped forehead profile. The fish's body ranges in colour from a handsome coppery-bronze with green reflections in clear water, though to pale, yellowish-white in muddy locations. Golden perch are sometimes very faintly barred or irregularly speckled, especially in clear water. The fish's underbelly is usually creamy-yellow, but may sometimes be a much brighter lemon-yellow, hence the fish's name.

Figure 3-3:
Golden
perch or
yellowbelly
are a
popular
freshwater
fishing
target
throughout
a huge slice
of inland
Australia.

Most golden perch taken by anglers weigh from 200 grams to 3 kilos, although in a number of lakes and dams, hump-shouldered specimens from 4 to 7 kilos are encountered on a reasonably regular basis.

Outback survivors

The golden perch is the most widespread and prolific of Australia's large inland native fish, occurring naturally in four states and both territories. The fish's original range encompassed most of the Murray and Darling River system, excluding the highest sub-alpine headwaters. Golden perch also occur naturally in the Dawson and Fitzroy drainage areas of central Queensland and Lake Eyre and the Coopers Creek system in Australia's arid interior. Golden perch are also found in a number of coastal rivers in northern New South Wales and southern Queensland.

In addition, stocks of these hardy fish have been introduced successfully into many dams and man-made lakes from Townsville to Perth.

Most golden perch or yellowbelly taken by outback anglers are hooked using the following natural baits:

- Bardy grubs
- Earthworms

- Shrimps
- Wood grubs
- Yabbies

These baits work well when presented on or near the riverbed and close to fallen trees and other structures. A willing striker of lures in clearer water, golden perch take a variety of artificial baits and even flies.

Perch on the plate

Many expert anglers rate golden perch as one of Australia's tastier inland native fish, although you need to be a bit choosy about which yellowbelly you eat.

Specimens weighing less than 2 kilos are generally superior in table quality to their larger kin. Also, perch from clean, slightly cooler water taste much better than those from hot, muddy waterholes or dams. A really big golden perch from a muddy, weed-filled lake is generally hardly worth eating and I recommend you give these larger fish their freedom.

Catching Murray Cod

The mighty, almost mythical, Murray cod is definitely Australia's best-known inland species and, as one of the three or four largest freshwater fish to be found anywhere on Earth, that level of fame is well deserved.

Unrelated to the true cod family of the Northern Hemisphere, old Murray is actually a distant member of the perch tribe, which makes the fish a second cousin of the golden perch (refer to the previous section) and Australian bass (refer to the section 'Banking on Bass', earlier in this chapter).

The Murray cod is robust and barrel-shaped with a cavernous mouth and small eyes set well forward (see Figure 3-4). The fish's colour varies considerably, depending on the cod's environment. Having said that, the majority of Murray cod are olive-green to yellow-green on the back, yellowish on the flanks and creamy-yellow or white on the belly. The back is overlaid with darker green or brownish mottling, which extends well down the flanks. The eyes are usually brown. The cod's second dorsal fin, ventral fin and tail ordinarily have white margins or edges.

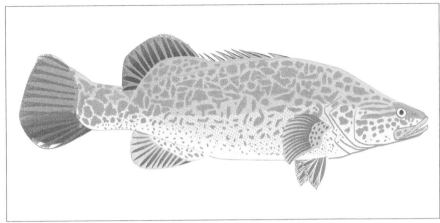

Figure 3-4:
The Murray
cod is
Australia's
largest
freshwater
fish.

Land of the giants

The Murray cod has the potential to reach more than 100 kilos in weight, but many decades have passed since specimens approaching that size have been recorded. Today, any cod over 40 kilos is considered to be a large fish indeed and most of those seen by anglers weigh from 500 grams to 10 kilos, with a few 10–40-kilo specimens still taken each year.

Native to the Australian outback, Murray cod were once found throughout most of the Murray and Darling Basin, with the exception of the cold, sub-alpine headwaters. Dam and weir construction, de-snagging (pulling out snags like fallen trees to improve river flow), pollution and over-fishing have reduced the species' range. Fortunately, cod are still present in reduced numbers throughout most of the fish's traditional habitat. Murray cod have also been introduced into many dams and reportedly have been introduced into a number of eastern flowing coastal rivers.

Traditionally, Murray cod were taken on heavy *set-lines* (strong lengths of line tied to trees or to sticks driven into the bank). The cod were baited with yabbies, whole fish, rabbit carcasses or even galah (parrot) breasts or pieces of kangaroo meat. Today, set-lines are illegal in most areas and anglers have come to appreciate the sporting qualities of these fine fish. Murray cod are more often sought on medium or even lightweight tackle baited with the following live baits:

- Bardy grubs
- Shrimp
- Worms
- Yabbies

Murray cod respond actively to lures, especially in clearer water. A slow, steady retrieve or walking-pace troll behind a moving boat is best when lure fishing.

Let them go, let them grow

Murray cod are regarded as one of Australia's most delicious outback table fish. The flavour of smaller cod is excellent, especially those taken from clearer streams. However, the fish tend to be rather oily or fatty at weights around 10–20 kilos and fish from very dirty water may have a distinct muddy taint to their flesh.

In recognition of the fish's increasing scarcity and slow growth rates, many sport fishers release most cod, keeping only the occasional fish for the table. In many areas, Murray cod are protected during spawning by a closed season that usually runs from September until the end of November.

Seeing whether the Trout Are About

Although trout are one of Australasia's best-known freshwater fish, the slippery critters aren't native to this part of the world. Instead, trout were introduced from the Northern Hemisphere during the 1800s and have thrived in a number of the cooler Australian rivers, creeks and lakes as well as in large areas of New Zealand.

Two species dominate trout populations in Australia and New Zealand — the North American rainbow trout and the European or British brown trout. While similar in appearance and habits, these species actually have quite different personalities (if I can be forgiven for using such an anthropomorphic term to refer to fish!). The rainbow, as befits the fish's Californian origins, is loud, brash and often reckless in nature. By contrast, the thoroughly British brown is a much more subdued, reserved and genteel fish.

Both the rainbow and the brown trout (see Figure 3-5) are characterised by relatively elongated bodies, a single, soft dorsal fin, a fleshy *adipose* fin (a small, meaty protuberance between the dorsal fin and tail) and the placement of the ventral fins well back on the belly. Take a look in Chapter 1 to get an idea of where these fins are located.

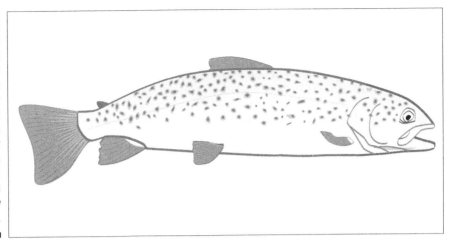

Figure 3-5:
Brown trout have proven to be extremely successful immigrants in the cooler Australian waters and also thrive in New Zealand.

Brown trout have a relatively large mouth and a squared off or slightly forked tail that either lacks spots or has a small number of relatively large spots along the upper edge. Brown trout are usually olive-green to dark brown on the back and flanks and cream or creamy-white on the belly. This base colour is overlaid with black and red spots, often with a lighter halo around each spot. The gill covers have large, widely-spaced spots.

In contrast, the rainbow trout has a slightly smaller mouth than the brown trout, and the fish's tail is usually a little more forked and is covered with small, dark spots. Most Aussie and Kiwi rainbow trout are olive-green to deep, steely-blue on the back, silvery on the flanks and silvery-white underneath. The back and flanks are overlaid with a thick peppering of dark spots and many rainbows have a bright crimson or pink slash along the flanks and gill covers, although this slash may be vague at times. As with all members of the trout family, these colours intensify during the spawning season (winter and spring for rainbows, autumn and winter for browns). *Note:* A closed season is in place for trout angling in many waters at these times. Always check your local rules and regulations before casting a line (see Chapter 26).

Trout and about

In their native Northern Hemisphere waters, both brown and rainbow trout have been known to reach weights of up to 20 kilos. Here in Australia and New Zealand, most trout caught by anglers weigh from 200 grams to 3 kilos, with record-breaking fish (particularly browns) occasionally approaching the 10-kilo mark.

In Australia, trout prefer cool, clean rivers, creeks, lakes and dams mainly in alpine and sub-alpine areas. The fish's distribution in mainland Australia is limited to the higher, cooler areas of New South Wales, Victoria, the Australian Capital Territory, South Australia and southern Western Australia. Both species are much more widespread and prolific in Tasmania and on both islands of New Zealand, although only in very isolated pockets north of Auckland. Brown trout have been especially successful immigrants in many of these regions and viable, self-supporting or wild populations now exist in a number of areas.

You can usually catch trout on light tackle and fairly fine lines baited with the following:

- Earthworms
- Grubs
- Insects and insect larvae, such as mudeyes (dragonfly larvae)
- Shrimps

Baits are best float-suspended or very lightly weighted, rather than anchored to the bottom and smallish hooks tend to work best. However, always check first to see whether bait fishing is allowed where you're fishing for trout, because some areas (especially in New Zealand) are designated as lure-and-fly-only or, even, fly-only waters (see Chapter 26).

Trout respond well to lures — you can cast and retrieve from the shoreline of a lake or river or slowly troll behind a moving boat. Trout are also ideally suited to fly fishing — a technique that originated many centuries ago in Eastern Europe with this group of fish as the primary target.

Swish fish dish

Trout are widely regarded as good or even excellent table fare, although a few specimens tend to be a little dry, while others have a slightly muddy taint.

Trout flesh varies from white or pale pink to bright orange or even red, depending on the individual fish's diet. The more strongly-coloured orange or red flesh is generally the tastiest and most sought-after. Trout flesh is ideally suited to being smoked, pickled or sugar-and-salt cured as *gravlax*, a traditional Northern European dish.

Finding Freshwater Salmon

A couple of species of true salmon from the Northern Hemisphere have been trans-located to our Antipodean waters, with mixed success. The two most important varieties are the Atlantic salmon and the chinook or quinnat salmon. Of these, the chinook or quinnat has had the greatest impact on Australasian angling.

In the chinook salmon's native waters, which stretch around the rim of the Northern Pacific basin from Japan, China and Eastern Siberia to Alaska, Canada and as far south as northern California, on the American west coast, these impressive salmon are the largest of all the migratory salmonid (trout/salmon) species, occasionally approaching 50 kilos and regularly topping 15 kilos. Salmon in Australasian waters are usually much smaller, but 20-kilo specimens have been recorded in New Zealand.

These true salmon look a lot like a big trout, but have a more deeply-forked tail, smaller eyes, a very large mouth, a dense peppering of small, dark spots on their upper body and a black lining inside the mouth. The chinook's colouration is typically metallic silver with a green or steel-blue back and dark spots (see Figure 3-6), but mature salmon become very dark all over as they approach their biologically-programmed spawning time (usually in autumn or early-winter).

Figure 3-6: Chinook (quinnat) salmon, originally transplants from North America, are now self-sustaining in New Zealand's South Island.

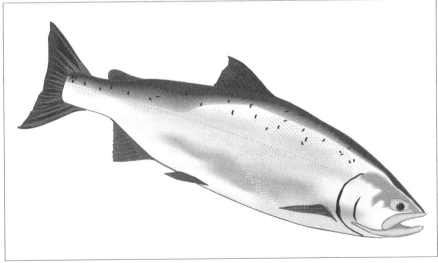

To complete their life cycle, chinook salmon must migrate from the rivers of their birth into the open ocean to grow and feed for three to five years before returning to the very stream where they were spawned in order to re-start that cycle.

Introduced chinook salmon are established and able to complete this circle of life in only one place on Earth outside the natural range of the species — around the South Island of New Zealand, where they're almost always called quinnat salmon. Here (particularly on the east coast of the South Island), the salmon grow to maturity in coastal waters before ascending major rivers to spawn and die. Established salmon *runs* or spawning migrations are present in many South Island rivers and although most of these runs require top-ups from time to time with hatchery-bred fingerlings, a few are very close to being self-sustaining.

Elsewhere in Australasia, land-locked, non-breeding populations of usually much smaller chinook or quinnat salmon occur only as put-and-take stocks in a few Victorian lakes.

Desperately seeking salmon

Chinook or quinnat salmon respond to many of the same fishing techniques as trout, with a greater emphasis on the use of metal spinners, spoons and jigs or large wet (subsurface) flies, all of which are described in Part III.

When salmon are feeding on small fish, prawns, squid and other organisms in the ocean, bays and harbours, these fish can often strike aggressively at lures or (less frequently) take natural baits such as pilchards or cut fish pieces. However, as soon as salmon head upstream on their late-summer and autumn spawning runs, these predators effectively cease feeding and only strike rather reluctantly (and perhaps from instinctive habit) at lures or flies that are presented right across their fishy noses.

The most effective way to catch spawn-run quinnat salmon is to cast a relatively heavy spinner, spoon or sliced metal lure up and across the current flow in the river and bring the lure back just slightly faster than the speed of the water's flow, keeping this offering as close as possible to the river bed without constantly hanging it up or snagging ... not always an easy task! Many, many casts and retrieves may be required before a salmon throws caution to the wind and grabs your lure, but the wait is worthwhile when you finally connect with that big, silvery torpedo of a fish!

To die for

Sadly, life is short for chinook salmon. Following a year or so in the stream of their birth, these fast-growing fish move downstream into the ocean, migrating up and down along the coast or well out to sea and feeding ravenously for three to five years before ascending their home river to complete their brief but intense life cycle.

After spawning on shallow gravel beds well upstream, usually in late-March, April or May (at least here in the Southern Hemisphere), all adult quinnat salmon die within a few days or, at most, weeks. Their decaying carcasses line the banks of some of these spawning rivers by early-winter.

When mature salmon enter the lower estuaries in February or March, they're typically bright, metallic silver and their flesh is a delectable orange colour. At this time, salmon make superb table fare. However, as they forge their way upstream over the following weeks, their scales darken, their fins become ragged and their flesh softens and loses some of its orange intensity and accompanying flavour.

Fresh-run quinnats newly arrived from the sea are superb fighters and highly rated for their edible qualities. Both aspects suffer over the following weeks, and by the time the legal salmon fishing season closes (a date which varies from area to area or even between rivers) these once mighty fish may not be worth either catching or eating. So, intercept your salmon early in the lower reaches of these rivers. And then you're in for a major treat!

Part II
Tackling the Right Gear

Glenn Lumsden

'And I'll need a bottle of wine. Preferably something that goes with fish.'

In this part . . .

*I*n many ways, this part is the most important part of the whole book because it looks at the equipment you need to catch fish. If you're an accomplished angler, you may find a few of the sections in this part overly simplistic, but I do hope you read through the information anyway (or at least scan these chapters), because you're sure to find a few new and useful tidbits. On the other hand, if you're a beginner to fishing, every section includes information that's sure to set you on a successful angling path. Chapter 5 is suited to novice and accomplished anglers because this chapter looks at the all-important rod and includes a section that may well answer any questions you have about choosing the correct tackle for various forms of angling.

Chapter 4

On a Hook and a Line

In This Chapter

▶ Getting the point about hooks

▶ Lining up the best fishing line

*T*he purest form of fishing is a simple business. To catch a fish, all you need is a length of line with a hook attached at one end. Sure, a bit of bait on the hook helps, as does having a reel to store your line and a stick or rod to control the rig, but none of these items is truly essential.

Anglers in ancient times had no choice but to keep fishing rigs simple. Centuries ago, lines were fashioned by plaiting vines or rolling or plaiting plant fibres, animal hairs and the like. At the end of the line, the ancient anglers lashed a piece of bone, a splinter of fire-hardened wood or a shard of stone. This device, called a *gorge*, was intended to jam inside the mouth of any fish silly enough to bite the gorge and hold on for long enough. In many cases, bait was unnecessary, especially if the gorge was jiggled about to imitate a living, kicking critter (obviously, fish were pretty dumb in those days!).

In time, anglers of old worked out that pieces of sea shell made the most successful gorges and rudimentary lures, thanks to the shells' shiny colours. Your smarter-than-average primitive fishermen realised that a curved or bent piece of broken shell was more likely to catch in the mouth of a fish. The fish hook was born!

Interestingly, the olde English name for this fancy bent or curved gorge was *angle* (see Figure 4-1), hence the name of the sport today — angling. Now, that's a wonderful piece of trivia you can use to dazzle your friends!

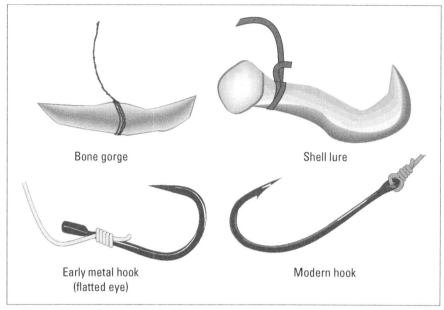

Bone gorge

Shell lure

Early metal hook
(flatted eye)

Modern hook

Figure 4-1:
The
evolution
of the fish
hook.

Looking at Hooks

A lot of water has flowed under the metaphorical bridge since our Neanderthal whiz kid fashioned the first crude, curved lure from a shiny sliver of shell and out-fished everyone else in the village. With the coming of the various metal ages, making strong, sharp angles or hooks became easier and, for centuries now, metal has been the accepted material for making fish hooks.

Line has also advanced far beyond woven vines and plaited horsehair, but the overall concept remains unchanged and any modern kid with a length of string and a bent pin is closely emulating our ancient ancestors.

Keeping an eye on the basics

Most modern fish hooks (see Figure 4-2) have the following easily recognisable parts:

✔ **Eye:** An opening through which to thread and tie the line.

✔ **Barb:** A sharp projection facing in the opposite direction to the point of the hook intended to stop the hook from slipping out once the point has found its mark.

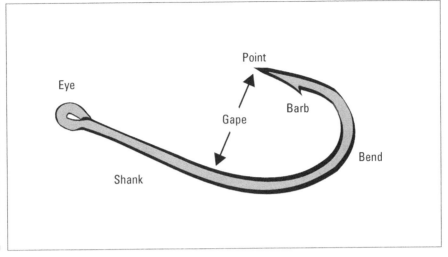

Figure 4-2:
The
anatomy of
a modern
fish hook.
Styles,
shapes and
sizes vary
enormously,
but most
modern
hooks share
the basic
features
shown here.

- **Bend:** The curved or bent section of the hook that gives the hook its distinctive shape.
- **Gap or Gape:** The width between the point of the hook and the shank.
- **Shank:** The stem or shaft of the hook.

The earliest recognisable fish hooks didn't include an eye for attaching the hook to the line. Instead, the most primitive of gorges were simply lashed or bound directly to the end of the line. The next development in the evolution of hooks was the inclusion of a lump, an indent or a flattened section at the top of the shank to provide a more secure connection to the line. (Hooks with flattened or *flatted* shanks and no eyes are still available, but aren't popular in Australia and New Zealand.)

The next evolution was the addition of eyes and barbs and, by this time, fish hooks began to look similar to modern hooks. Ordinarily manufactured by blacksmiths and cottage industry craftsmen, the shapes and styles of hooks varied from place to place, so regional names were often used to describe specific hooks. You can still find hooks with, for example, the English, Scottish and Irish town and county names of Carlisle, O'Shaughnessy, Limerick and Aberdeen.

In the late-1800s, a horseshoe nail manufacturer, O. Mustad and Son of Norway, became the first mass producer of hooks, eventually automating the process. Many people believe that this early hook manufacturer can be blamed for the convoluted sizing system (see the next section) that still applies to fish hooks.

Making sense of the sizing system

Hooks range from tiny little bits of metal intended to catch tiddlers up to giant contraptions that appear to be capable of stopping an ocean-going ship. Every size of hooks has a corresponding number that refers to the width of the gap or gape of the hook rather than the overall dimensions of the hook (refer to Figure 4-2 to remind yourself what the gape is).

The most confusing part of the sizing system is the fact that the smallest hooks have the biggest numbers. For example, a No. 24 hook is a little bigger than the head of a pin, whereas a No. 12 hook is larger and is just about perfect for catching yellowtail, mullet and garfish, while a No. 2 hook is significantly larger again and is excellent for targeting bream and perch.

The seemingly backwards sizing system, with the hook gape increasing as the number describing it decreases, continues until we hit the No. 1 hook, which is a useful, all-purpose size for catching flathead, drummer and trevally in saltwater or bass and yellowbelly in freshwater.

Hooks larger than the No. 1 are described by an ascending series of numbers followed by a slash and a zero. For example, the next size up from a No. 1 is the 1/0, next is the 2/0, next the 3/0 and so on (see Figure 4-3). The biggest hooks — used for catching sharks, marlin and giant tuna — are in the 18/0 to 20/0 range and are big enough to look right at home hanging from the derrick of a crane on a building site.

From ought to nought

As a matter of interest, Australians pronounce the larger hook sizes as *one-oh, two-oh, three-oh* and so on; whereas, in America, the same sizes are called *one-ought, two-ought* and *three-ought* and so on (*ought* being, in theory, an abbreviation of the word *nought*).

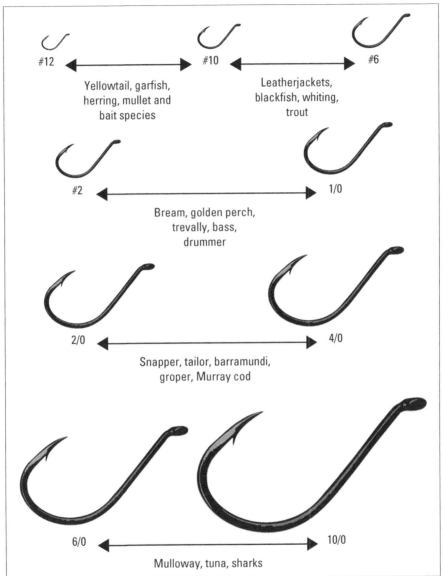

Figure 4-3:
Hooks
ranging in
size from
a No. 12
to 10/0.

Choosing your hook collection

The vast majority of fishing situations encountered by Australian anglers are more than adequately covered by hooks in the range of sizes Nos 12–10/0. Hooks smaller than No. 12 are mainly used by trout fly fishers making imitations of tiny insects or anglers targeting very small fish to use as bait, whereas sizes larger than 10/0 are the sole province of heavy tackle game fishers.

Because the variation in size between each hook number is small, you can easily skip sizes when putting together a basic collection of hooks. The following ten sizes cover the vast majority of popular Australian angling situations: No. 12, No. 10, No. 8, No. 6, No. 4, No. 1, 2/0, 4/0, 6/0 and 8/0. If you only intend to fish in freshwater or in estuaries, bays and harbours, you can also skip the 6/0s and 8/0s.

When buying your first set of hooks, just purchase a small number of hooks in each of the above ten sizes. The next question is which shape or pattern of hook best suits your needs and I deal with this in the next section.

Picking a pattern

The bigger manufacturers of hooks offer catalogues that list thousands of hook patterns, each in dozens of different sizes. To a large extent, however, you can fish successfully using no more than a handful of patterns in about ten different sizes.

Hook patterns differ according to the length of the shank, the thickness of the metal and the shape of the bend, the point, the barb, the eye and the kirb (also called offset). A hook with a *kirb* or *offset* has an *angled point*, meaning that the point isn't in line with the shank and eye. Kirbed or offset points are claimed to offer slightly better hooking efficiency than straight hooks, but there's really not much in it.

Being wise about size

The size of the hook you use is more important than the pattern of the hook, the length of the shank or whether the hook has an upturned or down-turned eye (see the section 'Picking a pattern'). More often than not, bites are missed or fish hooked and lost because the hook was the wrong size.

First, make sure that the size of the hook matches the dimensions of the bait. For example, a small hook carrying a large piece of bait is unlikely to secure a solid hold on a biting fish. On the other hand, a very large hook carrying a small bait looks unnatural and can scare away timid fish.

Second, the size of the hook should match the weight and strength of the tackle, especially the line. For example, it's simply too difficult to set or drive home a large hook when using extremely light line, whereas heavy line is likely to straighten out the curve of a small hook or tear the hook from the fish's mouth before the catch can be landed.

Third, the final consideration is matching the size of the hook to the size of the target fish, but this correlation is actually less important than many people imagine. If this point concerns you, remember that you can catch a big fish on a small hook, but a small fish is unlikely to fall foul of a big hook!

Hooks come in specialist patterns such as *doubles*, *trebles*, *wide gapes*, *bait-holders* and *long shanks*. You can also buy *open-eyed* models for *ganging* or *linking* the hooks together (see Chapter 12). When a specialist hook is required, I point this out in each specific case throughout this book.

For most situations, I recommend you choose from the most popular modern hook patterns, which are the Suicide or Octopus, the Aberdeen, the Carlisle, the French or Viking, the O'Shaughnessy and the Kahle or wide gape hook (see Figure 4-4). Watch out for the fact that different makers of hooks use different names or model numbers to describe similar hook patterns. For example, Mustad calls the wide gape hook a Big Mouth, whereas the Aberdeen shape is occasionally referred to as a *perfect bend*.

Going barbless

These days, some anglers choose to go fishing using hooks that don't have barbs. This approach makes unhooking your catch without injuring the fish (an especially important consideration in *catch-and-release* angling — see Chapter 15) much easier. As a bonus, if you're unlucky enough to get a hook stuck in your own flesh, getting it out is much easier and less painful! A few catch-and-release competitions even stipulate the use of *barbless* hooks by competitors, to enhance the survival prospects of fish returned to the water.

A few companies now offer a limited range of barbless hooks in their vast catalogues, although many anglers create do-it-yourself barbless patterns by crushing the existing barbs flat using a pair of long-nosed pliers.

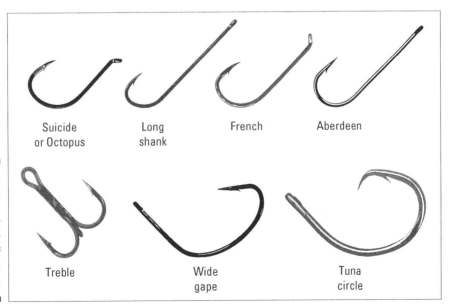

Figure 4-4: A selection of the more popular styles or patterns of hook in use today.

Shop and stock

Hooks come in boxes or packs containing 25, 50 or 100 hooks or in smaller batches of 10, 12 or 20. You can buy hooks individually if you want to have a few hooks in an odd size or unusual pattern, but hooks are generally cheaper per unit when purchased in bulk.

All hooks, including the so-called *stainless* models, rust after prolonged exposure to water and salt air. To minimise rusting, keep your hooks in a watertight container and dispose of rusty hooks immediately by wrapping the hooks in a scrap of aluminium foil or thick plastic (so the hooks don't prick an unsuspecting friend) before tossing these rejects in the garbage.

Note: I recommend you keep bulk boxes of hooks at home, away from the corrosive elements, and give the hooks a light spray of aerosol lubricant before putting the main supply in storage.

Almost certainly you're going to lose a few more fish after hooking up while using barbless hooks, especially if the species involved likes to jump clear of the water and shake its head while on the line (trout and barramundi being two excellent examples). However, you may consider the loss of an occasional hooked fish a relatively small price to pay for the reduction in damage to the fish and — potentially — to your own hide!

One way of reducing the number of fish lost when using barbless hooks is to make every effort to keep a tight line when bringing a fish in and to avoid creating any significant slack in the line.

You don't need to let yourself become bogged down in all the subtleties and nuances of hook shape and style, especially early on in your fishing career. Remember that all hook patterns catch fish and the different bend shapes, shank lengths and wire gauges merely suit various types of bait and target species slightly better than others, which is why so many patterns are available. I recommend you don't worry about all that for now, remembering that I cover most of the specific situations that require a certain style of hook in the various sections of this book.

Sharp-sighted

Many modern fish hooks are marketed with the claim that the hooks have been *chemically sharpened*. This term simply means that the hook has been mechanically ground or sharpened in the normal manner and then etched in a caustic acid bath to remove any imperfections, rough spots or burrs formed during the grinding process. Chemically sharpened hooks are generally much keener when new than traditional, machine-sharpened hooks.

Originally used mostly by fly fishers and specialist freshwater anglers, chemically sharpened hooks are now popular with a wide cross-section of recreational fishers because the hooks work more efficiently with timid fish and hard-jawed species.

Chemically sharpened hooks do cost a little more, but most anglers agree that the extra expense is justified in terms of increased catches.

Learning Your Lines

Although you can catch fish using a piece of string or cotton — and people in remote subsistence cultures still occasionally use woven vines or plaited animal hair lines for landing dinner — chances are that your fishing rig includes bought fishing line, which is available in a wide range of thicknesses and types.

The most popular type of fishing line is made from a plastic known as nylon and is usually called nylon *monofilament* or just *mono*. The word monofilament refers to the fact that the line consists of a single strand of extruded nylon, in contrast to the old-fashioned *multi-strand*, *braided* or *woven* lines such as *cuttyhunk*, *Dacron* and *linen line*.

Although enormously popular, nylon monofilament no longer has a monopoly in the fishing line business. Fancy new extruded plastic formulas such as *co-polymers* and so-called *fluorocarbons* are becoming increasingly popular; and, during the 1980s, an exciting family of multi-strand lines known as *gel-spun polyethylene* or *GSP* lines burst onto the fishing market and revolutionised the recreational angling scene (see Figure 4-5). Today, although still not as widely popular as nylon lines, GSP *super lines* and a range of the fancier nylon derivatives such as fluorocarbons account for a significant and growing share of the fishing line market. The following sections look at the type of line best suited to your needs.

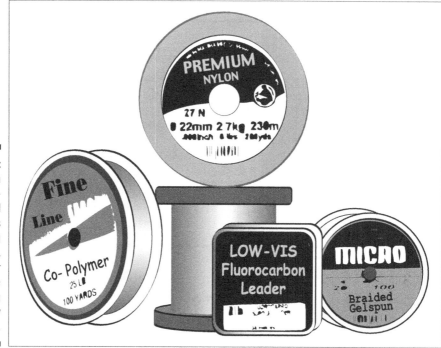

Figure 4-5:
Nylon mono-filament still dominates fishing line sales, but newer varieties are becoming increasingly popular.

Nattering about nylon

The single most important advancement in fishing technology was the advent of reasonably cheap and hard-wearing nylon monofilament line, which came on the market in the middle of the last century.

Modern nylon fishing line is relatively thin (given the line's strength), supple, resilient, fairly stretchy and available in a wide range of colours. Nylon line is ideal for most types of fishing and is reasonably affordable, although the price varies considerably from one brand to another.

For a higher price, you can buy the more advanced nylon-based monofilaments such as the co-polymer lines and fluorocarbons. The makers claim these more advanced lines are harder wearing and less visible to fish than ordinary nylon and, to a certain extent, I believe the claims are true — although you may find it difficult to justify the increased cost for average, day-to-day fishing.

For most forms of fishing, a mid-priced brand of nylon monofilament line is fine, and is ideal for a newcomer to the sport. Pick a variety of line that has a neutral colour (such as green, brown or clear) and is of the finest *diameter* and the lightest *breaking strain* you think you can use for the type of fishing you intend doing. (For more information about line diameter and breaking strain, see the sidebar 'Taking the strain' and the section 'Speaking of strength and length', later in this chapter.)

Gasping over GSP

One of the more significant trends in fishing over the past two decades has been the introduction of *gel-spun polyethylene (GSP)* super lines. The base material for GSP is a polyethylene gel — a fancy plastic polymer — that is spun to realign the carbon atoms and increase the bonding strength of the material. The resulting micro-fibres are then braided or fused together to produce line that's incredibly thin for the strength of the line and that has very little stretch.

This type of line was first available only in a braided configuration, but is now also available in a *heat-fused* or *welded* form widely known as *fusion* line.

When first developed, this very strong, light, low-stretch fibre was used to make protective clothing, rigging for yachts and even string for high-performance kites. Before long, anglers twigged to the huge potential of GSP.

The first GSP fishing lines were braided or twisted together — a slow and expensive process. Later came heat-welded lines, which, although not quite as thin and supple as the braids, are cheaper to produce and easier to handle.

Both kinds of GSP lines — braided and fused — offer significant benefits over nylon in the important area of strength-for-thickness. In fact, GSP lines are up to three times stronger than the best nylon monofilaments of a similar diameter!

Being able to reduce a line's diameter without reducing the strength allows anglers to fit more line on a reel and, as I mentioned earlier, finer lines also suffer less drag from wind or water and are less visible to fish.

In addition, GSP lines stretch less than nylon monofilaments, which can stretch as much as 25 per cent (or even 30 per cent) before breaking. In comparison, the percentage that GSP lines stretch can be measured in single digits, allowing the angler to be more in tune with what's happening to the hook, lure or fly, which in turn leads to better bite detection, faster and harder hook-setting capabilities and increased control over hooked fish.

Taking the strain

The label on a spool of fishing line usually indicates both the line's diameter and the manufacturer's estimation of the line's breaking strain, although sometimes only the breaking strain is displayed.

Breaking strain is the approximate weight a length of the line without knots can support. Many manufacturers undervalue the breaking strain of the line on the label, so you can assume that a length of line with a breaking strain of 4 kilos can withstand 5–6 kilos of strain before snapping — until you tie a knot in it, anyway.

The only major exceptions to this rule are lines that have *pre-test* or *tournament grade* on the label. Pre-test and tournament grade lines are intended to meet the stringent requirements of record-keeping bodies and tournament

committees and are designed to break at, or slightly under, the stated test strength. A pre-test tournament line rated at 4 kilos may actually test out at 3.5 kilos breaking strain, so watch out for the words pre-test and tournament when shopping for line.

You can successfully take on the vast majority of fishing in Australian and New Zealand waters using lines with stated breaking strains 2–25 kilos. When you go shopping for line, remember that, with care, you can land a fish much heavier than the line's rated strength. Lighter, thinner lines have the benefit of being less obvious to the fish and less susceptible to wave and wind action than heavier lines, resulting in more bites and more fish being hooked. My motto is: Fine lines catch more fish.

On the negative side, GSP lines are relatively expensive and tying strong knots in GSP line is a little more difficult than tying similar knots in nylon. Also, although GSP lines stand up well to abrasion against fairly smooth surfaces such as boat hulls and fish bodies, GSP line can be easily cut by contact with sharp edges such as oysters, fish teeth and rock ledges.

GSP lines (both braided and fused) are more successful than nylon monofilament in extremely demanding situations that require minimum stretch and maximum strength for a given diameter. Examples of demanding fishing include:

✔ Bottom fishing in deep water

✔ Lure and bait fishing for hard-fighting fish species

✔ Some types of trolling

Generally, GSP lines aren't especially suitable for beginners in the same way as is nylon line (which is a much more forgiving type of line). For this reason, GSP line is unlikely to completely replace nylon monofilament line or even displace nylon as the top-selling form of fishing line — at least in the foreseeable future. However, the share of the market commanded by GSP line is sure to grow over coming years as more experienced anglers begin to take advantage of the line's unique properties.

Speaking of strength and length

If you're a new chum to the sport or you fish in relatively undemanding conditions, nylon is the best choice of line, but you still need to decide on breaking strain and how much of this line you should buy. As a general rule, select a nylon line with a breaking strain at least two to three times greater than the better-than-average fish you're targeting. In other words, if your quarry is a bream weighing 0.5–1 kilo, try a line in the 2–3 kilo breaking-strain range. (***Note:*** If you do opt to buy GSP line, you can choose an even stronger breaking strain without sacrificing the advantages of a fine diameter.)

Fishing line is typically sold on *spools* containing 100, 125, 250, 300, 500 or 1,000 metres of line. The label on the spool of your reel or the box the reel comes in usually includes data on how much of a particular strength of line you need to correctly fill the reel. You need to buy at least that much line in a single length (see Chapter 10 for details on how to fill your reel with line).

Later in your angling career, you may consider the long-term savings involved in purchasing a bulk spool of 500–1,000 metres of line rather than the 100–300 metre *filler packs*.

Some specialist tackle shops can also fill your reels for you from enormous bulk spools, charging you accordingly for the amount of line used and, possibly, for their labour. This option can be handy for busy occasional anglers.

Drawing a line in the sand

No discussion of fishing lines is complete without a mention of the threats posed to the environment and wildlife by lost or discarded line. Some forms of fishing line can take centuries (literally!) to break down when discarded. This long-term issue is especially true of the GSP varieties (refer to the section 'Gasping over GSP', earlier in this chapter). During that time, lengths of lost line can easily entangle birds, turtles, dolphins and other creatures, which sometimes causes horrific injuries and even death.

As anglers, we need to minimise the amount of fishing tackle — including line — that we leave in the natural environment. Here's how:

- ✔ If your line becomes *snagged* or stuck on the seabed, always try to break the line as close as possible to the snagged end. If you must cut the line, again, do so as close to the snagged obstruction as practical, to minimise the length of line left in the water.

- ✔ Never discard line off-cuts or tangles when you're fishing. Always bundle them up, bring them home and dispose of them in your non-recyclable household garbage — after first sealing the scraps in an old plastic bag.

  Better still, check out the location of the few recycling stations around these days that collect old fishing line and return it to plastics' manufacturers for re-use or recycling. In New South Wales, for example, T*Angler*Bin (www.oceanwatch.org.au/TAnglerBinProject1.htm) offers a statewide recreational fishing line recovery scheme. Check out similar opportunities in your region by entering **fishing line recovery** on your search engine.

- ✔ When you dispose of line in your household garbage, you can further reduce the chances of it entangling wildlife at landfill sites by wrapping the line into a tight coil or *hank* and then cutting the entire coil in several places using sharp scissors, in order to produce a multitude of very short lengths or off-cuts.

- ✔ Choose to use a biodegradable line. At least one brand of biodegradable line is available on the market (called Bioline), and more are sure to be offered in coming years. (See Chapter 17 for more about the concept of biodegradability.)

Time lines

Modern nylon monofilament and gel-spun polyethylene (GSP) fishing lines are pretty tough, but neither is indestructible. Fishing line is constantly exposed to all manner of abrasive and damaging forces as the line is pulled across rocks, sand and submerged timber, as well as being regularly soaked and dried, stretched and relaxed, coiled and uncoiled.

Long-term damage to line is also caused by ultraviolet radiation from sunlight and exposure to various chemicals and pollutants in the air and water. Nylon, in particular, is easily weakened by exposure to sunlight and chemicals. You can fight this deterioration by storing your reels and line indoors or under cover when not in use, but eventually you're bound to lose the battle.

You need to replace fishing line on a regular basis to avoid unexpected breakages when fishing. Experienced anglers refill or top-up reels with fresh line at least once a year and I recommend you do the same.

Chapter 5

Hot Rods

A fishing rod is basically a stick that allows you to increase the radius of your casting area and exercise greater control over hooked fish. More precisely, a rod is a flexible shaft that's usually fitted with runners to carry the fishing line and includes a place to mount a reel.

You don't really need a rod to go fishing — a length of line and a hook are the only basic essentials — but being able to cast well beyond the shore or further from your boat increases your chances of landing that dream catch.

Rods have advantages over simple handlines. For example, rods

- ✔ **Allow you to reach beyond obstructions such as bushes and rocks:** A rod acts like an extension of your arm in these instances.

- ✔ **Keep your line off hard edges that may snag or cut a line:** The sides of a boat can saw into a line, while a boat's propeller is an annoying magnet lying in wait to snarl your line. Equally, barnacles and rusting nails on jetty pylons can play havoc with fishing lines.

- ✔ **Make useful bite indicators and act as shock absorbers:** These attributes come into play when hooking, playing and landing fish (see Figure 5-1).

- ✔ **Strongly enhance your ability to cast a baited hook, lure or fly out to where (hopefully!) your next catch is waiting:** Sure, you can cast a handline a reasonable distance, but in doing so you run the risk of looking like an out-of-control windmill and ending up with line wrapped macramé-fashion around your head and a baited hook for an ear.

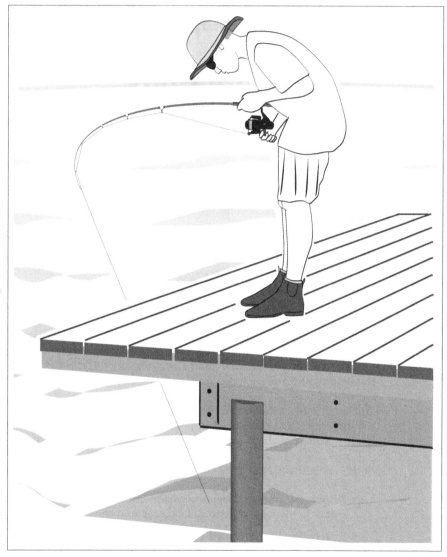

Figure 5-1:
A rod offers extended reach and improved direction in casting, acts as a useful bite indicator and is a shock absorber when playing and landing fish.

The upshot is that if you're even a little bit serious about taking up fishing, you need a fishing rod. In fact, if you're anything like me, you're bound to end up with a garage full of rods for every occasion. In this chapter, I explain the rod basics to prepare you for that moment when you venture into a tackle store to make your first — or fiftieth — rod purchase.

Casting into the Space Age

Before you hit the tackle shop, read this section to help you understand the rudiments of how a rod is put together, the various materials used to make rods and the names of all those different bits found on a rod. So that you're not put off by strange words or terms you haven't seen or heard before, I recommend you learn the basic lingo. At the very least, you can then nod knowingly when the sales assistant starts bandying around terms that sound as if you're having a tech-design lesson instead of planning a fishing expedition.

As in so many fields, the manufacture of fishing rods underwent a major revolution with the arrival of plastics and, in the 1930s, *fibreglass* (more correctly known as glass-reinforced plastic or GRP). Fibreglass, that marvellous stuff used to make surfboards and many boats, is still the material of choice for most fishing rods — with good reason.

Fibreglass is strong, flexible, reasonably light and cheap. The earliest fibreglass fishing rods featured solid *blanks* (the word blank simply means the shaft of the rod). In the 1960s, hollow or tubular fibreglass blanks were introduced to make fishing rods even lighter.

Glass versus graphite

Fishing with a hollow fibreglass (or *glass*) rod is a lot more fun (not to mention easier on the arms) than wielding a heavier solid rod. Hollow or tubular fibreglass rods are also significantly more responsive than the solid varieties because they more readily register and transmit the vibrations, tugs and nibbles of timidly biting fish.

In the 1970s and 1980s, manufacturers began using more advanced materials to make fishing rods, including substances created for the aerospace industry. The most notable of these super substances is a type of carbon fibre known as graphite.

Graphite is stronger and lighter than fibreglass and is therefore a real boon to many sports people, including golfers who use club shafts made of graphite, and anglers. Unfortunately, rods made of graphite are more expensive than fibreglass rods and are apt to break more easily than fibreglass.

All fishing rods, whatever the construction material, make excellent conductors of electricity, especially when wet. As a result, you should be extremely careful not to wave longer rods around near power lines and to never, ever hold a fishing rod up in the air during an electrical storm. At the first hint of lightning, stow your gear and head for shore or shelter ... fast!

Fittings and fixtures

The various fittings and fixtures on fishing rods have evolved over time. As soon as reels were added to the angling equation, a *reel seat* or *winch mount* was needed to attach these line holders securely to the blank, as well as *eyelets* or *runners* (occasionally called *guides*) to carry the line along the blank to the tip. Like blanks, the fittings and fixtures gradually became lighter, stronger and more affordable in the wake of the plastics revolution.

The number of runners and type of reel seat, handles or grips and butt section on a rod depends on the rod's intended application — not to mention the preferences of the maker and the ever-changing fashions of fishing (see Figure 5-2).

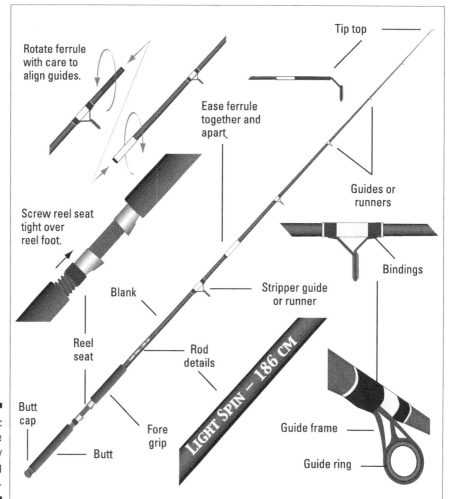

Figure 5-2: The anatomy of a fishing rod.

We've come a long way since the stick!

Through the ages, fishing rods were made from all manner of materials. The earliest examples were simply branches lopped from trees, lengths of bamboo or sections of cane with a length of line tied to the thin end.

The manufacture of fishing rods became increasingly sophisticated with the advent of laminated timber and split cane.

Various metals have even been tried as rod-building materials and one creative example was seen immediately after World War II when the steel whip antennas from surplus army tanks enjoyed a brief burst of popularity in fishing circles. Understandably, the trend had a limited lifespan.

To resolve these drawbacks, many manufacturers today build composite rod blanks from a combination of fibreglass and graphite in various proportions. These types of composite tubular rods now dominate the fishing-rod market, mainly because of their suitability to the needs of most anglers — you and me included.

Inner-line alternatives

As an example of the variety of rods on the market today, one style has no runners. Instead, the line travels up the inside of the tubular blank and exits at the top. Called *inner-line rods*, this innovative design certainly has a place in the sport, but the system also has a number of annoying glitches. For starters, knots and connections in the line don't pass easily through these rods, and you need a special wire pull-through device to thread them up each time you re-rig. For these reasons, inner-line rods have been slow to catch on in Australia and New Zealand. However, the recent introduction of a new generation of inner-line rods may see a gradual increase in their popularity in this part of the world.

Choosing the Right Rod for You

When you walk into a well-stocked tackle store, you're confronted by a vast and often bewildering array of fishing rods. Don't be daunted! Trust me when I say that finding the right rod to catch the fish you hope to take home for dinner is not all that hard (particularly if you read this chapter).

The majority of rods on display in fishing shops feature tubular blanks with a composite graphite/fibreglass construction. These fishing rods have a seat for the reel, rubberised or cork handles, from 2 to 9 runners bound in place with thread along the blank and a special runner at the top end or rod tip called — rather unimaginatively — a *tip-top*. The runner located closest to the reel is called a *stripping guide* or *stripper* and has a bigger diameter than the other runners.

While most rods fit this basic description, you're now faced with choosing the rod's length, taper and so on. The following are the main items to consider:

- ✔ **Diameter:** Rods come in a staggering array of blank *diameters*, which simply means the overall thickness of the rod's shaft.

- ✔ **Wall thickness:** Rods come in a range of blank *wall thicknesses*, which is the term for the thickness of the fibreglass or composite wall of the blank or shaft.

- ✔ **Length:** Rods range from little more than 1 metre to well over 4 metres.

- ✔ **Runners:** The great majority of rods have *runners* and, ordinarily, the number and placement of the runners depends on the rod's intended type of fishing.

- ✔ **Taper:** The gradual thinning of the rod from the bottom to the top is known as the rod's *taper*, which can vary enormously from rod to rod.

To familiarise yourself with the difference between rods, take a trip to your local tackle shop (with your *Fishing For Dummies* bible) and spend a bit of time comparing the rods on display.

One of the first items you're bound to notice is that rods have just about as many price differences as design differences. For example, you can pay less than $50, or more than $500, for rods that appear (at first glance) to be identical. Understanding the relative pros and cons of various materials and fittings used to make the rods can help you to decide whether a certain rod is value for your hard-earned money.

Sinking the myth of the general-purpose rod

Sadly, no such beast as an all-round or general-purpose rod exists — despite the best efforts of a number of manufacturers and their advertising agencies to convince you otherwise.

A rod that may be perfect for casting little lures out to catch trout and bream or floats and tiny baited hooks to land garfish and mullet is totally unsuited to heaving huge sinkers into the surf when pursuing mulloway and sharks or battling tuna and marlin from an ocean-going game boat. All fishing rods — even the so-called general-purpose rods — have their strengths and weaknesses and are best suited to a particular set of applications.

As well as coming in a range of lengths, weights, strengths, thicknesses and tapers, different fishing rods are designed to go with different styles of reel (I talk about reels in all their wondrous diversity in Chapter 6).

For now, all you need to remember is that certain rods are designed specifically for use with *threadline* (or *spinning*) reels, others are for *sidecast* reels and still others are made for use with *overheads* (I explain the differences between these *reels* in Chapter 6). I mention this variety here, though, because you need to know what type of reel you want to use before you buy a rod. In other words, read this chapter and the next one before you go shopping.

Knowing where you're fishing and what you want to catch

From the dozens of rods facing you in the tackle shop, how do you know which is the right one for you? The answer becomes simpler after you work out the angling style that best matches your plans. Are you going to be fishing

- ✔ For small fish or big fish?
- ✔ From a boat or off the riverbank or seashore?
- ✔ In fresh or salt water?
- ✔ With lures, bait or fly?

As a general rule, longer rods are best when fishing from the shore, especially where lengthy casts may be required. In a boat, shorter rods tend to be more convenient and effective because trying to swing a four-metre rod about when you're stuck in a small boat with a couple of hapless companions can at best be tiresome and at worst dangerous!

Meeting the major rod families

Before deciding on the right rod, you need to be able to recognise the main types of fishing rods. Because fishing rods and their various reels are a mix 'n' match concept, I talk about reels in this section as well as rods, but to really delve into the world of reels, check out Chapter 6 before you venture out to the tackle shop to buy your first combination.

I group the main contenders into eight families of fishing rods and match them with the range of fish that each family of rods is best suited to catch. Chances are that your first fishing rod (and maybe your first half dozen when the bug bites) is included in these eight broad groupings.

Spinning rods — single-handed

Ultra-light and light single-handed spinning rods are occasionally called *flick sticks*. Designed to hold threadline (spinning) reels, single-handed spinning rods are usually 1.6–2 metres in length. These rods are perfect for catching smaller fish such as trout, perch, whiting, garfish (piper) and bream.

Spinning rods — double-handed

Medium to heavy double-handed spinning rods (see Figure 5-3) are designed for use with bigger threadline reels. Usually 2–3.5 metres in length, double-handed spinning rods are ideal for tackling slightly larger fish, including tailor, salmon (kahawai), trevally, flathead, snapper, barramundi and Murray cod.

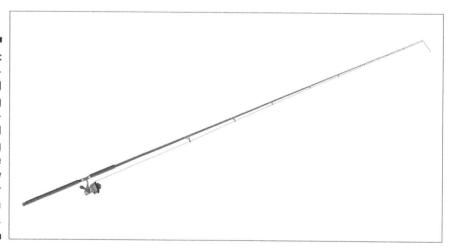

Figure 5-3: A double-handed spinning rod. Single-handed spinning rods are generally shorter and have a shorter butt.

Plug (or baitcaster) rods — single-handed

Single-handed *baitcaster* or *plug rods* are designed for use with small overhead reels called baitcasters or with *closed-face* (*spincast*) reels (I talk about these reels in Chapter 6). Most are 1.6–2 metres in length and are the tool of choice of many specialist bass and Murray cod anglers.

Single-handed plug rods are also useful for catching flathead or smaller barramundi, or even snapper and school kingfish, depending on where you fish. Single-handed plug rods may be fitted with either a straight butt and conventional reel seat or a *pistol grip* handle (see Figure 5-4). Pistol grips are extremely effective when accurate casting is required.

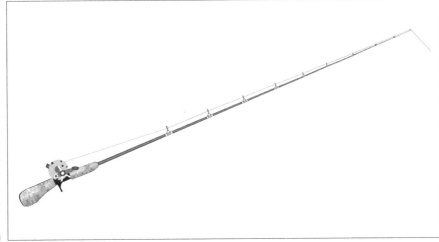

Figure 5-4:
A single-handed plug or baitcaster rod with a pistol-grip handle.

Plug (or baitcaster) rods — double-handed

Double-handed plug rods are designed for use with larger overhead reels. Normally 1.8–2.2 metres in length, these rods are perfect for targeting snapper, mulloway, small tuna and big barramundi, especially from boats.

Sidecast rods

Sidecast rods (see Figure 5-5) are mostly used for casting from the ocean shore. These rods are relatively long (anywhere from 3 metres to 4.2 metres), have short butts and large diameter line guides and readily handle tailor, salmon (kahawai), snapper, trevally, mulloway and a host of other species.

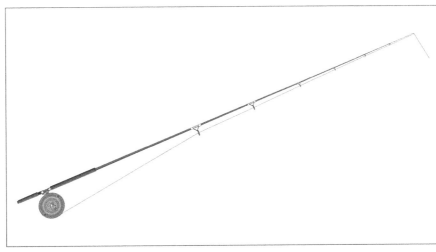

Figure 5-5:
Sidecast rods are long (usually more than 3 metres), have short butts and large diameter guides.

Boat, jig and trolling rods

Boat, jig and trolling rods are typically short (1.4–2 metres) and can be used with threadline, overhead, sidecast or centrepin reels (see Chapter 6) where casting isn't important. Depending on the design, you can use these types of rods to catch anything from whiting and flathead to snapper, barramundi, kingfish and tuna.

Game rods

Game rods are specialist boat rods for use with big overhead reels (see Figure 5-6). Most are 1.6–2.2 metres in length and often feature fancy (and expensive) *roller runners*. These special runners are fitted with little wheels to reduce wear and tear on the line during lengthy battles with big, fast fish. Game rods are used to catch a range of game and sport species from tuna and mackerel to sailfish, marlin and sharks.

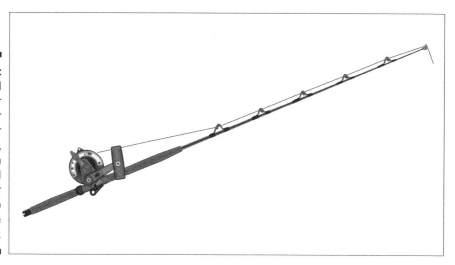

Figure 5-6: A game rod is similar to other boat, jig or trolling rods, but is often equipped with roller runners to reduce line wear.

Fly rods

Fly rods are specialist tools that are usually between 2.6 metres and 3 metres in length and carry 7–9 line runners (see Figure 5-7). The uppermost of these runners are often lightweight *snake guides* made from hardened wire. Fly rods are designed for use with fly reels and are built to match specific fly line weights, because in fly casting the mass of the line is what carries the fly out to the fish, rather than a *sinker* or *float* (I describe the process of fly casting in more detail at the end of Chapter 8, and also in Chapter 13).

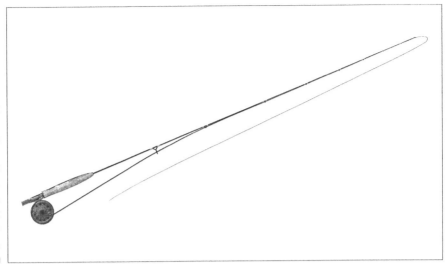

Fly rods and the special lines they cast are rated differently to other forms of fishing tackle and are described using a numbering system created by the American Fishing Tackle Manufacturers' Association (AFTMA), which later came to be known as the American Sportfishing Association (www.asafishing.org). Fly rod weights theoretically range from Nos 1 through 20, although most fly rods sold in Australia fall between No. 4 and No. 15 in this weight scale. To give you some idea how this system works:

- A No. 4 or No. 5 rod is ideal for catching trout or mullet.
- A No. 7 or No. 8 is good for bass or small barramundi.
- A No. 12 is suitable for big, strong saltwater fish such as tuna.

Buying a rod — shopping around pays off

When selecting the right rod for your specific requirements, you can rely, at least in part, on the advice of the sales staff in the tackle or sporting goods store. Taking time to shop around and compare information at different outlets is a key to gathering the knowledge you need, because the advice can be surprisingly inconsistent from one place to the next. Watch out particularly for the guy or girl behind the counter who's all talk and little substance.

What about a rod-and-reel combo?

Many manufacturers offer matched rod-and-reel outfits, also known as *combos*, at highly competitive prices. Combos are also created by individual retail outlets or fishing-tackle chain shops, often to suit local conditions.

Combos take the guesswork out of correctly matching the right rod to the correct reel and can also save you money, so consider these when you first tackle the tackle shops.

As a rule, steer clear of extremely cheap combos and so-called kid's sets. These are often assembled using inferior quality or discontinued gear. Expect to spend about as much on a reasonable combo outfit as you would on a medium- to high-quality reel. While you're at it, check to see whether the manufacturer offers a spare parts back-up or any kind of warranty.

These days, many rod manufacturers print valuable data on the shaft of the rod itself, just above the top handle or *fore grip*. A number of companies also add a swing-tag with additional printed information. By reading these labels, you can discover:

- ✔ The best line strengths for use with that particular model
- ✔ The length of the rod
- ✔ The maker's suggested casting weights

As well, manufacturers often include advice on which type of fishing the rod is suited to and which species of fish you're most likely to catch using the rod. *Note:* imported rods naturally come with advice that applies to American, European or Asian fishing conditions and may be of limited relevance to Australian and New Zealand anglers.

Seven Rods for Seven Situations

A fun way to find the best fishing rod for your location and for the fish you want to fry is to take a dream trip around a few of the country's finest fishing spots! In this section, I introduce you to seven pretty smart anglers who know how to buy the right rod for the right conditions.

Harbour bream

Harry lives in Sydney and wants a rod to catch bream and the occasional flathead and whiting from the harbour, Botany Bay and the Hawkesbury River. As well, he wants to take the rod on his annual holiday to Yamba in northern New South Wales, so he needs a rod to suit all those locations. He settled on a smallish threadline (spinning) reel and a 3-kilo nylon line.

Harry lives in an upstairs unit and often catches the bus to go fishing along the harbour shoreline or, occasionally, he hires out a boat with his fishing mate. For this reason, Harry needs a rod he can store easily and carry on the bus.

The ideal rod for Harry is a two-piece tubular fibreglass or fibreglass/graphite composite model about 2 metres in length with five to seven runners and a light, sensitive tip.

In the shop, this rod, which can be used both single- or double-handed, is likely to carry a label indicating that the blank's best suited to lines in the 2–4 kilos breaking strain range with casting weights from 4 grams to 15 or 20 grams. Fortunately, the market has many rods in this range, so Harry can choose from a wide range of prices and brands.

Piece of the action

A number of modern rods are made in a one-piece format, while others feature multi-piece, take-apart designs with two to six separate sections. A few are even telescopic, with each section sliding inside the next.

Multi-piece and telescopic rods are obviously much easier to store and transport than one-piece designs, especially in lengths over 2 metres.

The choice between one-piece and multi-part or telescopic construction largely comes down to convenience. The *joints* (also known as *ferrules*) in today's fishing rods are so well made that the joints do little to detract from the strength, feel and performance of the assembled rod.

If a multi-piece rod best suits your lifestyle and personal needs (especially if you travel a lot), then that's what you should buy.

Bay whiting

Rhonda is a budding Melbourne angler, who's fortunate to have a friend with a boat. She has a yen to catch the delicious King George whiting in Port Phillip and Westernport bays and she's keen also to have a crack at the annual run of *pinkies* (small to middling snapper) that enter these bays every spring.

Acting on advice from her boating friend and the staff at the local tackle store, Rhonda chooses a medium threadline (spinning) reel and fills the reel with a premium quality 5-kilo nylon line. Now to choose a rod!

Rhonda's needs are best suited by a 2–2.2 metre, double-handed, threadline (spinning) rod with a moderately light tip but with enough stiffness in the lower two-thirds to handle the weight of the big sinkers occasionally needed in the swift tidal currents of Westernport. This stiffness in the bottom part of the rod is also perfect to help her deal with the pinkies and even a larger snapper, should she be lucky enough to hook one.

Rods such as Rhonda's are plentiful on the tackle store shelves and most are two-piece, making storage and transportation easy.

Taupo trout

Con lives in Auckland and has been toying for years with the idea of trying fly-fishing for trout in the streams and lakes around Lake Taupo, in the centre of New Zealand's North Island. Now he's about to take the plunge.

After carefully shopping around and reading plenty of magazine articles on the subject, Con opts for a No. 6 weight outfit (I briefly describe the special numbering system for fly tackle in the section 'Fly rods', earlier in this chapter) and has already bought himself a sweet little fly reel, a bunch of Dacron backing line and a weight-forward No. 6 weight floating fly line (I describe these types of reels, backings and lines in Chapter 4 and Chapter 6). Now he's about to buy his first fly rod.

Con wisely decides to buy the best rod he can afford and is planning to spend at least $500 after accepting professional advice that the rod is the most important part of the entire fly-casting process and that he's much better off learning with a high quality rod.

Con's choice for his first fly rod is a 2.7-metre, fully graphite, No. 6 weight from a well-known manufacturer that offers an excellent warranty and replacement service in the event of a breakage. As he's planning a fishing holiday to New Zealand's South Island, Con opts for a four-piece travel version of the rod and I just know he's set for many years of pleasure from his new fishing gear.

Bight mulloway

Barry lives in Whyalla, South Australia, and has been fishing locally for years, but now he's decided to venture west to the beaches of the Great Australian Bight in search of giant mulloway (jewfish) and the big whaler sharks he's heard so much about.

Barry has already mastered the nuances of casting with an overhead reel and decides to use a large overhead filled with a 14-kilo line to take on the mulloway, sharks and big salmon that swim the Bight.

He shops around, but can't find a high quality overhead rod to suit his specific needs, so he decides to have one custom built to his specifications at a local tackle store. This process involves Barry selecting a blank, in consultation with the shop's resident rod builder, and choosing the necessary fixtures and fittings needed to turn the rod into a perfect product of choice.

Barry's mulloway rod ultimately measures 3.2 metres in length and is of a heavy, robust construction that allows him to cast large baits and heavy sinkers, then do battle with powerful mulloway weighing up to 30 kilos or even a 2 metre-plus shark. His customised rod is fitted with a long, wooden *sand spike* at its butt end that can be jammed into the sand or into crevices in rocky headlands. As the rod is to be carried on the roof of his four-wheel drive vehicle, Barry is opting for the strength and simplicity of one-piece construction.

Herring special

Linda, 12, is a budding angler who lives in Mandurah, in southern Western Australia. She loves catching tommy rough (called herring in the West) from the Peel estuary and in the Dawesville Cut. Linda's dream is a new fishing rod and reel for Christmas.

Linda's parents are taking advice from the local tackle store proprietor who suggests buying a matched combo consisting of a 1.8-metre, two-piece, hollow fibreglass, single-handed spinning rod and a small threadline reel pre-filled with a 3-kilo line. The proprietor explains that this particular rod has a short section of solid fibreglass at the fine tip, extending around 40 centimetres down the rod. This feature makes the rod more durable and less likely to break than a rod that's completely hollow. The light tip also helps Linda cast small sinkers and feel for the soft nibbles of the herring.

Barra buster

Leon has just moved to Darwin to take up a new job and is eager to catch a barramundi. Even better, Leon's new boss has a boat and wants to take him barra fishing. Leon has no gear for this type of angling and has no idea what to buy.

After discussing his needs with several locals and the staff of a large tackle store, Leon decides against buying one of the baitcaster reels he sees in so many magazines and on TV fishing shows because he's never cast an overhead reel before and doesn't feel he has time to learn. Instead, he opts for a medium threadline (spinning) reel.

To go with his reel, Leon chooses a one-piece, 1.8-metre, double-handed, spinning rod with a moderately light tip, a *fast taper* (in other words, the rod features a rapid transition from being quite thin and whippy at the top to relatively thick and stiff at the bottom) and it carries six runners.

The rod's label, found just above the rubberised fore grip, states the rod is best suited to lines with breaking strains of 5–8 kilos and for casting weights from 8 grams to 20 grams. Leon decides to use a 7-kilo line and buys several highly recommended barramundi lures that each weigh 10–15 grams. This rod is ideal for his needs.

Bass specialist

Youlla is from Brisbane and has fished in saltwater since she was a schoolgirl. Recently, however, she's decided her targets are to be bass and golden perch in the man-made freshwater lakes of south-eastern Queensland. Now Youlla's ready to buy her first specialist bass rod.

Youlla has already fished with a borrowed baitcaster or plug outfit and, after just one or two minor line tangles, she's quickly mastered the skills of casting the small, overhead reel. As a result, Youlla is opting for a single-handed baitcaster or plug outfit and has already bought a high quality baitcaster reel, and she fills the reel with an 8-kilo braided gel-spun polyethylene (GSP) line (I describe the attributes of this line in Chapter 4).

The rod Youlla eventually chooses to complete her specialist bass-and-perch outfit is a 1.65-metre, single-handed, one-piece, graphite/glass composite plug rod with a pistol grip handle. Light but powerful, this rod is ideally suited to accurately casting the 7–15 gram lures Youlla plans to use.

Balancing Your Tackle to Match Your Rod

I guess now is as a good a time as any to introduce you to the rather elastic concept of *balanced tackle* — a term widely used in fishing literature, but rarely explained in anything beyond vague approximations and exceedingly broad brushstrokes.

Put simply, all the bits and pieces of gear that you use in your fishing should roughly match each other, creating a balanced outfit (see Figure 5-8). In other words, a little teeny-weeny reel filled with fishing line the thickness of a spider's web has no place hanging off a ruddy great rod that would look right at home holding up a couple of telephone lines!

Fine lines, small hooks, little reels and fish you can pick up without giving yourself a hernia all go best with light, whippy rods you can easily hold and swish about in one hand. Conversely, thick lines, big reels and seriously large fish demand rods with the bending characteristics of a pool cue.

The tricky part of finding the right balance is the fact that length has little to do with the balance equation when dealing with rods. Most of the lightest, most sensitive rods (such as fly rods and specialist blackfish or luderick rods) are extremely long — typically around 3 metres or more.

Figure 5-8:
The concept of balance in fishing tackle is important for successful fishing.

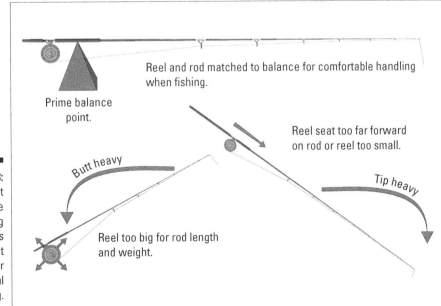

Reel and rod matched to balance for comfortable handling when fishing.

Prime balance point.

Reel seat too far forward on rod or reel too small.

Butt heavy

Tip heavy

Reel too big for rod length and weight.

By contrast the heaviest, most powerful rods (such as the big game rods used to catch sharks, tuna and marlin) are relatively short — often under 2 metres.

When considering the balance factor in relation to rods, think more about the physical weight and thickness of the rod itself and how easily the rod is going to bend under load.

So-called light and ultra-light rods are not only feather-like to hold, these types of rods are also thin (especially at the tip) and easily bent. These rods are best used with small reels, fine lines and little hooks.

Understanding Your Rod Action

The technical side of fishing includes the concept of *rod action*. Basically, this means the way a rod bends under load, when casting and also while playing and landing a fish (see Figure 5-9).

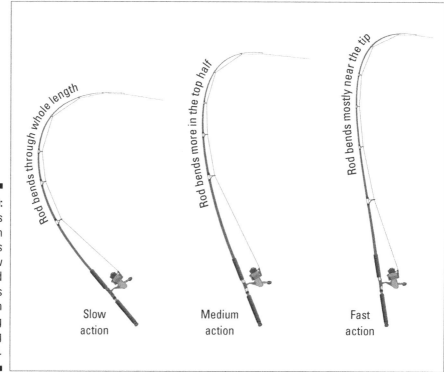

Figure 5-9: A rod's action dictates how the rod behaves when casting and playing fish.

Rods that bend fairly evenly from tip to butt and form a clear **U** shape are said to have *slow* actions. These rods are also often described in books and magazines as having *parabolic* or *progressive* tapers. On the other hand, rods that bend most near the tip or in their top one-third, forming a sort of inverted **J** under load, are deemed to have a *fast* or even a *radical* action.

Rods with slower, more progressive actions tend to be more forgiving (because the rods bend more easily), both when casting and while fighting fish. A forgiving, medium-slow action can be really handy when you're a beginner, while expert anglers may prefer radically fast actions for specialist applications.

Looking After Your Rods

Thankfully, most modern fishing rods don't demand a huge amount of maintenance. However, you can benefit from learning the habit of removing reels from rods when not in use and taking multi-piece rods apart for storage to prevent the various bits from gumming together (and creating one-piece rods!).

A quick hose down after fishing and an occasional wipe with a wet, soapy cloth is worthwhile — especially if you fish in saltwater. I sometimes take my rods into the shower with me after a hard day's fishing, but I've been told this is a tad extreme.

Rods are best stored horizontally on pegs or racks. You can stand your rods in a corner as a convenience option, as long as the rods are completely straight — because storing rods bent or under load can make rods stay that way ... forever.

Prolonged exposure to direct sunlight degrades rod finishes and ultimately weakens the blank material, so avoid leaving your rods on the roof of the car or out in the backyard for long periods.

Oh, and while you're at it, don't do what a mate of mine did and leave your fishing tackle lying on the front lawn. He thought he'd lost his favourite surf casting rod ... until he mowed the grass. Crunch ... Ouch! That's certainly one way of turning a one-piece rod into a multi-piece.

Ten top ways to break a rod

If you fish on a regular basis, you're sure to eventually break a rod. Believe me, I know this fact from bitter experience. As soon as you accept this truth, the experience becomes less traumatic when the inevitable finally happens. Unlike diamonds, rods are not forever!

Surprisingly few rods are actually broken while hooking, playing and landing fish. The majority of fractures are directly due to operator error and many fractures take place well away from the water — during storage, transportation or while showing off your pride-and-joy to admiring friends.

Note: Fishing rods are relatively fragile and can and do break. Rods don't have to be handled like eggs, but these fishing friends do deserve a modicum of care and respect. Otherwise you may as well go back to using a stick. The following are ten ways to easily break a rod:

- Allow the rod tip to hang over the side of a boat while coming alongside a jetty or bank.

- Drop a heavy tackle box on your rod while it's lying on the floor of your boat.

- Entrust your rod to airline baggage handlers without packing the rod in a sturdy (make that bomb-proof) tube or case.

- Grab the tip and bend the rod sharply to demonstrate the action.

- Hit a tree branch or boat awning while casting.

- Leave your rod on the lawn and run over your beloved pole with the mower.

- Lend your rod to a mate.

- Slam your rod in a car door.

- Step on the rod or leave the rod where someone else can step on your fishing friend.

- Try to break a snagged line by jerking upwards with the rod.

Chapter 6

The Reel Deal

In This Chapter

▶ Understanding how fishing reels work

▶ Focusing on the seven main types of reels

▶ Taking care of your reels

A fishing reel is primarily a device for recovering and storing line, but a number of styles are also designed to help you cast the line.

Like rods, reels aren't absolutely necessary to the fishing process (refer to Chapter 5), yet reels are so helpful when it comes to catching fish and also increase the enjoyment of fishing so significantly that many modern anglers regard reels as essential items rather than luxuries.

Every fishing reel has a *spool* of one type or another on which to store the line. With the exception of the simple *handcaster* or *hand spool* (which you use without a rod), all reels feature a *handle* or *crank* that you can turn to recover the line and a *foot* that you use to mount the reel onto a rod. Most modern reels also have a *drag* or *slipping clutch* of some sort that allows the fish to pull the line from the reel's spool under a pre-set tension to prevent the line from breaking.

Fishing reels vary enormously in size, shape, design, construction materials and, naturally, cost. In fact, modern fishing reels — especially premium, high-quality models built from space-age materials — don't come cheap and in many cases reels cost more than rods and are likely to be the most expensive piece of fishing equipment you own. For this reason, I recommend you spend plenty of time choosing the right reel for your purposes and maintain your reels to achieve a long lifetime of trouble-free service.

As with many other fishing products, I advise you to buy a reel from one of the bigger, better-known manufacturers, which typically offer warranties, after-sales service and spare parts backup.

In most instances, you need a separate fishing reel for every rod you own and the cost of each reel should be at least the cost of the corresponding rod. In other words, if you outlay $100 or $150 on a rod, figure on spending at least that much on a suitable reel. (The only major exception to this general rule is in the area of freshwater fly-fishing, because high-quality fly rods typically cost three or four times as much as basic freshwater fly reels.)

This chapter looks at the seven main styles or families of reels, but first up I use the most popular type to explain how reels work.

Spool School

The reel that dominates Australian angling today is the *threadline* or spinning reel (see Figure 6-1), which is occasionally irreverently referred to as an eggbeater or coffee grinder due to the reel's unique appearance and action.

The threadline is known in certain highbrow fishing circles as a *fixed-spool* reel because the spool doesn't rotate as the line is being retrieved. Instead, the line wraps around the stationary spool by means of a *rotor head* carrying a *bail arm* and a *bail roller* to feed the line onto the spool. The spool also remains stationary when casting, with the line feeding off in loops over the *spool lip*. The spool only rotates when a hooked fish pulls out the line under pre-set pressure against the drag or clutch.

None of this technical mumbo-jumbo is especially important to you, me and the mullet, and all you really need to know is that the threadline reel's design makes casting an absolute breeze because you don't have to control a rapidly rotating spool that's hell bent on throwing off great tangles of loose line! (Check out the section 'Avoiding line tangles', later in this chapter.)

Threadline or spinning reels are so immensely popular because the design is extremely easy to use — even for complete beginners and kids — and suits most of the common styles of fishing, using either bait or artificial lures in freshwater or saltwater. This kind of reel is absolutely brilliant for using finer lines, casting light weights and catching smaller fish. On the negative side, threadline reels don't cope well with thick, strong line or heavyweight fish.

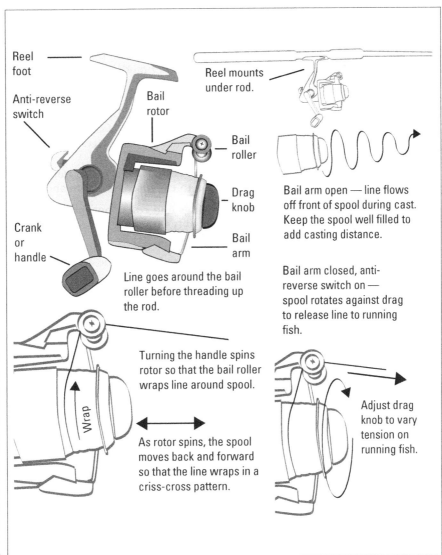

Reel foot

Anti-reverse switch

Bail rotor

Reel mounts under rod.

Bail roller

Drag knob

Crank or handle

Bail arm

Line goes around the bail roller before threading up the rod.

Bail arm open — line flows off front of spool during cast. Keep the spool well filled to add casting distance.

Bail arm closed, anti-reverse switch on — spool rotates against drag to release line to running fish.

Turning the handle spins rotor so that the bail roller wraps line around spool.

Wrap

As rotor spins, the spool moves back and forward so that the line wraps in a criss-cross pattern.

Adjust drag knob to vary tension on running fish.

Figure 6-1: The anatomy of a threadline reel, which is far and away the most popular style of reel in use today.

Choosing your eggbeater

Because threadline reels, or eggbeaters, are so popular, every major reel manufacturer offers a range of different models, with new designs appearing every year.

Threadline reels cost from $25 to over $1,000, an amazing price range that has little to do with the physical dimensions of the reel or the size of the fish the reel is intended to catch. Instead, the price is dictated by:

- **Materials used to make the reel:** The materials range from cheap plastic and die-cast metals to expensive graphite and titanium.

- **The number of ball bearings and roller bearings included in the reel:** Generally speaking, the quality of bearings also goes up with price.

- **The reel's level of 'sex appeal':** Some reels look like accessories from a Star Wars movie, while others have all the aesthetic appeal of the Soviet era.

- **The type of warranty offered by the manufacturer:** These vary from very limited one-year warranties to much more comprehensive three- to five-year-plus warranties.

As a general guide, if you spend somewhere between $100 and $400, you can end up with a quality threadline reel that (with a minimum of tender loving care) you can continue to use for many years.

Handy hints

Most modern threadline (spinning) reels are ambidextrous, meaning you can easily swap the crank handle from the right to the left side of the reel, often without the use of any tools. Other styles of reel are available in either right- or left-handed versions, while a few (especially large overheads and game reels) are only offered with a right-hand drive.

Which hand you use to wind or crank your reel has been an ongoing argument in fishing circles for years. Many experienced anglers (myself included) prefer to crank small to medium threadline (spinning) reels and most fly reels with their non-dominant hand (in other words, the left hand for a right-handed angler

such as myself). This method allows efficient, single-handed casting without having to swap the outfit from one hand to the other after each cast. That said, the choice is entirely yours; so, if you prefer to crank a reel with your dominant hand and swap hands after casting, go right ahead!

Most anglers start out winding reels using the dominant hand and a percentage later experiment with reels with the opposite drive. The bottom line is that fishing is supposed to be fun and you should use your gear the way that feels best for you; so, never let yourself be bullied by the so-called 'experts' into doing everything their way!

Taking a long line

One interesting twist on the long-established threadline theme over the past couple of decades has been the advent of so-called bait runner or bait feeder models from several manufacturers.

These specially-adapted spinning reels (see Figure 6-2) feature a switch or lever which you can engage to effectively *free-spool* the reel. Free-spooling is a technique that allows the line to pull off the spool against minimal tension while the bail arm is still in the closed position. (Don't worry, I explain all this terminology and how those bits work elsewhere in this chapter!) Biting fish can easily pull the line from the reel under a minimum of tension. This tension may be adjusted using a knob, usually located on the rear of the reel. To re-engage the gears and strike the fish, an angler may either manually trip the lever or simply rotate the reel's crank handle.

As their names imply, *bait runner* or *bait feeder* style spinning reels are especially useful when bait fishing for species that are more easily and securely hooked when these fish are allowed to swim off some distance with the bait before the angler attempts to strike or set the hook.

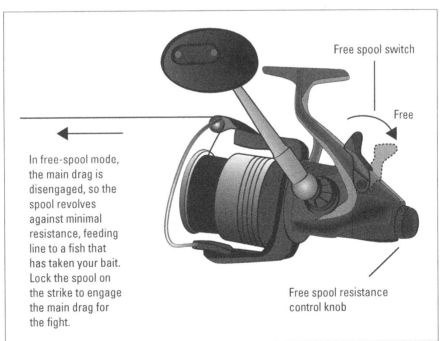

Figure 6-2:
Bait runner or line-feeder style reels have a lever that effectively acts as a free-spool mechanism, which allows biting fish to easily pull line from the reel under minimal tension.

In free-spool mode, the main drag is disengaged, so the spool revolves against minimal resistance, feeding line to a fish that has taken your bait. Lock the spool on the strike to engage the main drag for the fight.

Free spool switch

Free

Free spool resistance control knob

If you plan on bait fishing, definitely talk to the staff in your tackle shop about the potential advantages of having a bait runner function on your spinning reel. Better still, have them demonstrate its use to you.

Avoiding line tangles

Because threadline reels (and the closed-face or spincaster reels I describe in the section 'Closed-face reels', later in this chapter) are fixed-spool designs, the beasts do have one bad habit: As the line rolls off over the lip of the spool when casting (or back onto the spool when retrieving), the line can become twisted. When retrieving line, this problem may be aggravated if the line slips against the drag or if you're using a bait or lure that spins in the water.

Line twist causes tangles and nobody (with the possible exception of fishing line manufacturers) likes to do the tangles tango. Luckily, if you take the following easy precautions, you can limit the number of twist-induced line tangles:

✔ **Apply tension:** Whatever type of reel you use, always maintain a light tension on the line when retrieving the line. This action is especially important when bringing in an empty line or one carrying a light weight. You can achieve this result by pinching the line lightly between the thumb and forefinger of your rod-holding hand when winding in.

✔ **Use swivels:** Always incorporate at least one swivel (see Chapter 7) in every rig you use when fishing, especially with threadline, spincaster and sidecaster reels.

Even if you use my tips, chances are you may still occasionally experience annoying line twist. To remove twist from a line, try one of the following:

✔ **Untwisting a fishing line from a boat:** Remove all the hooks, sinkers, lures, swivels and other items attached to the line (this gear is known as _terminal tackle_) and then trail the line behind the boat while motoring slowly ahead. I recommend you let out at least as much line as the length of your longest cast, and trail (or _troll_) the line for at least 5–10 minutes to allow the twists to unwind.

As you trail the line, be careful to make sure the line doesn't become tangled in the boat's propeller!

✔ **Untwisting a fishing line from a bridge or jetty:** As above, remove the terminal tackle and feed out the line, letting the current or tide untwist the line.

 ✔ **Untwisting a fishing line anywhere else:** As above, remove the
    terminal tackle from the line and walk the affected length of line out
    across a grassy field, park or yard and rewind it onto the reel under
    light finger tension.

I explain all the other characteristics of threadline reels in the next section,
while working through the major reel types or families.

Seven Deadly Reels

Seven major families of fishing reels are in widespread use around the world
and each style has a place in Australian and New Zealand fishing, although a
couple of types aren't widely used in this part of the world.

In this section, I look briefly at each main style of reel, listing them in order
of design complexity, starting with the simplest and working up to the most
sophisticated. (To find out which reel — and corresponding rod — is most
likely to best suit the types of fishing you want to do, refer to the sample
scenarios in Chapter 5.)

Handcasters

When I was a kid, my mates and I wrapped our handlines around empty
soft-drink bottles. With the line secured around the bottle's waist, the
bottle is held at the neck and the base is pointed in the direction you want
your rig and baited hook to end up. After whirling the sinker around your
head a few times to generate momentum, you then lob the lot out towards
your target (retaining your grip on the bottle, of course!). Certainly, this is a
crude form of casting (and rather hazardous to bystanders!), but the system
does work; whereas the accuracy of the operation is nothing to write home
about, casts of 10–15 metres are achievable with a relatively heavy sinker.
(If we didn't catch 'em, we still had a chance of knocking 'em out with the
sinker!)

In the early 1970s, solid cork cylinders became popular as handline
holders because the rig was light to carry and floated, making retrieval
after a slip-up easier. Unfortunately, the cork cylinder fad coincided with
the introduction of chunky, cork-heeled platform shoes that became so
fashionable a worldwide shortage of cork resulted and persists to this day!
(Oh, the memories . . .)

Handline technology leapt into the age of fantastic plastics with the advent
of the Australian-designed circular handcaster (see Figure 6-3).

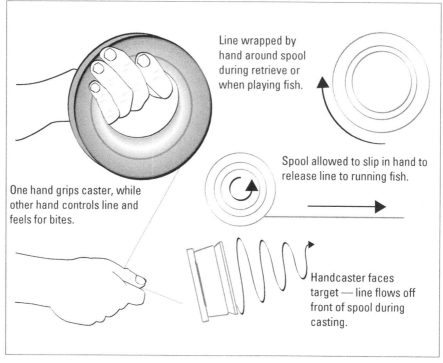

Line wrapped by hand around spool during retrieve or when playing fish.

Spool allowed to slip in hand to release line to running fish.

One hand grips caster, while other hand controls line and feels for bites.

Handcaster faces target — line flows off front of spool during casting.

Figure 6-3: Plastic handcasters or hand spools are excellent devices for storing and casting handlines.

Shaped like a doughnut, plastic handcasters often have a central crosspiece that can be used as a handle when casting. The best handcasters have smooth lips and slots around the base to hold hooks — an excellent safety feature. Plastic handcasters are handy for storing line and allow quite effective casts to be made using the tried-and-proven soft-drink bottle method described at the beginning of this section.

Handcasters are cheap, functional and last a lifetime if stored out of the sun between fishing trips. Plastic hand spools come in a variety of colours. However, I suggest you buy bright yellow or red hand spools, because yellow and red objects are much easier to see in long grass or on river banks and jetties and are therefore less likely to be left behind when packing up after fishing.

Centrepin reels

Centrepin reels are the simplest form of reel designed to fit on a rod and have been around since Adam was a small boy. In fact, chances are centrepin reels were the first style of reel ever used and, backing this up, basic versions of the reels can be seen in Chinese art dating back well over 1,000 years.

Geared for action

With the exception of handcasters and most centrepin, fly and sidecaster reels, modern fishing reels have internal gearing.

The gears are designed to multiply the angler's winding effort and thereby speed up line recovery. In other words, one turn of the reel's crank handle is translated through the gearing into more than one turn of the spool or rotor head. The degree of multiplication is called the gear ratio and is described by numbers such as 4:1 (pronounced four to one) or 5.2:1, which simply means that the spool or rotor makes 4 or 5.2 rotations for every single turn of the crank handle. (If you're a cyclist, you're already one crank ahead in your understanding of this technical aspect of gearing ratios!)

Gearing is a boon to anglers, especially when using smaller reels, because the gearing greatly reduces the amount of time it takes you to wind in a length of line or bring in a fish. Gearing also allows you to make a lure travel quickly through the water, giving it enough action and life to attract the attention of hungry fish.

Gearing does have a number of disadvantages. Because of the laws of physics, with a faster style of gearing or a higher gear ratio, the crank handle becomes more difficult to use under pressure, which in turn creates more wear and tear on the teeth of the gears. This becomes quite noticeable in reels with gear ratios higher than 5:1 and is one reason why you should *pump and wind* (see Chapter 14) when fighting or *playing* a big fish.

Unless you plan to become involved in a specialist form of fishing such as *high speed spinning* (retrieving metal lures very quickly to catch tuna, kingfish and other fast-swimming saltwater predators), I recommend you choose a reel with a gear ratio between 3.5:1 and 5.5:1.

Centrepins are *revolving spool* reels that are designed to hang underneath the butt or handle of a fishing rod. The spools turn on a fixed axle or shaft attached to a *back plate* that has a reel foot at the top to allow the reel to be fitted to a rod. Few centrepin reels have gears, so the *retrieve ratio* is 1:1 (in other words, one rotation of the handle results in a single turn of the spool — for more on gearing, refer to the sidebar 'Geared for action'), making line recovery relatively slow, especially in the case of smaller diameter reels.

Centrepin reels are relatively useless for casting — unless you're something of an expert (or a masochist!) — because controlling a spinning centrepin spool during a cast takes considerable skill and dexterity. For this reason, many users of centrepin reels pull the relevant amount of line off the reel, allowing it to form a neat pile on the ground, and then make a gentle, pendulum-style *lob cast* with the rod.

More advanced centrepin reels have a rudimentary drag or a *clicker* that you can activate via a sliding button on the back plate. However, when a fish takes out line, the spool and the crank handle spin around — often rather violently — leading to the reel's nicknames of *knuckle-buster* or *knuckle-duster*. Other monikers for the centrepin reel family include *Nottingham* and *Scarborough* after the English towns where some of the earliest models of centrepin reels were first made.

Today, with one notable exception, you rarely come across the old style of centrepin reels, although a few die-hard luderick or blackfish specialists (myself included!) still swear by the design. The major exception is in the area of fly-fishing because fly reels are basically modified centrepins, although many are much more sophisticated than the knuckle-busters of old.

Expensive modern fly reels (see Figure 6-4) — some of which can cost more than a thousand dollars apiece — have drilled spools to reduce the reel's weight and allow ventilation and quick drying of the line. Modern fly reels also have sophisticated drags or clutches and, in some instances, *anti-reverse* systems to immobilise the handles as the line is pulled from the spool and internal gearing for quicker retrieval of the line.

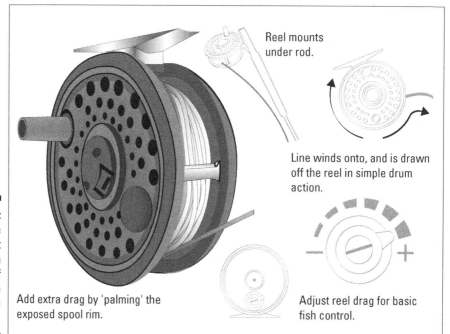

Figure 6-4:
Fly reels are the most common form of centrepin reel used today.

Reel mounts under rod.

Line winds onto, and is drawn off the reel in simple drum action.

Add extra drag by 'palming' the exposed spool rim.

Adjust reel drag for basic fish control.

Sidecast reels

Angling historians have been arguing for years whether the sidecast system was invented in Australia or England. Whichever the source (I'm on the Old Dart's side), sidecast reels have certainly found a home — and a legion of enthusiastic fans — on Australia's surf-pounded beaches and ocean rock ledges. Giving the design even more of an Aussie edge, the name of the largest Australian manufacturer of sidecasts — Alvey — has become a generic title for this type of reel, just as Esky has come to mean insulated cooler. Sidecasts have been a little slower to take off in New Zealand, but do enjoy a following in some surf fishing circles in the land of 'chilly-bins' (Eskies) and 'jandals' (thongs).

A sidecast reel (see Figure 6-5) is a centrepin reel with a spool that you can twist on the fixed base and reel seat through 90 degrees to face forwards, which allows you to make a fixed-spool style cast, with the line peeling off over the spool lip. When you complete the cast, you can turn back the spool to the original position and rotate it using a crank handle or handles to recover line. A simple, but brilliant, system!

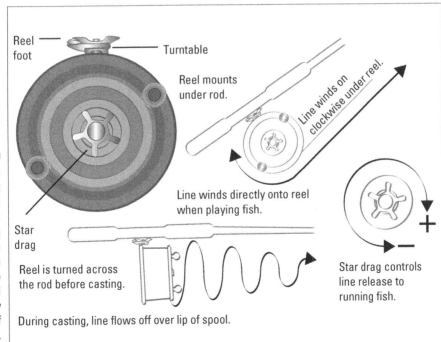

Figure 6-5: Sidecast reels have become something of an Australian icon due to their rugged simplicity and ease of use.

Reel foot

Turntable

Reel mounts under rod.

Line winds on clockwise under reel.

Line winds directly onto reel when playing fish.

Star drag

Reel is turned across the rod before casting.

Star drag controls line release to running fish.

During casting, line flows off over lip of spool.

Sidecast reels hang underneath the rod and offer all the robust simplicity of centrepin reels (refer to the previous section) combined with the smooth, easy casting of threadline reels. For this reason, sidecast reels have become extremely popular with anglers fishing in harsh environments such as from surf beaches or ocean rocks, especially when light weights need to be cast considerable distances, when big fish are likely to be hooked or when a fast retrieve speed is less important than sheer cranking power.

Sidecast reels are offered in a variety of configurations, with quite sophisticated drag systems, anti-reverse mechanisms, *ratchets* (clickers) and even, in a few instances, gearing to increase the retrieve speed. However, all sidecast reels have the same innovative turntable assembly that allows you to rotate the spool for casting.

Sidecast reels are quite competitively priced and most models fall into the $100 to $250 price range, which is very good value when you consider that one can easily last a lifetime!

Closed-face reels

Closed-face reels, also known as spincast or spincaster reels (see Figure 6-6) are fixed-spool fishing reels designed to sit on top of a rod, rather than hang underneath the rod (hence the name *overhead* reel). As the name implies, closed-face reels are characterised by having a cover over the spool, which is usually a dome of metal or plastic with a hole in the front for the line to feed through. Many models are quite cheap (well under $100) but more expensive spincasters costing up to several hundred dollars are also available.

Figure 6-6: Closed-face or spincaster reels are simple to use and provide excellent accuracy in casting.

Line release button — press to cast.

Drag control

Reel mounts on top of pistol grip rod.

Turning the crank draws line in through the hole in the front housing.

To cast a closed-face reel, the angler simply depresses a large button with his or her thumb and holds the button down until the moment the line releases to execute the cast. (I describe this casting process in detail in Chapter 13.)

Closed-face reels are arguably the easiest of all reels for a beginner to master and are extremely accurate for casting over short- to medium-range distances and yet the design has never become popular in Australasia. The reasons for the lack of acceptance of closed-face reels include the following:

- ✔ Generally slow retrieve speeds
- ✔ Limited space for line
- ✔ Poor durability, especially in a saltwater environment
- ✔ Relatively rough and unsophisticated drag systems

All of the above problems make closed-face reels unsuitable for heavy-duty saltwater fishing, but the design is still useful for lighter freshwater and estuary applications. If you intend on doing a lot of short-range, accurate casting in fresh water or estuaries, especially with lures, definitely consider using a closed-face reel.

Threadline reels

As I mention in the section 'Spool School', earlier in this chapter, threadline reels are fixed-spool reels that hang underneath the butt or handle of a rod. Threadline reels have a spool, a crank handle (that you can usually switch from one side to the other and thereby control with either your left or right hand), a slipping clutch or drag and internal gearing that typically gives the reel a line recovery ratio in the order of 4:1 up to about 6:1 (refer to the 'Geared for action' sidebar).

Threadline reels are easy to operate, come in a wide range of sizes, and you can use this type of reel for most styles of fishing with either baits or artificial lures. The reels are especially useful if you're targeting species weighing up to 10 or 15 kilos and when you use a line with a breaking strain in the range 1–15 kilos (I explain line strengths and their ratings in Chapter 4). You can also use threadline reels for tackling larger game in relatively experienced hands, but they're less than ideal for this purpose, due to the considerable force imposed on the line where it turns at 90 degrees to pass around the bail arm and bail roller. If you intend fishing specifically for larger fish with heavy lines, overhead reels or sidecast reels are more useful than threadline reels.

The positive aspects of threadline or spinning reels include the following:

✔ Threadline reels are readily available in a wide range of styles (ranging in price from less than $60 to well over a grand).

✔ Threadline reels are extremely efficient for casting light weights.

✔ Threadline reels are designed with simplicity in mind.

The drawbacks of threadline or spinning reels include these issues:

✔ The line has a tendency to twist (refer to the 'Avoiding line tangles' section, earlier in this chapter).

✔ The reel design has a reduced ability to handle heavier lines and large, active saltwater fish.

Baitcaster reels

Baitcaster or plug reels (see Figure 6-7) are revolving drum, overhead reels. This means that the reel sits on top of a rod handle and has a spool that spins when casting, recovering the line (by turning via internal gearing) and yielding line to a strong fish by using the slipping clutch or drag.

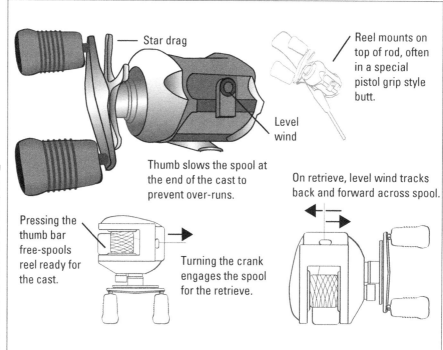

Figure 6-7: Baitcaster or plug reels are revolving drum, overhead reels with a line-laying level-wind device.

Star drag

Reel mounts on top of rod, often in a special pistol grip style butt.

Level wind

Thumb slows the spool at the end of the cast to prevent over-runs.

Pressing the thumb bar free-spools reel ready for the cast.

Turning the crank engages the spool for the retrieve.

On retrieve, level wind tracks back and forward across spool.

Baitcasters tend to be fairly expensive reels, costing from just over $100 to well over $1,000, depending upon their quality.

The name baitcaster is actually a rather inappropriate misnomer for this style of reel because at least a half of the baitcasters sold in Australia and New Zealand are used for casting lures rather than natural baits! (I explain what a lure is, how a lure works and how a lure differs from a bait in Chapter 8.)

At first glance, baitcasters or plug reels (refer to Figure 6-7) look very much like smaller versions of the overhead reels that I describe in the last part of this section. However, baitcasters differ from other overhead reels in that the design includes a *level-wind* device on the front of the reel (a rather cunning little line carrier that tracks back and forth across the face of the turning spool to neatly distribute the retrieved line onto the spool).

The level-wind mechanism is driven by an *Archimedean screw* that turns and drives the line carrier as the spool rotates (go ahead and impress your friends with this great piece of trivia that links to the famous Greek mathematician with a penchant for overfilling his bathtub!).

Baitcaster reels have a reputation for being something of an 'expert's' reel because the design is slightly more complex and difficult to master than a threadline reel, a closed-face reel or a sidecaster reel. The difficulty arises because the spool spins during casting and this spinning can easily become out of control, leading to *over-runs*, *backlashes* and all sorts of nasty tangles (often called *birds' nests*). That said, modern baitcasters are nowhere near as difficult to handle as their predecessors; if you can see clear advantages in owning a baitcaster reel, don't be put off by the reel's reputation. (I explain how to cast a baitcaster reel in Chapter 13.)

The positive aspects of baitcaster reels include

✔ Excellent casting accuracy (as soon as you master the spinning spool)

✔ The ability to easily handle large, active fish (baitcaster reels are especially popular with anglers using lures to pursue species such as barramundi, bass, sea-run chinnok (quinnat) salmon and Murray cod)

The downsides of baitcaster reels include

✔ An inability to cast very light weights (especially into a breeze)

✔ The need for a little practice and continued concentration on the part of the operator

If you're going to spend a lot of time casting or trolling lures that weigh more than 10–12 grams and your target fish are occasionally going to exceed 5 or 10 kilos (you hope!), then I recommend you try a baitcaster reel.

Overhead reels

Overhead reels (also called *multipliers* or *revolving drum reels* in older literature) are really no more than grown-up baitcaster reels (refer to the previous section). They have grown-up prices to match; generally starting at a couple of hundred bucks and going skywards from there.

The biggest examples of overhead reels are very grown up indeed and seem almost as large (and heavy) as the old surf rescue belt reels still occasionally seen on Aussie and Kiwi beaches in summer nostalgia-driven re-enactments. These mega-models are called *game reels* and are used with thick, strong line for tackling heavyweight sharks, tuna and marlin. Overhead game reels cost a small fortune (up to several thousand dollars), are virtually impossible to cast (and are, therefore, mostly used for boat fishing) and aren't likely to be of great interest to angling novices.

At the opposite end of the scale are overhead reels that are the same size as large baitcaster reels (see Figure 6-8). The only obvious difference between large baitcasters and small overhead reels is the presence of a line-laying, level-wind device on most baitcaster reels and the lack of this mechanism on most other overhead reels. The similarities between the two reels often leads to a semantic argument about whether or not a bigger overhead with a level-wind is in fact a baitcaster reel — not that this matters much to the fish!

Figure 6-8:
Overhead reels excel at casting long distances (at least in experienced hands) and are superlative tools for catching big, strong fish.

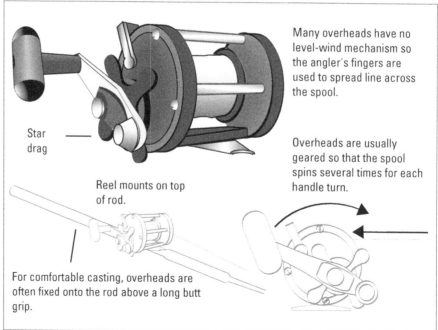

Many overheads have no level-wind mechanism so the angler's fingers are used to spread line across the spool.

Star drag

Overheads are usually geared so that the spool spins several times for each handle turn.

Reel mounts on top of rod.

For comfortable casting, overheads are often fixed onto the rod above a long butt grip.

Made in America

As with many inconsistencies in the modern English language, we Kiwis and Aussies can blame the Americans for applying the name baitcaster to a type of reel an angler mostly uses with lures.

In the United States, both natural and artificial offerings intended to fool fish into biting are often called baits. As a result, an ideal reel for casting lures goes by the name of baitcaster!

Overhead reels have internal gearing with retrieve ratios ranging from around 3:1 up to 7:1 and an in-built clutch or drag mechanism that operates by an external star wheel (called a *star drag*) or via a quadrant lever (called a *lever drag*). Many overhead reels also have a clicker or ratchet (sometimes referred to as a *strike alarm*), which operates by an external button or switch.

Overheads share the same strengths and weaknesses as their smaller siblings, the baitcasters, and have a similar reputation for being a bit of an 'expert's' reel. That said, when it comes to belting out a really long cast with a heavy lure or sinker and then doing battle with big, strong fish such as snapper, mulloway and sharks, no other reel matches the quality of an overhead reel (with the possible exception of a large sidecaster). Overhead reels are also superb for most forms of offshore boat fishing, from trolling to deep water *bottom bouncing* and *jigging* (I describe these forms of fishing in Chapter 22).

Reel Respect

Reels generally require a bit more maintenance than rods because reels have a more complex assembly with various moving parts. (Swim on back to Chapter 5 for all you need to know about keeping your rods in good nick.)

The best way to look after your reels is to remove the devices from your rods whenever the gear isn't in use (including the time spent in your vehicle). As this section explains, I also recommend you wash and lubricate your reels from time to time and have the reels serviced once a year by a qualified technician.

Store your reels in a cool, dry place well away from direct sunlight and, while you're at it, make a note of the make, model and any serial numbers for your household contents insurance policy, in case of theft or fire.

Don't faucet

After a fishing trip, you can wash your reels while still attached to the rods. However, if you use a hose or tap, be careful not to direct a high pressure jet of water onto the reel because this often forces saltwater, salt, sand and dirt into the internal workings of the reel. Instead, use a fine spray or a trickle of slow-flowing water to rinse off your fishing gear. Better still, fill a basin or bucket with warm, soapy water and use a soft cloth dipped in this water to gently wipe over your reels, paying particular attention to any nooks and crannies where nasties may gather. After rinsing the reels, wipe the remaining water off with a soft, dry cloth.

Oil toil

After every three or four outings, I recommend you add a drop or two of fine machine oil to the reel's external moving parts, including the handle knobs, bail arm assembly, bail roller, level-wind device and so on. Sewing machine oil is excellent for this purpose, although specialist reel lubes are also available. An occasional squirt of the reel's exterior with an aerosol lubricant is also a good idea. However, try not to spray too much of this stuff onto the spool or the fishing line itself as the chemicals in some lubricants may degrade nylon fishing lines (and many people believe that the smell of chemicals on your line can put some fish off biting).

Pro-active

Every year or two, or any time your reel begins to make funny grinding noises or is stiff and lumpy to turn, take the reel to a reputable tackle shop and have the device serviced by an expert.

You can certainly do this job yourself at home if you have even a modest level of mechanical aptitude, but in this age of specialisation and out-sourcing, why bother? Unless you're the sort of person who changes the oil in your car and can rebuild a cranky lawn mower, I recommend you avoid the headaches and pitfalls of reel servicing and pay an expert to handle the job. The more expensive and complex the reel, the more the use of an expert makes sense. Though this service may cost you from $50 to $100 or more (depending on whether or not any parts need replacing) your reels (and probably your hip pocket) are going to thank you in the long run.

Chapter 7

Terminal Tackle

. . . .

. . . .

*A*ll the bits and pieces of gear that you can tie to the end of your fishing line or attach somewhere along the length of the line are collectively called *terminal tackle*. This name is a happy coincidence because it indicates that the items are used at or near the end of the line and that the same gizmos can prove fatal to fish (you hope!).

Common items of terminal tackle include the following:

✔ Fish hooks (which are looked at in detail in Chapter 4)

✔ Flies

✔ Floats

✔ Leaders

✔ Lures

✔ Rings

✔ Sinkers

✔ Swivels

✔ Traces

Don't worry if you're not sure what some of these items are, because I explain each in detail in this chapter and the following chapter, providing you with enough information to choose and use each device — and to avoid being bamboozled by jargon-spouting tackle shop staff!

Sinkers Away!

Sinkers are weights made from lead, lead-alloys or other heavy materials. Sinkers include either a hole or channel, an eyelet or a ring to hold the line. *Shot* are smaller versions of sinkers and include a split on one side, allowing the line to be inserted before the shot is squeezed shut.

You can add sinkers or shot to a fishing line to serve a number of purposes, the most important being to

✔ Balance or ballast a float so that the float's movement clearly indicates bites

✔ Hold a bait at a desired level in the water

✔ Keep the line and rig beneath the surface in a strong current

✔ Provide additional weight to aid in casting

✔ Sink a rigged line down towards the bottom of the river, lake or sea

In most fishing scenarios, if you can avoid thinking of sinkers as anchors, you're more likely to use them in a way that enhances your catch rather than shoos them away! You're going to catch a lot more fish because your bait behaves far more naturally in the water.

Thinking small

Many anglers erroneously think that a sinker is designed to hold the bait firmly in one place and keep the line tight so that bites can be easily felt. The fact is that most bites register just as easily when the line is slightly slack and far fewer fish shy away from a bait that is allowed to move about in a natural way, at the whim of the current and tide.

In nearly every case, the smallest sinker you can use in the circumstances is the best. In other words, this is one area of life where smaller (or lighter) is almost always better. (Remember the adage: Less is more.)

The shape and design of the sinker is less important than the sinker's weight because the shape merely allows you to finetune your rig. A number of shapes are designed for special functions. You can see some of the most common and popular sinker designs in Figure 7-1.

Figure 7-1: A range of common sinker styles.

Ball sinker

Bean sinker

Barrel sinker

Snapper sinker

Split shot

Picking a sinker shape

For most day-to-day fishing needs, *ball, bean* and *barrel* are ideal. The performance of each is so similar that you can pick whichever shape appeals the most.

As well as the common sinkers, the following sinker styles have useful applications in certain forms of fishing:

- ✔ **Snapper lead:** This type of sinker is designed to sink fast, straight and without spinning and travel through the air with little wind resistance, making the snapper lead extremely suited to deep-water fishing or long-distance casting.

- ✔ **Star sinkers and helmet sinkers:** These sinkers are designed to have excellent grip in sandy seabeds, especially when strong cross currents are flowing, making the styles useful for surf fishing on rough days.

Some specialist sinkers that were popular in years gone by have less relevance to angling today. *Spoon* sinkers, for example, have largely gone out of favour with modern anglers, even though this style is good for using over snaggy bottoms because the design makes the sinker ride up over obstructions when retrieved quickly. Other unusual designs such as the *channel* sinker or so-called *picker's doom* have also faded from general use and are mostly only found in museum collections or pictured in old books.

Using split shot

Shot, which are often called *split shot*, are small sinkers in the shape of a ball or bean with a slice or split rather than a central line channel. Shot are held in place by inserting the line into the split and then crimping or squeezing the gap shut.

Split shot are especially useful for finetuning the balance of a float or for providing a tiny amount of weight to the line at a set distance above a bait, fly or lure. Shot are also convenient to use because you can add the itsy-bitsy pieces of lead to the line at any time, without cutting and re-tying the rig.

Drawbacks of split shot include

> ✔ **Line damage:** If squeezed or crimped too tightly, shot can damage the line.

> ✔ **Shot damage:** Shot have a habit of rattling and banging about in tackle boxes so that the split closes up, making the shot useless.

The best type of shot are made from soft lead or lead alloy and come in a handy, circular dispenser with a sliding lid that allows you to easily select the size of shot. While soft lead shot are easier to use, many countries are phasing out soft lead shot because the material is harmful to the environment. (I devote an entire chapter to sustainable fishing and the future — see Chapter 17.)

Never clamp split shot onto the line by biting the shot or crushing the shot between your teeth! Not only can this common practice damage your teeth (as my dentist can attest), the method can also result in lead poisoning. Instead, use finger pressure or a pair of pliers to attach shot to the line. Equally, avoid placing sinkers in your mouth or touching food after handling sinkers — give your hands a quick wash first. This advice is especially relevant to your tiddler adventurers, who are more susceptible to lead poisoning.

Splitting the difference

Depending on the style of sinker you choose and the type of fishing you're doing, you can either fix sinkers in place on your line or allow them to run freely on the line. Split shot, which you attach by pinching them onto the line, and snapper leads, which you usually tie to the end of the line, are examples of fixed sinkers when used in the manner the manufacturers intended.

By contrast, for sinkers with a hole or channel through the middle — including ball, bean, bug and barrel sinkers — you can attach them so they simply slide up and down freely on the line. They can go either all the way to the hook or as far as a stopper such as a swivel or ring, a split shot or a knot (I discuss the various methods of attaching sinkers in Chapters 11 and 12).

Buying and making sinkers

Sinkers are numbered or sized in a variety of ways; however, most shops or sinker manufacturers number smaller sinkers (especially ball sinkers) starting with the designation 00 for the smallest and moving up to 0, then 1, then 2, and so on. The numbering on sinkers larger than 28 grams (about one ounce) usually switches to the weight in grams or ounces (for example, a four-ounce snapper lead or a 60-gram bean sinker).

Sinkers can be bought individually, in packages of tens or dozens or greater, with the number of sinkers in each pack varying according to the sinkers' individual size. Expect to pay anywhere from a few cents to several dollars per sinker, depending on their size and weight.

As a general rule, I recommend you carry a larger number of relatively small sinkers in your tackle box or kit rather than fewer heavier sinkers. By doing this, you can add extra weight to a rig by sliding two, three, four or even more small sinkers onto the line rather than adding a single large sinker. The advantage is that when you need just a small amount of weight, you can use just the one sinker.

Moulds are available for anglers who want to make sinkers from scrap lead or lead alloys. This is a money-saving alternative for anglers who use a lot of sinkers, but, be warned, because dealing with molten metal is messy, inconvenient and potentially dangerous.

Avoiding that sinking feeling

Because lead has potential health hazards, it's worth pointing out that this material most likely has a finite future in Australasian fishing, precisely because of those hazards.

Some countries have already outlawed the use of lead in shotgun pellets, sinkers and split shot, mainly because so much lead was being discarded into the environment and the metal was being accidentally eaten by swans, ducks and other creatures, sometimes leading to their death.

Almost certainly, the fishing industry is going to see lead phased out and replaced with other dense materials in sinker and shot manufacture over the coming decade or so. Meanwhile, you can do your bit (as can I) by minimising the amount of lead you leave in and around your aquatic environments.

Swivels' Turn

Swivels are brass or steel devices that have a rotating loop or *eyelet* at each end and a *barrel* or body in the middle (see Figure 7-2). The primary function of swivels is to prevent or reduce line twist and the tangles this twisting can cause. However, swivels also make convenient sinker *stoppers*, and are handy for joining bits of line together when *rigging up*.

Common types of swivels include the following, listed in order of simplicity, strength and cost (from just cents per unit for small barrel swivels to several dollars apiece for large ball bearing models):

✔ Barrel swivel

✔ Box swivel

✔ Torpedo swivel (designed to be used with thick, heavy lines)

✔ Various stainless steel ball bearing swivels (much more expensive than other types of swivels, but extremely strong and effective when used in demanding conditions)

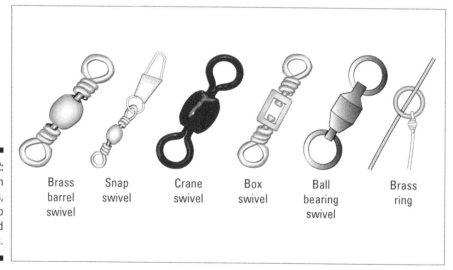

Figure 7-2:
A selection
of swivels,
clips, snap
swivels and
rings.

Brass   Snap   Crane   Box   Ball   Brass
barrel   swivel   swivel   swivel   bearing   ring
swivel   swivel

Switching swivels

As with sinkers, swivels are sized by number and the higher the number, the smaller the swivel. Generally, the smallest swivels that are practical to use are the No. 14 and No. 16 swivels. Box swivels are rarely available in sizes smaller than No. 10.

Swivels from No. 14 up to about No. 4 cover the majority of fishing situations, but a larger swivel such as a torpedo or ball bearing swivel, is recommended for chasing big, powerful fish. Often, the torpedo and ball bearing swivels are numbered according to the tested breaking strength of the swivel.

Discovering a few swivel secrets

The secret with swivels of any type is to choose the smallest size practical for the strength of line you're using and the size of the fish you're targeting. Only then do swivels spin as intended and actually remove or reduce twist in the line.

Bearing this in mind, beware using No. 14 or No. 12 swivels on stronger line because a big fish may well tear or pull a small swivel apart. As well, the fine wire used in the eyelets of tiny swivels can cut into thick line under pressure and cause the line to break at the knot.

In most cases, I recommend you choose a swivel on which the eyelet wire is about one and a half to two times as thick as the line you're using. The following are recommended swivel sizes for various line strengths:

- ✔ **Lines up to a breaking strain of 3 kilos:** Use No. 14 or No. 12 swivels.

- ✔ **Lines with a breaking strain of 4 kilos to 8 kilos:** Use No. 10 or No. 8 swivels.

- ✔ **Lines with a breaking strain of 9 kilos to 15 kilos:** Use No. 6 or No. 4 swivels.

Buying and keeping swivels

Swivels in the Nos 4–16 range are commonly sold in packets containing 12, 20 or 25 units. The more expensive torpedo and ball bearing swivels (which can cost several dollars each or more) are sold individually or in smaller packs.

As swivels are made of brass or stainless steel, relatively little preventive maintenance is necessary to keep the swivels in top shape. That said, sand and grit left lying in your tackle box can jam barrel swivels, and all swivels eventually corrode if used around saltwater. You can prevent corrosion by storing the swivels carefully and by occasionally spraying the swivels with a light coat of aerosol lubricant.

Quick Connection

Snaps, *clips* and *snap swivels* are devices similar to safety pins, are made of brass or steel wire and, commonly, are used to connect lures, leaders or even hooks to the line, especially when frequent changes of terminal tackle are necessary (refer to Figure 7-2). Snaps, clips and snap swivels also help artificial lures to swim more seductively in the water by removing the tight line-to-lure connection created by an ordinary knot tied directly to the lure's eyelet.

Adding a weak link

Snaps or clips are sold either individually or already attached to a swivel. This latter arrangement is usually called a snap swivel.

Some clips and snaps are rather weakly constructed and are unable to withstand the pressures exerted by large fish hooked on heavy tackle. Price is a fair guide to the quality and strength of snaps and clips (expect to pay from a few cents each to a dollar or two per clip, depending on the size and strength of the product), but no matter how high the quality, snaps and clips are always a potentially weak link in the fish catching chain and I recommend you only use the gadgets when absolutely necessary.

Enjoying the two-ringed circus

Anglers commonly use two types of rings: split rings and solid brass rings.

Split rings are similar to those found on a key ring and are made of brass, chromed brass or stainless steel and are mainly used for attaching hooks to lures. (You can pick these up for a few cents apiece, although really big, strong models can be pricier.)

If possible, don't tie a nylon line directly onto a split ring because the knot can easily slide into contact with the sharp ends of the coiled wire or, in rare cases, unwind completely out of the ring. If a lure you want to use has a split ring on the front eyelet or *tow point*, use a snap or clip to attach the lure to your line or fit a small solid brass ring to the split ring and tie your line to this.

Solid brass rings also make extremely useful connectors, spacers and sinker stoppers, especially when a swivel isn't required to stop the line from twisting. Solid brass rings are cheaper (a few cents each), lighter and stronger than swivels, but fail to prevent line twist.

Split and solid rings are both available in a range of sizes and are usually sold in packets of 10, 12 or more, although you can generally buy individual larger split rings.

Bobbers' Job

You use fishing floats primarily to suspend a bait at a predetermined depth below the surface of the water and to give a visual indication of bites.

Using stemmed floats

Several distinct styles of float exist (see Figure 7-3), but the most common type is the *stemmed float*, which has a shaped body of foam, cork or wood and a shaft of dowel, bamboo, plastic or metal. The float's shaft is fitted with either metal or plastic eyelets or carries lengths of tightly fitting plastic tube to hold the float to the line. I explain how to rig and use floats in Chapter 12.

Stemmed floats are extremely popular with blackfish (luderick) specialists on the east coast of Australia and are also often used by anglers pursuing drummer, bream, mullet, sweep and similar species. Kiwi anglers mostly use them for catching garfish or piper. Expect to pay anywhere from $2 to $10 apiece for stemmed floats.

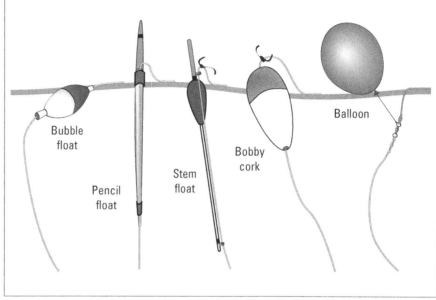

Figure 7-3:
Floats come in a wide variety of sizes and shapes — all designed to suspend the bait and provide a visual indication of bites.

Bubble float

Pencil float

Stem float

Bobby cork

Balloon

Light-stemmed floats that don't have a body are called *quills*, because the floats were originally made from porcupine quills or the stems of large feathers. Quills are best used in still or slow-flowing waters to present baits to trout, garfish, mullet and similar light- to middle-weight species.

Using floats without stems

Floats without stems mainly take the form of *bobby corks* (also called *bobbers*), *bubble floats* or even inflated balloons. The floats' sizes and uses differ enormously, as the following shows:

- ✔ **Bobby corks:** Made from foam, cork, timber or hollow plastic casing, most bobby cork style floats have a hole running through the middle to carry the line. Corks can be as small as a thumbnail or as big as a rockmelon and cost around $10 for a pack of five.

- ✔ **Bubble floats:** Made from clear plastic or soft, transparent rubber, bubble floats are fitted with plugs or slits so you can partially fill it with water to provide additional casting weight. The float attaches to the line by means of moulded eyelets or a central channel. Bubble floats are popular with many trout anglers using baits such as live mudeyes (dragonfly larvae), shrimps or worms. (Pay between $1 and $4 depending on size.)

- ✔ **Inflated balloons:** You can use heavy-duty balloons as floats to suspend large baits intended for sharks, tuna or marlin.

Fixing the position of floats

You can either fix a float in position on the line or allow it to run freely below a stopper — a piece of knotted line, wool or rubber on the main line or a swivel or ring tied into the rig. (The stopper is necessary to keep the line from sliding through the float, allowing the baited hook to run all the way to the sea, lake or river bed.)

Ordinarily, fixed floats are best for fishing at relatively shallow depths beneath the surface, whereas running float rigs are preferred by anglers wanting to present a bait deep below a float. I explain float rigging in detail in Chapter 12.

Most floats, especially the stemmed variety (see the section 'Using stemmed floats', earlier in this chapter), work best if the float is weighted or ballasted so that the float is at least three-quarters submerged and requires only a soft bite or pull on the line to sink the float beneath the surface. Insufficient weighting of a float can 'spook' fish and result in missing out on bites.

The Lure Cure

A *lure* or a *fly* is an artificial bait used to attract the fish. To put it more colourfully, a lure is a lie told by an angler to a fish!

Most lures and flies are intended to represent small fish, prawns, crabs, yabbies or insects when pulled through the water or allowed to drift either through or on the water. However, a number of types of lures and flies look like nothing on Earth (see Figure 7-4) and still manage to catch fish — sometimes!

An old adage states that many lures and flies catch more anglers than fish. In other words, the lures appeal more to human senses than to those of fish. While the saying has a certain truth, today's lures and flies on the tackle shop shelves are products of a keenly competitive market and most are efficient at drawing fish to your hook — under the right circumstances. (I discuss lure fishing at greater length in Chapter 8.)

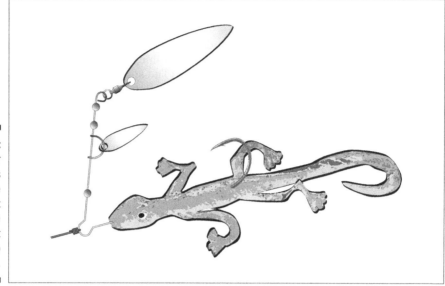

Figure 7-4:
A number
of lures
have bizarre
designs, but
still manage
to attract
the fish to
your hook.

Take Me to Your Leader

A *leader* or a *trace* is a section of line inserted at the working end of your line. The sections are constructed from a different material to your main line. Usually, the section of line is either heavier and stronger (called a trace) or lighter and weaker (called a leader) than the main line. Leaders and traces are often made from a different material to the main line, such as wire.

The following shows the reasons for using a leader or trace:

✔ **Leaders:** A length of lighter, finer line inserted directly ahead of the hook or fly reduces the chance of detection by more timid or sharp-sighted fish, especially in very clear water. The light pieces of line are often made of nylon and are sometimes tapered, especially in fly-fishing.

✔ **Traces:** A length of nylon, fluorocarbon or wire at the business end of the line prevents hooked fish from chewing through the line or abrading it with their teeth, gills, scales, spines or tails.

Using wire leaders and traces

Shop-bought wire traces are readily available from tackle stores and generally come in 20–40 centimetre lengths, are made of nylon-coated, multi-strand wire and have a swivel at one end and a clip or snap at the other end. Expect to pay around a dollar or three for traces.

These wire traces are adequate for use on light to medium tackle and for catching smaller fish with sharp teeth; however, this type of trace is prone to failure when using it to catch big, strong fish. To ensure quality, most anglers who regularly use wire or heavy nylon leaders eventually turn to making traces by hand.

At the light end of the spectrum, tapered leaders for fly-fishing are more trustworthy than many other commercially made leaders or traces and many experienced fly anglers use this type of factory-made product rather than tediously tying hand-made leaders.

Working with snells and snoods

Another popular product in some areas is the *pre-snelled* or *snooded* hook. This type of rig consists of a hook knotted to a length of nylon line (usually 20–50 centimetres in length) with a loop or swivel at the other end for attaching the gear to the rig.

Pre-snelled or snooded hooks are usually sold in packs of 6, 20 or 25 units. While the design provides considerable convenience, snells aren't generally favoured by more experienced anglers, who prefer to tie their own knots and construct their own rigs.

Tackling the shops

Terminal tackle is available in a bewildering array of shapes, sizes and designs, with some tackle shops carrying thousands of items of stock that fall under this heading. In reality, you need to buy only a tiny percentage of the different hooks, sinkers, lures, floats, swivels, leaders, lures and flies on the market. The trick lies in recognising the items best suited to your specific needs, then making do with the simplest selection possible.

Most serious anglers end up accumulating a large collection of terminal tackle — and then only using a fraction of the gear. If you're a fishing novice or want to try a new style of fishing or location, I recommend you restrict the amount of terminal tackle you buy. Instead, proceed slowly and carefully, only adding new items to your collection when you really need a different type of terminal tackle.

Chapter 8

Baits, Lures and Flies

*Y*ou really only need a hook and a length of line to catch a fish, but a tempting morsel (natural or otherwise) attached to the hook certainly helps!

The purpose of bait is to fool a fish into biting or swallowing a hook. Baits are divided into two broad categories — baits that are edible and baits that are not.

The second category includes artificial baits, better known as lures or flies. Man-made contrivances, artificial baits can be thought of as being counterfeit baits as opposed to natural baits (although the term 'natural' is used rather loosely by some anglers!).

The range of edible substances that can be pressed into service as fish bait is limited only by the imagination of the angler because fish are known to be tempted by a range of outlandish offerings. A few examples of weird and wonderful bait include boiled egg white, cheese, tripe, lollies, flower blossoms, chickens' intestines, spiders, slugs and a range of fruits and vegetables. This amazing variety has, however, nothing on artificial baits! I've heard of fish being seduced by clothes pegs, sections of drinking straw, bits of teased rope fibre and even torn strips of a desperate angler's underwear!

When considering why fish sometimes respond to what appear to be unlikely baits and lures, remember that the critters have no arms or hands. If a fish wants to examine an intriguing object, the fish usually does so with its mouth — often with fatal results (I explain this phenomenon and what I call the wet paint syndrome in Chapter 1).

A huge array of items can tempt fish from time to time. However, long-term angling success — especially on difficult species in hard-fished waters — is ordinarily enjoyed only by anglers who make something of a science of using the best, most natural and appealing baits or the best possible imitations. Think of the following adage, and you can't go far wrong: When choosing bait, fresh is good, live is better and the stuff you catch or gather yourself is best of all.

Seducing Saltwater Fish

Live and frozen prawns top the list of the most popular baits for catching saltwater fish, but an enormous range of other types of bait exist to help you in the battle to tempt a fish onto your hook.

Coming the raw prawn

The humble frozen prawn is without doubt the most popular bait among Australia's vast army of saltwater anglers. To a lesser degree, prawns can also be used quite effectively in freshwater environments.

Tens of thousands of packets of frozen prawns are sold every year from tackle shops, boat hire sheds, garages and general stores right around the country's coastline, with sales reaching peak levels during the school holiday periods.

Prawns are attractive to most species of fish and because of the popularity of frozen prawns as bait, more fish are caught each year using prawns than any other single bait type.

The method you use to attach the prawn to the hook can make the difference between success and failure. When using thawed or freshly dead prawns, I recommend you stick the sharp end of the hook into the prawn under its little tail fan. Work the body of the prawn around the bend of the hook bringing the hook point out under the bait's head among the prawn's front legs (see Figure 8-1). Usually, a prawn bait that lays straight in the water is more appealing to fish than an offering that's all curled up in a little ball.

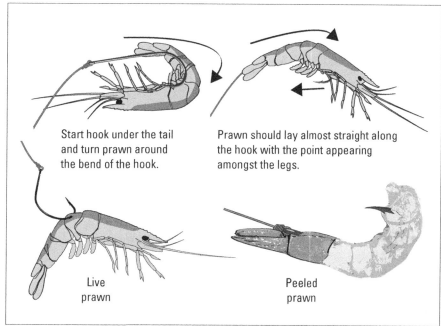

Start hook under the tail and turn prawn around the bend of the hook.

Prawn should lay almost straight along the hook with the point appearing amongst the legs.

Figure 8-1: Make sure you take the time to attach the prawn firmly to the hook.

Live prawn

Peeled prawn

While frozen prawns are reliable and convenient bait in many situations and catch plenty of fish, the icy crustaceans aren't necessarily the best choice. A rung above frozen prawns are live or extremely fresh prawns. Don't believe me? Spend a few hours one night in the shallows with a flashlight to attract and find the prawns and a scoop net to harvest the tasty morsels, and then put the juicy beasts to good use the next morning. I promise you that this method is sure to prove how truly deadly the old raw prawn can be!

Picking the best of the rest

Apart from the ubiquitous frozen prawn, saltwater anglers have the option of choosing from an incredibly wide range of baits. You can buy some types of bait (including squid, mullet gut, cockles, pilchards, whitebait and so on) frozen in packets at bait outlets. You're best to purchase other types of bait (including whole mullet, garfish and octopus) fresh from fish shops where the fish are intended for human consumption and are typically displayed in tip-top condition.

As with prawns, take your time when putting bait on the hook to make sure the bait is firmly attached and that it camouflages the hook (see Figure 8-2).

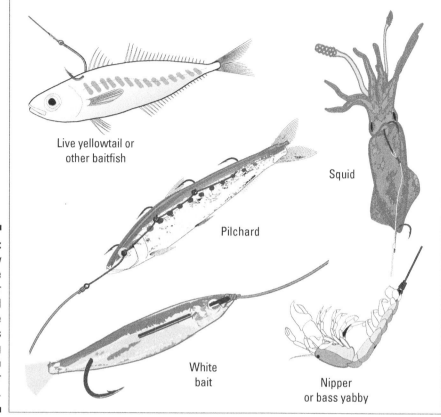

Figure 8-2:
A few effective saltwater baits and some of the best ways of placing the baits on a hook or hooks.

Live yellowtail or other baitfish

Pilchard

Squid

White bait

Nipper or bass yabby

Catching your own bait

The best baits for virtually all styles of fishing — in both saltwater and freshwater — are fresh baits caught by the angler (even experts can be fooled about freshness in bait shops). Saltwater baits that you can easily catch or gather include:

- ✔ Crabs
- ✔ Cunjevoi (also known as sea squirts)
- ✔ Mussels
- ✔ Pipis (cockles)
- ✔ Prawns
- ✔ Razor fish
- ✔ Saltwater yabbies (also known as nippers, pink nippers or bass yabbies)

✔ Shrimp

✔ Various burrowing marine worms (including sand worms, blood worms, squirt worms and red wrigglers)

✔ Various marine algae (including green weed, sea lettuce and sea cabbage)

Methods for catching or gathering fresh bait vary from species to species and place to place, but most require the use of your hands and one of the following four tools (see Figure 8-3):

✔ **Bait fish trap:** Sometimes called a poddy mullet trap, you can bait this type of trap with bread and place it in shallow water to snare little mullet and other species.

✔ **Fine mesh scoop or dip net:** You use this type of net to scoop up prawns, shrimps and small fish from the shallows.

✔ **Light handline or fine rod and reel rigged with tiny hooks:** You guessed it! Use this rig for catching small fish.

✔ **Nipper (or yabby) pump or worm gun:** This device is a siphon-like tube with a handle and internal plunger that you use to suck or blow worms and yabbies from burrows in the sand or mud.

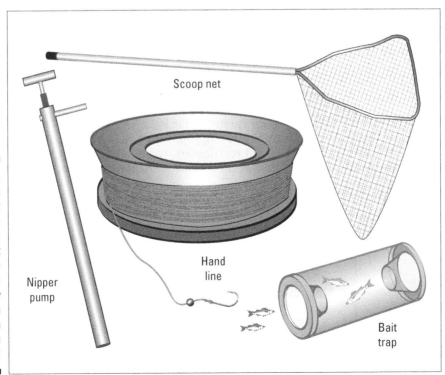

Figure 8-3: A few of the tools that you can use to catch bait — but be sure to check the legality of such devices in your area first!

Scoop net

Nipper pump

Hand line

Bait trap

Before you use fish traps, scoops, a rod and line or a worm gun to gather bait (or other devices such as cast nets and drag nets), be sure to check the current fishing rules and regulations in the state or territory where you're fishing (see Chapter 26). Many of these devices may only be used in specific locations, while various areas have laws regarding how much bait you can catch and which species you may harvest. Remember, ignorance of the law is no excuse!

Considering the great de-bait

Whether you buy packaged bait or go out and collect your bait needs fresh for yourself, your green conscience is going to thank you if you can take a moment to stop and consider the impact that all forms of bait harvesting — commercial and recreational — can potentially have on the natural environment.

By definition, most varieties of bait come from the broad base of the pyramid-shaped food chain. That posi makes these organisms extremely important to the wellbeing and even the survival of creatures higher up the rungs of that inter-connected ladder.

Over-harvesting of bait and the almost inevitable accompanying haul of *by-catch* (unwanted or non-targeted species that are often taken along with the bait) can be detrimental to the aquatic web of life. For this reason, anglers should always attempt to minimise their bait usage and to re-use or recycle any leftover bait, even if only as *berley* (material introduced into the water to attract and excite fish). It is also worth considering the use of artificial lures and flies in order to minimise bait consumption, particularly in vulnerable waters.

In addition, be sure to carefully check the local rules and regulations before gathering or harvesting your own bait supplies, and be especially aware of the often tight restrictions that apply in marine parks and designated habitat protection zones. (Chapter 26 lists various websites for you to peruse.)

Hurly-berley

Berley (also spelt burley) is the name given by Australian and New Zealand anglers to bait scraps and other edible matter introduced into the water in order to attract and excite fish. Berley is known as *chum* in North America and *ground bait* or *rubby dubby* in England.

Think of a berley trail as a stream of attractive smells wafting from the kitchen while a delicious meal is being prepared. The smells grab your attention and you start thinking about eating. Berley works the same way with fish!

Introducing berley into the water is most commonly done in saltwater, although you can use this system on inland lakes and streams.

The simplest form of *berleying* involves throwing unwanted bait scraps and pieces of fish already caught on the day into your casting area. You can take the process a step further by freezing leftover bait, fish offal and food scraps for use as berley on future outings.

Enhance a basic berley of bait scraps by adding cereals such as bread, boiled wheat, pollard or chicken feed pellets. Soak the dry goods thoroughly in a bucket of water first, and then mix with the bait scraps and, finally, distribute the mixture as evenly as possible into the area being fished. ***Note:*** If you're chasing deepwater fish, try adding some sand to the mixture to increase the sink rate of the berley.

Another worthwhile addition to most berley mixes is fish oil of some type. The most common varieties of fish oil used for berleying are tuna oil and pilchard oil, both of which are available commercially. Fish oils form a plainly visible surface slick (called a *berley trail*) and under ideal conditions the slick stretches for several kilometres, attracting fish from far and wide towards your baited hooks.

Tempting Freshwater Fish

A garden worm wiggling on a hook is one of the most recognisable images of the sport of angling — a piscatorial cliché that transcends the boundaries of language and culture. But successful freshwater bait fishing is more than simply sticking a worm on a hook, dangling the line in the water and hoping for the best!

Some of the popular saltwater baits described in the previous section also work in freshwater. In particular, fresh and frozen marine prawns are useful when pursuing species such as freshwater bass, golden perch (yellowbelly) and sooty grunter. Similarly, saltwater mussels are known trout tempters both in Australia and New Zealand, particularly in discoloured streams after flooding, and small marine bait fish (such as whitebait and even pilchards) appeal to target species such as larger trout and land-locked chinook (quinnat) salmon.

For the most part, however, freshwater anglers prefer to use specific freshwater baits. The following are the most popular of the freshwater baits:

- ✔ Bardy (witchetty) grubs
- ✔ Crayfish (freshwater yabbies)
- ✔ Earthworms
- ✔ Insects or the larvae and nymphs of insects
- ✔ Scrub worms
- ✔ Shrimps
- ✔ Small live fish (especially gudgeons and minnows)

Certain types of potential fish food — especially frogs and small fish — are banned as bait in some states and in most national parks, so you need to check with the authorities (see Chapter 26) before you set off to gather up some bait!

Best baits for popular fish

Matching the bait to the fish is a topic that anglers spend endless hours debating (pardon the pun!). That said, the most popular salt-water and fresh-water fish species (refer to Chapters 2 and 3) can each be caught using a range of specific baits.

Certainly, many, many other baits also work but the following list shows the tried and true types of bait:

- ✔ **Barramundi:** Small fish, prawns, fish pieces
- ✔ **Bass:** Crickets, shrimp, earthworms
- ✔ **Bream:** Marine worms, prawns, saltwater yabbies
- ✔ **Flathead:** Small fish, prawns, saltwater yabbies
- ✔ **Garfish (piper):** Bread, maggots, worm or prawn pieces
- ✔ **Golden perch:** Shrimp, yabbies, earthworms

- ✔ **Leatherjackets:** Worm or prawn pieces, squid strips, mussels
- ✔ **Murray cod:** Bardy (witchetty) grubs, yabbies, earthworms
- ✔ **Salmon (kahawai):** Pilchards, fish pieces, prawns
- ✔ **Snapper:** Squid, fish pieces, prawns
- ✔ **Tailor:** Pilchards, garfish, fish pieces and strips
- ✔ **Trevally:** Fish pieces, prawns, saltwater yabbies
- ✔ **Trout:** Mudeyes (dragonfly larvae), shrimp, earthworms
- ✔ **Tuna:** Small fish, pilchards, fish pieces
- ✔ **Whiting:** Marine worms, saltwater yabbies, squid strips

Man-made baits (such as packet, long-life, *putty-style mixtures* and so-called *bait eggs* made from flavoured gelatine) can be useful at times in freshwater angling, but are usually less productive than natural food items.

Desperately seeking supplies

Generally, freshwater baits are less easy to obtain through commercial outlets than saltwater baits, although an increasing number of worm farms now supply anglers with quality earthworms, tiger worms and scrub worms. The worms are usually sold in plastic tubs containing anywhere from 50 to 500 individual worms, along with a little soil, compost or leaf litter. Expect to pay a few bucks for a punnet of worms. Sometimes it's cheaper to buy them from garden supply outlets than bait shops!

You can also buy live crayfish (yabbies) and dragonfly larvae (mudeyes) and more exotic offerings such as maggots or *gents* at a number of specialist outlets found near popular freshwater fishing venues. The supply of this type of bait tends to be limited and may be expensive — up to a dollar or more per mudeye at times!

Because freshwater baits can be relatively hard to come across, freshwater anglers tend to be even more self-reliant than saltwater anglers and put a greater emphasis on gathering, catching or breeding bait.

Opening a can of worms

Luckily, many of the best inland baits are relatively easy to gather and you can find the various worms, in particular, in the following environments:

- ✓ **Earthworms:** Common varieties of worms are readily available in most gardens in the damp, rich soil under compost heaps or around drains and septic tanks.

- ✓ **Scrub worms:** Larger than earthworms, scrub worms live in leaf litter, fallen bark and other detritus along creek gullies, around cattle yards and alongside storm water drains.

- ✓ **Variety of other types of worms:** Other types of worms are best found in muddy soils around stockyards or under pats of soft cow manure.

Keen freshwater anglers may even consider setting up a worm farm at home to ensure a handy and endless supply of bait, especially during the hot, dry summer months when wild worms can be extremely hard to find. You can buy worm farms and starter stocks of worms at bigger gardening centres.

Trapping shrimps and crayfish

Catching shrimps and crayfish (freshwater yabbies) is fairly straightforward when you use a simple drum or tin perforated with a collection of small holes (see Figure 8-4). You can buy traps of this kind at most tackle shops, along with *witch's hats*, *hoop nets*, *dillies* and so-called *opera house* traps. Each of the trap designs tend to work equally well, and the choice is up to the buyer's personal preference.

Not all of the available trap designs are legal in all areas, so be sure to check the legality of each style of trap for use in the waters where you intend to fish. (Chapter 26 lists some useful websites for checking the rules.)

You can bait shrimp and yabby traps with a fish head, a few scraps of meat or even a bar of unscented soap (fair dinkum!). Weight the trap with rocks and place it on the bed of the stream or lake close to areas of submerged timber and weeds. Within a few hours, reasonable quantities of shrimps or yabbies are sure to have taken up residence in the trap.

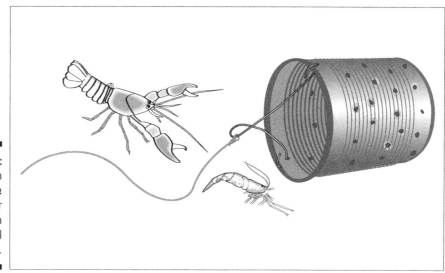

Figure 8-4:
You can easily make a shrimp or yabby trap from a small drum or tin.

Latching On to Lures and Flies

Fishing with lures or flies is the fastest growing sector of the sport of angling in Australia and New Zealand. This type of fishing has become popular for the following reasons:

- ✔ Catching fish on lures and flies is terrific fun!

- ✔ Fishing with lures and flies is an active and challenging sport.

- ✔ Lure and fly-fishing doesn't entail the mess and smell often associated with bait fishing.

- ✔ You can more easily unhook and release unwanted fish that you catch on lures and flies — with an increased chance that those released fish are going to survive. (For more on returning your catch to the water alive, see Chapter 15.)

A *lure* or *fly* is simply an artificial or counterfeit bait. Most lures and flies are intended to imitate small fish, prawns, crabs, yabbies or insects when pulled through the water or drifted on or in the water, although some look like nothing on Earth, yet they still catch fish (sometimes)!

Lures and flies vary enormously in price, from a couple of dollars each for smaller, simpler models up to $30 or even $50 for sophisticated imported lures, and even more for the large resin-headed trolling lures favoured by marlin and tuna specialists.

This section looks at the major lure types in use today and describes the groupings or families in Figure 8-5.

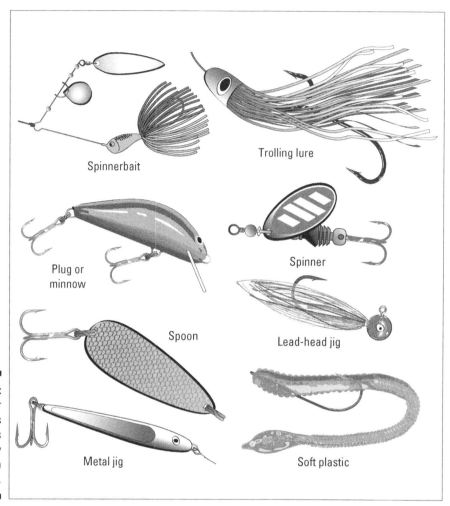

Spinnerbait

Trolling lure

Plug or
minnow

Spinner

Spoon

Lead-head jig

Metal jig

Soft plastic

Figure 8-5:
The major
lure groups
or families
used by
Australasian
anglers.

Bait-catching rigs

A bait-catching rig consists of a string of 3–7 small lures or flies, each
carrying a hook, rigged on short *droppers* (lengths of line attached to the
main line). A sinker or metal lure is attached to the bottom end of the rig
and a line tied to the top. You can then cast or lower the rig into the water
near bait schools and *jig* (jerk up and down), jiggle or steadily retrieve. The
rigs are extremely effective in the capture of bait species such as cowan-
young, garfish (piper), hardiheads, herring, pilchards, slimy mackerel and
yellowtail (also known as *yakkas*).

Bait-catching rigs also attract much larger customers at times, although landing a big salmon, tailor or kingfish on the tiny, fine gauge hooks and light lines typically used in this type of set-up is extremely difficult.

Before using any multi-hook rig such as a bait catcher, check the rules (Chapter 26) where you're fishing to see how many hooks are permitted per line. You may need to cut down or shorten the rig to reduce the number of hooks and comply with the law.

Lead-head jigs

Lead-head jigs are cast lead or alloy heads on a single, upwards-facing hook. The head is dressed with fur, feathers, synthetic fibres, shredded rubber or soft plastic tails and these lures can catch just about anything that swims if you use it in the correct way. Usually the correct way means casting the jig out, letting the lure sink towards the bottom, and then bringing the jig in with a stop-start jigging motion.

Metal jigs, slices and slugs

Made of brass rod or cast metal, metal jigs, slices and slugs are usually chrome-plated or painted. This family of lures work best in saltwater, especially if you can cast and retrieve the lures fairly rapidly.

As well as being cast and retrieved, metal jigs, slices and slugs are also good for trolling behind a boat to catch barracouta, bonito, mackerel, kingfish, pike, salmon (kahawai), tailor and many other predatory species.

Plugs and minnows

Plugs and minnows are lures shaped like fish or insects and are made from timber or plastic. Most plugs and minnows have a diving lip (also known as a *bib*) at the front. This bib imparts a swimming action to the moving lure and also causes the lure to dive down through the water when trolled or retrieved.

Plugs and minnows are available in sinking and floating models and range in size from a few centimetres to more than a half a metre in length, and are fitted with 1–3 sets of *treble* (three-pronged) hooks. Although expensive, plugs and minnows are extremely effective on a host of fish in both saltwater and freshwater. Popular target species include barramundi, bass, bonito, cobia, cod, flathead, kingfish, Murray cod, perch, salmon (kahawai), smaller tuna, trevally and trout. Small plugs and minnows can also tempt bream.

Poppers and surface lures

Poppers and surface lures are designed to allow you to create a fuss on the surface of the water, similar to that made by an injured small fish or drowning insect. Most poppers and surface lures float at rest and are fitted with 1–3 sets of three-pointed treble hooks.

Poppers and surface lures are particularly useful for catching bass in freshwater, while larger models work well on barramundi, cobia, kingfish, salmon (kahawai), tailor, tropical trevally and some of the tunas.

Soft plastics

Soft plastic lures are made from latex or rubber and come shaped as grubs, lizards, shads (fish shapes), worms, yabbies and other weird and wonderful critters. You can rig soft plastic lures in the same manner as natural baits or hang the lures on the back of lead-head jigs (see the section 'Lead-head jigs', earlier in this chapter) or spinnerbaits (see the section 'Spinnerbaits', later in this chapter). Most fish are known to chew on soft plastic lures from time to time.

Spinners

Spinners (also called *spinning blade lures* or *in-line spinners*), have a metal shaft or body and a rotating, spoon-like blade, with a three-pointed treble hook at the rear end. Some people call a whole range of different lures spinners, but the only style truly described by this title are spinning blade lures.

Spinners are most useful in freshwater where the lures tempt bass, perch, redfin and trout, although spinners also appeal to smaller saltwater species such as flathead, salmon (kahawai) and tailor.

Spinnerbaits

Spinnerbaits are weird-looking contraptions consisting of an arm in the shape of a coat hanger with a spoon-like blade on one end and a lead-head jig on the other end. Spinnerbaits usually have a *skirt* (a cylinder of rubber shredded to look like a long fringe) hanging over a single, upwards-facing hook.

Mostly used in freshwater, spinnerbaits are deadly on bass and Murray cod and also tempt barramundi, golden perch and saratoga. Kiwi anglers, also, can consider giving spinnerbaits a try on quinnat (chinook) salmon in coastal river mouths and estuaries.

Spoons

You can use spoons in both freshwater and saltwater and they come in a huge range of sizes, shapes, thicknesses, weights and finishes. The earliest spoons were literally made from the bowl of a teaspoon or tablespoon but, today, many different styles exist. Most spoons are made from metal and have a treble hook swinging from their rear end. You can either cast and retrieve spoons or troll them at a slightly slower pace than jigs or slices. The big family of lures known as spoons are effective on a wide range of fish, but are especially useful for tempting flathead, kingfish, pike, salmon (kahawai), tailor, freshwater salmon and trout.

Trolling lures

While all lures are suitable for trolling or trailing behind a moving boat, the large family of artificial trolling lures is designed specifically for this purpose. Most trolling lures have shredded, multi-strand plastic, vinyl or rubber skirts, giving the lure the vague impression of an octopus or squid, at least to our human eyes. Goodness only knows what fish think these lures are!

Trolling lures are incredibly variable in size, colour and head shape, except that virtually all are designed to have the line or leader run through the middle of the lure and one or more hooks attached behind. (I explain what a leader is in Chapter 7.) Used almost exclusively in saltwater, the lures are trolled at a fast speed to catch pelagic (ocean dwelling) species such as dolphin fish, kingfish, mackerel, marlin, tuna and wahoo.

Dispelling the Fly-Fishing Myth

Despite the mystique that often surrounds the subject, fly-fishing is really no more than a way of delivering a special type of artificial bait or lure (called a *fly*) to the fish.

Flies are made by binding the fur of animals, feathers of birds and various synthetic materials onto a hook. The resulting flies (see Figure 8-6) are so light that normal fishing gear makes casting them virtually impossible.

To cast the light lures, which is all flies really are, weight is incorporated into the line rather than the lure. This specially weighted fly line replaces the sinker or lure weight in normal fishing rigs and, instead, the mass of the line takes the fly out to the fish.

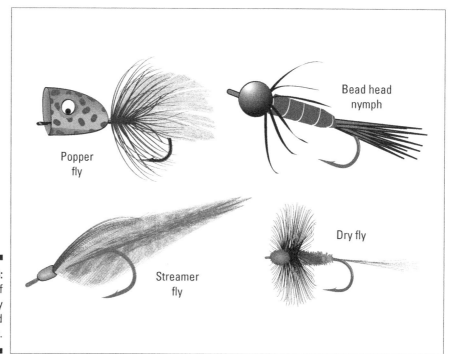

Figure 8-6: A range of common fly styles and patterns.

Popper fly

Bead head nymph

Streamer fly

Dry fly

Matching the hatch

Lovers of the sport of fly-fishing have a useful piece of terminology to describe the process of closely imitating natural food items when choosing a bait or lure — *matching the hatch*. The term refers to the insect swarms (also known as hatches) that are so important to trout anglers, but the concept is just as valid to a tropical lure caster pursuing barramundi or a game fisher trolling for marlin.

When trout feed heavily on just one type of insect (for example, ants or mayflies), the fish can become incredibly single-minded and often refuse to eat anything else. Many other kinds of fish exhibit similar behaviour, from bream gorging on prawns to tuna eating tiny whitebait. So, if you suspect that the fish you're chasing are keyed in to a particular food source, you'd be crazy not to try to match it!

Lining up your target

Because the casting weight in a fly line is 10 metres or so long (as opposed to mere centimetres in a regular sinker weight), you can't cast the line in the same manner as a sinker or lure. Instead, the way to perform this graceful manoeuvre is to sweep the rod back and forth through the air as the line extends beyond the rod tip, thereby forming a travelling wave in the line to transmit energy. The fly line is relatively thick and tapered at each end to facilitate this wave-forming process.

Earning frequent flyers

Traditionally, all fishing flies were made of natural fur and feathers and used almost exclusively to catch trout and salmon. Nowadays, flies are made from all manner of natural and synthetic materials and are tied or manufactured in sizes that appeal to everything from small trout to large tuna, kingfish and billfish (marlin and sailfish).

Flies for fishing in both freshwater and saltwater fall into the following two broad categories:

- **Dry flies:** This type of fly floats on the water. The category includes floating insect imitations and *popping bugs*.
- **Wet flies:** This type of fly sinks or dives beneath the surface of the water. The category includes *nymphs* and *streamers*.

Fly-fishing is a huge subject and has enough facets to easily fill a book the size of this one, but don't let this fact put you off the sport. Remember that fly-fishing is just another style of angling — not a religious cult or a secret society! If you're interested in trying your hand at fly-fishing, go right ahead — the sport isn't really as hard as the so-called experts say.

Part III
Using Your Equipment the Right Way

'Wow! Check out this season's new lures and hooks!'

In this part ...

Time to go fishing! This part is all about taking the equipment discussed in Part II, preparing the gear for a fishing expedition and, then, actually going fishing.

A number of sections in this part are designed exclusively for novices (for example, Chapter 9, which covers how to mount a reel onto a rod, and Chapter 10, which goes into how to spool line onto a reel). If you're confident that you have this type of information down pat, you can simply glance at the illustrations to confirm your knowledge.

Chapters 11 and 12 are designed for novices and accomplished anglers alike because the chapters include a number of new twists to tying knots and setting up a fishing rig.

Chapters 13 and 14 are must-reads for all anglers because the chapters deal with casting and hooking, playing and landing fish and include a ton of tips that are sure to improve your performance in the field — even if you're an old hand at the game.

Chapter 9

Creating Your Fishing Kit

. . . .

In This Chapter

▶ Fitting your reel to your rod

▶ Dealing with reeling options

▶ Organising your terminal tackle

▶ Gathering together the tools of the trade

▶ Assembling a collection of health and welfare accessories

. . . .

*I*f you work your way through Part II of this book, you have enough
information to go out and buy all the necessary basics to allow you to
take off and enjoy the wonderful sport of recreational fishing.

After bringing all the goodies home, chances are that you're not entirely
sure what to do with at least some of the gear. Not to worry! The aim of
this chapter is to help you organise your equipment and put the necessary
bits and pieces together so that you can finally hurl out that first cast and
(hopefully!) haul in a whopper!

Assembling the Rod and Reel

Like a horse and carriage or love and marriage (hey, don't blame me, I didn't
write the song!), rods and reels are intended to go together. The end result
is called an *outfit* or *combo* in trendy fishing parlance.

Your rod and reel need to complement each other (refer to Chapter 5 and
Chapter 6), but chances are you brought the gear home from the shop as
separate items. So, now's the time to connect all the nuts and bolts and
see how your new combo feels (the following steps kick off by assuming

you have a multi-piece rod — if your rod is fixed, simply jump to the second step):

1. **Fit the rod sections together.**

   If the rod is multi-piece, fit the sections together first, making sure the rod runners or guides line up neatly and that the ferrules (joints) are pushed firmly into place.

   If the rod is longer than 2 metres, you may prefer to fit the sections together outside to reduce the chance of knocking precious heirlooms off the mantelpiece, poking a pal in the eye or sticking the rod tip into the spinning blades of an overhead fan!

2. **Attach the reel to the rod.**

   You fit the reel foot to the reel seat or winch mount on the rod (refer to Chapter 5 and Chapter 6). Here's how:

   • **Slip one end of the reel's foot under the fixed (non-moving) hood of the reel seat.**

   (To work out which way around to fit the reel, see the next section, 'Reeling with Choices'.)

   • **Turn the screw fitting adjacent to the other hood to tighten the sliding hood firmly into place over the opposite end of the reel foot (see Figure 9-1).**

   Make sure to turn the screw sufficiently so that the fitting is firm, but not too tight — to ensure you can easily remove the reel from the rod at a later stage.

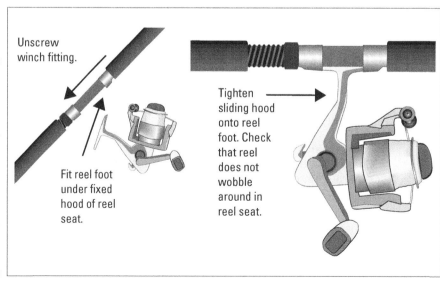

Figure 9-1: Lock the reel foot in place on the rod by turning the screw fitting to tighten the sliding hood of the reel seat over the reel foot.

Unscrew winch fitting.

Fit reel foot under fixed hood of reel seat.

Tighten sliding hood onto reel foot. Check that reel does not wobble around in reel seat.

By the way, this moment is a bad time to discover that the reel you chose doesn't fit into the seat on the rod you bought! This miss-fit is a rare occurrence, but has been known to happen, and is something worth checking in the shop — before you hand over your dough!

Reeling with Choices

Which way around does the reel go? Hey, this question isn't as silly as it sounds and the next person to fit a reel backwards on a rod certainly isn't going to be the last (and I speak from embarrassing experience)!

If you have a threadline reel (spinning reel) or closed-face reel (spincast reel), you can easily see which way to place the reel:

- ✔ **Closed-faced or spincast reel:** Align the reel so the conical hood and the hole where the line exits from the reel point straight up the rod.

- ✔ **Threadline or spinning reel:** Place the reel so that the bail arm and the rotor are in front, towards the tip of the rod.

Baitcaster reels, overhead reels, sidecast reels and centrepin reels (including fly reels) are potentially a little more confusing than threadline reels or closed-face reels; however, the following should give you enough info to do the job:

- ✔ **Baitcaster reels or plug reels:** Baitcasters and plugs have a level-winding device, which goes to the front, facing up the rod.

- ✔ **Centrepin reels and fly reels:** Centrepins and fly reels are ambidextrous, which means you can use the reels either with your left or with your right hand. If you put a centrepin reel or a fly reel on the rod the wrong way and tighten the drag or slipping clutch, turning the handle becomes difficult, which is a good indication that the time is nigh to look embarrassed and turn the reel around.

 When swapping a centrepin reel or fly reel from right- to left-hand drive or vice versa, you usually need to make minor internal adjustments. The aim is to make sure that the drag, slipping clutch, clicker or check only operates when the line is being pulled out by a fish and not when you're winding the line in.

- ✔ **Overhead reels:** The vast majority of overhead reels (including baitcaster reels and game reels) are sold in right-hand drive configuration and are designed to sit on top of the rod. Therefore, unless you specifically ordered a left-handed model, your overhead reel sits on top of the rod with the handles on the right as you look towards the rod's tip.

✔ **Sidecast reels:** Most sidecast reels are right-hand drive, although you can order a left-handed sidecast reel. ***Note:*** The line feeds onto the bottom of the spool on all sidecast reels, centrepin reels and fly reels, not the top, and right-handed models crank or turn in a clockwise direction. As a result, sidecast reels hang under the rod with the handles on the right.

When you're happy that you've correctly fitted the reel to the rod, you can skip straight to Chapter 10 and fill the reel's spool with line and come back to the rest of this chapter (which looks at dealing with your other fishing accessories) later.

Organising the Whole Box and Dice

After you attach the reel to the rod, the next aspect you need to think about is where you're going to store your growing collection of hooks, sinkers, swivels, floats, lures and other terminal tackle, and how you're going to transport the necessary gear to your fishing spot.

While you can easily take care of this job with specially designed tackle boxes, the question is whether to own one big tackle box or a bunch of smaller utility-style boxes consisting of flat trays with lids.

 Unless you intend to always fish from a boat or at a few specific locations where you can park your vehicle close to your casting spot, I strongly recommend that you opt for a collection of relatively small tackle containers rather than a single big one.

Boxes earn brownie points

I prefer to sort my essential fishing gear into around three units, using the smaller utility trays and boxes to create a handy modular system for carrying gear. For example, the smaller of the boxes can hold the little hooks and sinkers for chasing smaller target fish or going freshwater and estuary fishing. A second container can hold larger items of terminal tackle — which is more useful when you head offshore or onto the rocks, beaches and jetties to cast a line for bigger fare — while a third tray can hold your lures or flies.

Occasionally, you may only need to take one of the boxes with you when you go fishing. At other times, you may need two or even all three of the boxes.

TIP

For convenience, you can place the boxes in a shoulder bag, a small backpack or a haversack (see Figure 9-2), which can also hold your lunch, camera, sunscreen lotion and spray jacket. If you use a bag system, make sure to firmly close the lids on the tackle boxes before placing the utility boxes in a carryall. Otherwise the contents may spill out inside, making a tragic mess!

Figure 9-2:
This well-equipped angler is ready for anything!

Buckets can do the job

A large plastic bucket is a handy storage item for the mobile angler. You can buy tall, white, plastic buckets with tight-fitting lids at most tackle shops.

You can use a bucket:

- For storage:
  - Store your modular tackle boxes, knife and other bits and pieces when travelling.
  - Store your catch on the way home. If possible, add ice to the catch to keep the fish fresh.
  - Store your bait and berley.
  - For sitting on! I recommend you find a bucket with a lid because this can be more comfortable than an upturned bucket that may rock because of the raised handle.

If you keep your eye out, you may be able to find a tall, white, second-hand bucket, but chances are the bucket was originally filled with plaster, bulk catering sauces or chemicals. If this is the case, be sure to give the bucket a thorough scrub with hot, soapy water and let it air for several days before using the bucket for fishing.

Taking Along the Tools of the Trade

When you're out fishing, as well as your rod-and-reel combo or handline and some terminal tackle, you're going to occasionally need a range of other tools and accessories. Fishing tools can be roughly divided into essential and non-essential items.

Essential items

The essential tools for the angler in all situations are

- At least one sharp knife
- A pair of long-nosed pliers for safely removing hooks from fish

While not essential for all types of fishing, certain methods of landing fish require a *landing net* or *gaff* to secure the catch. (I discuss how to use nets and gaffs in Chapter 14 and a range of bait gathering tools in Chapter 8.)

On the cutting edge

If you're even halfway serious about fishing, you're going to need at least two styles of knives:

✔ **General-purpose knife:** Choose a budget-priced, general-purpose model with a reasonably stiff, stout blade. Even better is a knife with fish-scaling and rope-cutting serrations on the back of the blade and a built-in bottle opener (it's thirsty work out there!).

You use the general-purpose knife for cutting bait, trimming line, gutting fish and opening oysters. Ideally, carry the general-purpose knife on a belt in a stout sheath (remember to remove the belt while travelling on public transport!). When a fishing mate asks to borrow a knife (and this is bound to happen!), this general-purpose knife is the knife to offer up because its loss isn't going to be the

end of the world if it becomes lost or broken.

✔ **High-quality filleting knife:** Choose a knife with a long, slightly curved and moderately flexible blade — and spend as many bucks as you can afford!

Your higher quality knife needs to be kept wickedly sharp and should only be used for filleting your catch. Keep your best knife in a sheath in your bag or backpack and never, ever lend this knife to gear scroungers!

Ideally, both knives need to have stainless steel blades, non-slip handles and stout plastic sheaths (leather doesn't cope well with constant exposure to saltwater). Remember also that sharp knives are safer than dull knives because you don't need to push and hack as much with a keen blade, greatly reducing the risk of accidents.

Non-essential items

Less essential but, nonetheless, useful items of fishing equipment include

✔ **Camera:** Record your catch — and your smile!

✔ **Fish scaler:** This handy device greatly speeds up the fish cleaning process by quickly removing those pesky scales should you decide to leave the skin on your catch. (See Chapter 16 for how to skin and scale your fish.)

✔ **General-purpose knife:** I recommend you carry your general-purpose knife in a strong, plastic sheath or pouch hooked onto the same belt as the little bucket. (See the sidebar 'On the cutting edge'.)

Always remember to pack your knives away out of sight before entering a shop or travelling on public transport and store your knives in your check-in luggage, never your cabin luggage, when travelling by plane.

- **Pair of line clippers:** Carry this treasure on a light lanyard around your neck. Ordinary fingernail clippers can do the job, but are likely to rust after extended exposure to saltwater. Special line trimming scissors (sometimes called *braid scissors*) are also very handy.

- **Small plastic bait bucket:** Hook this timesaver onto a belt. A small bucket is handy for keeping a supply of bait at your fingertips as you move around (walking back and forth to your gear every time you lose a prawn to nibbling fish can be excessively annoying!).

- **Spring balance:** Knowing instead of guessing the weight of your catch helps to keep your fishing experience truthful when the time comes to share the adventure.

- **Tape measure or ruler:** Use this tool to stay on the right side of the law when it comes to minimum and maximum fish lengths. (See Chapter 26 for more information about rules and regulations when fishing.)

- **Torch or flashlight:** To find your way home after that 'just one last cast' moment takes you beyond twilight hours, or for baiting up and re-rigging in the dark.

Being Safety and Comfort Conscious

A range of other items you need to take with you on a fishing outing aren't directly involved in the fishing process, but are worth mentioning because the bits and pieces are vital to your personal health, wellbeing and comfort. In fact, if you choose to leave the following items (listed in alphabetical order) at home, chances are you're not going to enjoy your fishing expedition:

- **First-aid kit:** Give serious consideration to carrying a well-equipped first-aid kit in your boat or vehicle and a smaller kit on your person if you travel off the beaten track.

  If you plan on spending many hours fishing in out-of-the-way places, you should think about doing an approved first-aid course through the St John Ambulance organisation. (You can book online at www.stjohn. org.au). You may well end up saving someone's life as a result — perhaps even your own!

- **Food and water:** Take enough food and water to last you at least twice the amount of time you plan to spend out fishing (on the assumption that more often than not, you're out for longer than planned and that the weather is sure to deteriorate!).

✔ **Insect repellent:** You may not need anti-bug juice everywhere you fish, but where it is needed, leaving the repellent at home can really spoil your outing! If you fish in the tropics, the outback or in one of New Zealand's sandfly-rich southern forests, be sure to pack a high-strength repellent with plenty of the active ingredient DEET.

✔ **Life jackets:** When planning a boating fishing trip, make sure to do a check on life jackets — that you're carrying sufficient for all on board, they're accessible and in good condition.

✔ **Mobile phone:** Your phone can be a great communications and safety link, but if you're headed somewhere remote (or way offshore), consider also carrying an electronic position indicating radio beacon (EPIRB).

✔ **Sensible footwear:** Most forms of fishing are undertaken on uneven, rocky and otherwise hazardous ground, which is why you need to wear good quality, sensible shoes (see Chapter 21).

✔ **Sunglasses:** Fishing is often undertaken in bright conditions, so sunglasses are a necessity to both protect your eyes and give you better vision. Most anglers prefer glasses with polarising lenses because of the way the glasses cut the glare from the water's surface, making it easier to see fish, rocks, weed beds and deeper holes.

✔ **Sunscreen:** Cancer Council Australia's 'Be Sunsmart' campaign slogan is particularly relevant to anglers. Whenever you venture out in the sun, slip on a long-sleeved shirt and long, lightweight pants, slop on plenty of sunscreen lotion — with at least a SPF 15-plus rating, slap on a broad brimmed hat, seek shade if possible and slide on the sunnies mentioned earlier.

✔ **Warm, weatherproof clothing:** So often the day starts out sunny and deteriorates into a mess of clouds and rain, and if you're clothes don't suit the weather, you're going to become uncomfortable.

Follow the scout motto 'Be prepared' and take the right equipment with you on your fishing expedition and your day is bound to be more successful!

Chapter 10

Spooling Up

. . . .

. . . .

*W*ith a basic collection of tackle purchased and assembled, the time has almost come to head off fishing, but first you need to put some line on the shiny new reel.

After you fit your rod to your reel (refer to Chapter 9), the next step is to fill the spool of the reel with fishing line.

Spooling up is an easy enough process but, if you do manage to make a muck of the job, your fishing life is bound to become a misery of twisted line, impossible tangles and lost fish! So, even though filling a reel with line appears to be obvious and straightforward enough for a toddler to master, take a few minutes to read this chapter and study the illustrations to avoid hassles down the track.

Feeding the Line to the Spool

Line is bought by the spool and the first step of the process that the experts call *spooling up* is to find the end of the line. I detail the best types of line for various types of fishing in Chapter 4. The end of the line may be covered with a small piece of tape, may be knotted back over itself or may be trapped in a little slit on the edge of the plastic spool. If the end of the line is kinked or damaged in any way or is covered with sticky goo, grab a pair of scissors and cut off half a metre or so.

Now you're ready to fill your reel with line.

For all styles of rods and reels, take the end of the line and pass it down through the line guides or runners on your rod, starting at the rod's tip and ending with the stripper or stripping guide. (I describe the components of fishing rods in Chapter 5.)

Your next step in the spooling-up process depends on the style of reel, so the following explains how to spool up for three of the most popular types of reels:

- **Baitcaster reel or plug reel:** If you're filling a baitcaster reel or plug reel that has a level-wind device fitted to the front of the reel (refer to Chapter 6), you pass the end of the line through the little ceramic or metal line carrier on the level-wind device before you tie the line to the spool. This can be a bit fiddly to achieve on smaller reels.

- **Closed-face reel or spincaster reel:** To spool up this type of reel, unscrew the conical spool cover from the top of the reel, pass the line through the hole in the cover (from the front), tie the line to the spool and then screw the cover back into place. (I explain the various parts of spincaster reels in Chapter 6.)

- **Threadline reel or spinning reel:** To spool up this type of reel, you need to open the bail arm first, tie the line to the spool and then close the arm over the line (see Figure 10-1).

Moving the bail arm into the open position before tying on the line is vital to make sure the line winds in when you turn the reel handle.

Figure 10-1: When spooling up threadline reels, you need to open the bail arm before tying the line to the spool.

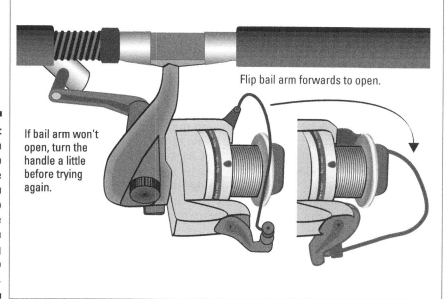

Flip bail arm forwards to open.

If bail arm won't open, turn the handle a little before trying again.

For all other reels, the process of spooling up is pretty straightforward and you simply tie the line directly to the middle of the spool, being careful to check whether the reel has any obvious line guides or line paths. If so, pass the line through the guides and then check the track the line follows from the spool to make sure the line doesn't touch any sharp or rough surfaces or go around any crazy corners (if this happens, you're doing something wrong!).

Tying One On

You can use a range of knots to attach the line to the centre of the reel's spool (by the way, this part of the reel is also called the *arbor*). However, from my experience, the no-nonsense knot that stands out as being the best for attaching the line to the reel is the *uni knot* (see Figure 10-2).

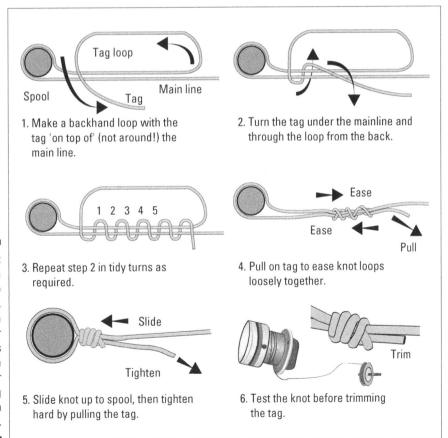

Figure 10-2: To attach the line to the spool, take the line two or three times around the spool arbor before tying a five-turn uni knot.

1. Make a backhand loop with the tag 'on top of' (not around!) the main line.

2. Turn the tag under the mainline and through the loop from the back.

3. Repeat step 2 in tidy turns as required.

4. Pull on tag to ease knot loops loosely together.

5. Slide knot up to spool, then tighten hard by pulling the tag.

6. Test the knot before trimming the tag.

(I describe knots, including the uni knot, in detail in Chapter 11, where I include lots of neat, easy-to-follow diagrams on how to tie each variety.)

Tying for testing times

Hopefully, you're not going to see your uni knot on the arbor again for quite some time (at least until you put new line on your spool a few months or a year from now). However, this seemingly unimportant connection may become extremely important when hooking a big fish or dropping your rod.

Hooking a big fish

A particularly big, strong fish can rip all of the line from your reel — despite the resistance imposed by the reel's drag system (refer to Chapter 6).

Fortunately, *getting spooled* or being *clean spooled* doesn't happen very often (despite the colourful tales you may hear to the contrary).

Chances are that if a fish is big enough to clean spool your reel, the fish is also big enough to snap the line well before the line runs out. If the line holds, however, that little knot joining the line to the spool may prove to be critical — that is, the difference between the fish swimming free and you landing it.

Dropping your rod

The knot you use to tie the line to your reel also becomes important if you drop your rod and reel overboard or off a jetty or rock ledge while the reel is in the free-spool setting or (on a spinning reel) the bail arm is open. If you're lucky enough to be able to grab the line at such a calamitous moment — or someone else hooks your line out of the water for you — you're going to have to pull all the line off the submerged reel into a big pile and then haul the rod and reel up from the depths of Davy Jones's locker. Once again, that connection between line and spool is extremely important at this point!

Tying up loose ends

The best way to connect the line to the spool's arbor is to use a uni knot (refer to Figure 10-2). ***Note:*** I suggest you wrap the line around the centre of the spool a few times before you tie the final part of the knot. This repetition is necessary to prevent the connection from slipping, sliding and spinning on the reel's arbor. After you tie the knot, lick it to lubricate the line with saliva and then pull the line tight. (I discuss this rather strange habit of licking knots, and why you should do so, in Chapter 11 — the knot-to-be-missed chapter of this book!)

When tightening the uni knot, pull on both the main line and the *tag end* of the knot several times until the knot snugs tightly down onto the reel. The next step is to use a pair of scissors (not your teeth!) to trim the tag end to around 1 centimetre from the knot. After tying the uni knot, you're best to test the connection thoroughly by pulling firmly on the line. If the knot is going to slip, you may as well find out now!

Winding Up the Process

After tying a brilliant uni knot, you can begin spooling up. A range of often confusing literature exists about the best ways to pull the line off the holding spool, including dragging the line over the side of the spool for some types of reel or pulling it directly off the spool for other types of reel. If you come across such information, the best thing to do is forget it! That kind of nonsense advice is all tripe! The best way to take the line off the holding spool is to insert some type of axle, such as a piece of wooden dowel, in the hole in the holding spool (see Figure 10-3).

The ideal axle for holding the spool and allowing the spool to spin is either a thin piece of wooden dowel or a metal rod, but a long screwdriver shaft, a knitting needle or a chopstick can do the job just as well. You can even use a pen or a pencil when winding line off relatively small spools.

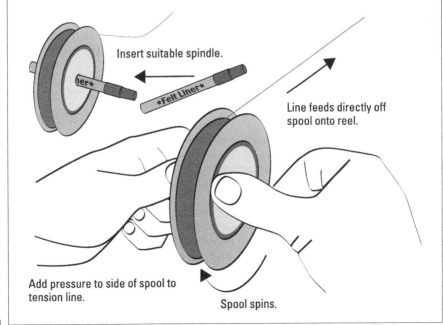

Figure 10-3: Despite arguments you may hear to the contrary, the best way to hold the spool when filling all styles of reel is to use an axle.

Insert suitable spindle.

Line feeds directly off spool onto reel.

Add pressure to side of spool to tension line.

Spool spins.

Spooling your resources

Spooling up is made ten times easier if you have someone to help you hold the spool of new line. Over the years, I've become adept at holding the spool axle between my toes while winding on the line, but this method isn't always practical — especially if you either need to apply extra tension to the line (see the following section) or have an awkwardly long rod.

Ask your assistant to hold the spool of new line by the makeshift axle and sit or stand directly in front of you a little more than the length of the rod away. You hold the rod and, pointing the tip of the rod at the spool, turn or crank the reel handle to pick up the line.

Watching as the tension rises

Whenever you wind line onto a reel without a weight (such as a sinker, a lure or a hooked fish), you have to apply some sort tension to the line. The tension ensures the line feeds neatly onto the reel, with firm, tight wraps and no loose loops or knots. The process of adding tension is especially important when first spooling up because winding line on loosely, when you fill a reel, can lead to all sorts of headaches later.

If the line you're filling your reel with has a rated breaking strain or strength of less than about 5 kilos (you find this information printed on the side of the spool), you can apply the necessary tension by running the line between the fingers of your rod-holding hand as you crank the line onto the reel. The preferred method of applying pressure with your hand is to squeeze the line firmly between the pad of your index finger and the ball of your thumb.

With lines much heavier than a rated breaking strain of 5 kilos, you need to apply extra tension, which is where your assistant begins to earn his or her keep.

The assistant can apply a slight amount of tension by pressing on the ends of the spool with his or her hands. This slight amount of pressure, combined with your own finger pressure, offers enough resistance for lines with a breaking strain of up to around 8 kilos.

Be aware, though, that your assistant is quite likely to cry out in pain after a short period because the friction between skin and spinning plastic can really heat things up! To avoid this problem, the assistant can wear a pair of light gloves or place a piece of fabric, such as a towel, between his or her hands and the spool rim.

You need to apply considerable pressure (more than you may imagine) when spooling up lines that have a stronger rated breaking strain than 8 kilos — particularly the gel-spun polyethylene (GSP) lines that I describe in Chapter 4. Lines with breaking strains of 24, 37 or 60 kilos that heavy-tackle game anglers use need a serious amount of pressure and, to achieve this level, a couple of strong assistants wearing oven mitts or thick gardening gloves (to press against the spool ends) is a necessity. Generally, if you don't raise a sweat spooling 300 metres or so of heavier line onto a reel, you're not packing it down tightly enough!

Avoid running the line itself through a towel or a gloved hand to add tension because the abrasion can severely damage fishing line (especially nylon monofilament), causing it to break when you hook a fish. Instead, always apply additional tension or pressure to the spool rims rather than directly to the line.

Working out when to stop

For most forms of fishing, you need 100–500 metres of line on your reel. The box or paperwork that comes with your reel usually indicates how much line of a particular strength or thickness the reel holds. ***Note:*** This information is only intended as a rough guide.

How much line you can actually fit onto the spool is dictated by the line's thickness and how tightly you tension that line while spooling up. Added to these specificities is perhaps the most vexing issue when spooling up, which is when to stop adding line, because under-filled or over-filled reels perform poorly and eventually have problems.

When considering how much line to put on your reel, remember that you can more easily take a little line off an over-filled reel spool than put more on an under-filled one — especially after you've cut the line!

If the reel you're using peels the line off over the lip or edge of the spool during a cast (as with threadline reels, sidecast reels and closed-face reels), make sure that the reel has plenty of line. Too little line has the result of dramatically reducing your casting distance and your ability to effectively use lightweight sinkers or lures.

The design of threadline reels, sidecast reels and closed-face reels requires you to fill the spool until the *line load* is just a few millimetres below the spool lip. The following explains what happens if the spool has too little or too much line:

- **Too little line on the spool:** Affects your ability to make a good cast.

- **Too much line on the spool:** Loose loops spew off the front of the reel, creating ugly tangles (fittingly called *birds' nests* by experienced anglers).

With revolving drum reels such as baitcaster reels, overhead reels, game reels and centrepin reels, the level of the line load is slightly less critical, but you still need to fill the reels to within a few millimetres of the spool lip for optimum performance (see Figure 10-4).

When you finish filling the spool to your satisfaction, stop winding and use scissors to cut the line. Keep any remaining line left on the plastic spool because the line is bound to be useful later for all sorts of purposes, including topping up your spool or making leaders (refer to Chapter 7).

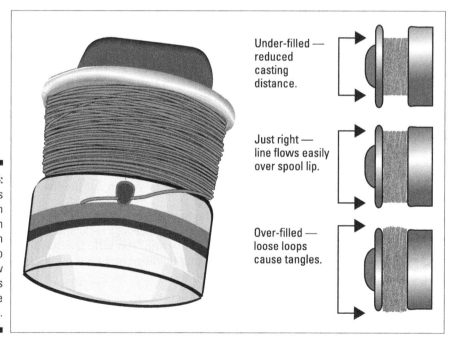

Figure 10-4:
Most reels perform best when filled with line to within a few millimetres of the spool lip.

Under-filled — reduced casting distance.

Just right — line flows easily over spool lip.

Over-filled — loose loops cause tangles.

Topping up the spool

As you use your rod, reel and line, the amount of line diminishes as you cut off line from knots, discard lengths of damaged line, cut off tangles or trim the line due to snags or breaks. Eventually, the amount of line reduces to the point that the reel's casting performance begins to suffer or you don't have enough line left on the reel to fish effectively.

At this point you have three options:

✔ **Join a section of new line to the end of the old line on the reel and top up the line load.** The option of joining new line to the end of the old line is called *top-shotting* and is an effective way to add line. However, for the system to work well, your original line load needs to be considerably diminished — by up to one-half the length of the original line — to avoid a weak point at a crucial part of the line. For this reason, consider discarding extra good line before top-shotting or use one of the other options described here. This method is good if you're on a tight budget.

✔ **Pull the old line off the reel, discard the line and start again with a new line load.**

✔ **Wind the old line off your reel onto another spool, place a small amount of new or spare line on the reel, then join your old line to this and crank it all back onto the reel.** This option involves the use of *backing*, which is anything placed on a spool underneath the main line load. This extra material can be any type of line, such as string or wool, but the preferred material is fishing line (even old, slightly worn line). Be sure to securely connect the original line to the backing.

Using backing is a bit more fiddly and time consuming than top-shotting because you first need to wind all of the original line off your reel onto another reel or line holder (such as a handcaster, an empty spool or a bottle). However, the end result is better because the connecting knot is buried deep on the spool, where the knot is unlikely to cause problems. This method also helps the budget — and your conscience if you don't like wasting resources.

The best knots to use for top-shotting and backing are the full blood knot or the double uni knot (see Chapter 11). Ideally, you need to add enough line to the reel's spool so that the connecting knot is rarely seen in the course of day-to-day fishing. When you add less line, the knot is constantly encountered while fishing and may adversely affect the reel's casting performance. The knot may also break on a big fish, because even the best knots are rarely as strong as the main line.

Spooling up is a simple enough operation, but you need to do the job carefully because your line load plays a vital role every time you go fishing — your line is the vital connection between you and that prize catch!

Chapter 11

Top Knots to Know

*T*he two most important keys to successful fishing are a sharp hook and a strong knot. The most sophisticated tackle, the freshest bait and the best local knowledge all count for nought if you overlook this pair of all-important basics.

Lines that mysteriously break and big fish that manage to swim free are common symptoms of failed knots. Too often, anglers blame problems of this nature on tackle, claiming the line was of poor quality or too light to handle the load. In the vast majority of cases, breakages and lost fish can be traced back to knot failure.

Scores of knots are suitable for fishing, but a handful of proven knots stand out as being the strongest and easiest to tie, even in adverse conditions such as wind, rain, cold and darkness. This chapter describes the essential knots you can put to use in every fishing situation.

Meeting the Major Knot Families

Hundreds of knots exist, but you only need to learn half a dozen knots (at most) and use the knots as your personal knot tying system. (Figure 11-1 shows the components of a typical knot.) The knots you choose are likely to be based on one of the major families of modern knots that I describe in this chapter.

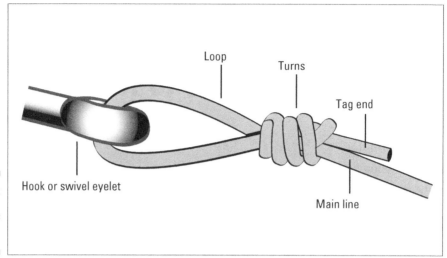

Figure 11-1: The anatomy of a knot.

Two distinct families or groups of knots form the basis of two excellent knot systems. One family is built around the blood knot and the other around the uni knot.

Both systems are extremely useful, but the majority of experienced anglers believe that the uni knot system is just a fraction stronger and more reliable than the blood knot system. Despite this favouritism, lots of anglers (myself included!) continue to fish happily for many, many years using a blood knot system; so, the choice is yours.

Try both knot families and see which of the systems you like best, taking note of which of the two types you can tie more easily, especially under adverse conditions. The ultimate test of any personal knot tying system is whether you can make it work in the dark with cold, wet, numb fingers. (For example, while I can use the blood knot system under trying circumstances, I have trouble with the uni knot system in the dark, cold or rain.)

Tying In with the Blood Knot Family

The blood knot system is based on the half blood knot, which is quick and easy to tie and is almost as strong as the uni knot.

When using the blood knot system, the trick is to use sufficient turns (or wraps) of line, to lubricate the turns with saliva or water when drawing the knot tight and to tighten and test the knot thoroughly before trimming the *tag end* (refer to Figure 11-1).

Half blood knot

The *half blood knot* (also known as the *clinch knot*) is a widely used knot for tying hooks, swivels, rings, lures and flies to the end of a line.

The following steps take you through the tying of a half blood knot (see Figure 11-2):

1. **Pass the end of the line through the eye of the hook, swivel, ring or lure.**

2. **Wrap the tag end back around the main line 5–8 times.**

   As a general rule, thicker line requires fewer turns than thinner line, while the slippery gel-spun polyethylene (GSP) line requires even more turns.

3. **Poke the tag end back through the main loop (see Figure 11-2).**

4. **Lubricate the entire knot with saliva.**

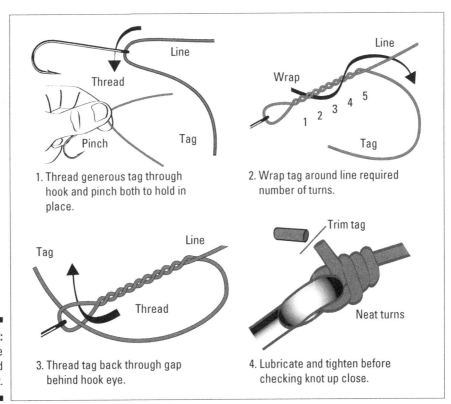

Figure 11-2: Tying the half blood knot.

1. Thread generous tag through hook and pinch both to hold in place.

2. Wrap tag around line required number of turns.

3. Thread tag back through gap behind hook eye.

4. Lubricate and tighten before checking knot up close.

5. **Draw the knot tight by pulling evenly on both the tag end and the main line first and then on the main line alone.**

The knot needs to be extremely tight and should then be tested using steady pressure on the main line.

6. **Trim the tag end.**

Leave a half a centimetre of line as a tag — for final insurance that the knot stays in one piece under stress.

Improved half blood knot

If you're likely to hook a big, strong fish or you're using the extremely slippery GSP type of fishing line, the basic half blood knot can be improved to reduce the possibility of the knot slipping. The end result is called, rather unsurprisingly, the *improved half blood knot* (see Figure 11-3).

Knot good enough!

Losing a big fish through knot failure is one of the most disappointing moments in angling. Knots fail for two main reasons:

- **The knot slips.** Slipping occurs as a result of insufficient turns or wraps of the line or because the knot wasn't tightened properly. A slipping knot can either slide undone or can generate enough friction within itself to literally melt the nylon fishing line.

- **The turns of line in the knot cut into another part of the knot.** Knots fail as a result of cutting when one turn of the line digs directly into the main line or across another strand of the knot. This problem happens as a result of insufficient turns or wraps of the line or when turns of line cross over each other at right angles.

The end result of both types of failure is the same: another story about the 'one that got away'!

A classic example of a knot that's likely to fail on both counts — by slipping and by cutting — is the *granny knot* (also known as an *overhand knot*). The granny knot is one of the worst knots to use in any type of fishing line because the granny knot effectively halves the breaking strength of the line!

You can test this lack of strength for yourself by tying a granny knot in the middle of a length of light line and then pulling on the line until the knot breaks.

Granny knots may be okay for tying up presents, but the granny knot really has no place in fishing! (Having said that, I show you (in the sections 'Looping the loop', 'Shock leader knot' and 'Slim and beautiful') some special knots that employ granny knots in their construction, but these are the exceptions that make the rule.)

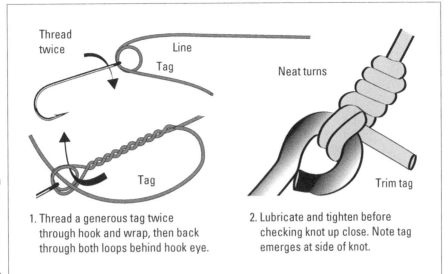

Thread
twice

Line

Tag

Neat turns

Tag

Trim tag

Figure 11-3:
Tying the
improved
half blood
knot.

1. Thread a generous tag twice
   through hook and wrap, then back
   through both loops behind hook eye.

2. Lubricate and tighten before
   checking knot up close. Note tag
   emerges at side of knot.

The improved half blood knot is made in the following way:

1. **Pass the end of the line twice through the eyelet of hook, swivel, ring or lure.**

2. **Take the tag end back around the main line 5–8 times.**

3. **Pass the end of the line back through the doubled loop formed at the eyelet (see Figure 11-3).**

4. **Follow Steps 4 through 6 in the half blood knot numbered list earlier.**

Full blood knot

The *full blood knot* makes use of a pair of half blood knots to join two lengths of line together. The full blood knot is an extremely useful knot when you need to cut a tangled or damaged section from the middle of your line or when you want to top your reel up with a length of fresh line, as described in Chapter 10.

The full blood knot works best when connecting lines with a similar or identical thickness and breaking strain. The full blood knot is less trustworthy when joining lines of dramatically different diameters.

Here's how to join two lines using a full blood knot:

1. **Cross the lines over each other at least 20 centimetres back from the tag ends.**

2. **Take the tag end of one line and wrap it around the other line five times, and then pass the tag end back between the two lines (see Figure 11-4).**

3. **Repeat Step 2 with the other line, this time passing the tag end through the opening in the middle of the knot in the opposite direction from the first tag end (see Figure 11-4).**

4. **Lubricate the entire knot with saliva and steadily tighten the knot.**

   This part of the process can be a bit tricky because you need to pull on both the main lines and the two tag ends at the same time — at least as you begin to tighten the knots (an extra pair of hands comes in handy at this point!). After the knot begins to snug down, you can safely release the tag ends.

5. **Tighten the lubricated knot using firm, steady pressure on both main strands of line.**

6. **Test the knot by pulling quite hard on the lines a couple of times.**

7. **Trim the tag ends to half a centimetre in length.**

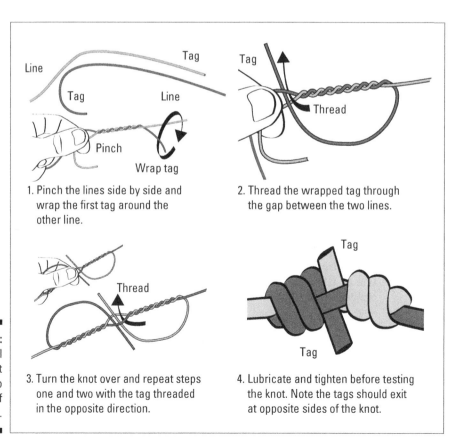

Figure 11-4: Tying a full blood knot to join two lengths of line.

1. Pinch the lines side by side and wrap the first tag around the other line.

2. Thread the wrapped tag through the gap between the two lines.

3. Turn the knot over and repeat steps one and two with the tag threaded in the opposite direction.

4. Lubricate and tighten before testing the knot. Note the tags should exit at opposite sides of the knot.

Meeting the Uni Knot Family

The uni knot (also known as the *hangman's noose* or *grinner knot*) forms the basis of an extremely viable alternative to the half blood knot system and is preferred by many experienced anglers.

Uni knot

The uni knot is

- ✔ Marginally stronger than the half blood knot
- ✔ Less likely to slip than the half blood knot
- ✔ Easier to use with thick, stiff fishing lines

Checklist for tying knots

A number of basic rules apply to the tying of all successful fishing knots:

1. **Check the working end of the line for nicks, chafes and flat spots before you begin to tie a knot or make a rig.**

   You can check the line by running the end of the line through your fingers or across your tongue to check for damage. This test is especially important if the previous rig is broken off on a snag or by a fish.

   Cut off any damaged sections before setting up the rig again.

2. **As you tie the knot, be sure to thoroughly lubricate it with water or saliva.**

   The best time to lubricate the knot is half way through the tying process. The best way to lubricate the knot is to give the knot a quick lick with your tongue.

3. **Tighten the knot using slow, steady pressure, avoiding any sudden jerks.**

   Make sure you snug the turns of the line tightly down against each other.

4. **Test the knot by increasing the pressure smoothly until the force exerted is at least half the breaking strain of the line.**

   This step is critical in making sure the knot is tight enough to hold. (Not sure how much pressure to exert? In the case of, say, a line with a breaking strain of 10 kilos, imagine how much muscle you need to lift up a 10-kilo bag of spuds and halve that amount of energy.)

5. **Trim the tag end from the knot, leaving half a centimetre for any slight slippage under load.**

   Leave the tag end cut a fraction shorter than half a centimetre when using extremely light lines and a shade longer when using heavy lines.

The following explains how to tie a uni knot:

1. **Pass the end of the line through the eye of the hook, swivel, lure or fly and form a backhand loop with the tag end alongside the main line (see Figure 11-5).**

2. **Wrap the tag end around the two parallel strands from 3 to 7 times, and then pass the tag end through the loop of line.**

   Three turns are sufficient when using extremely thick, heavy lines, but most anglers prefer four or five turns when using lighter lines and up to six or seven wraps when using slippery GSP lines.

3. **Lubricate the turns of line with saliva.**

4. **Tighten the knot slowly and steadily.**

   Tighten the knot by pulling on both the tag end and the main line to begin with, then on just the main line.

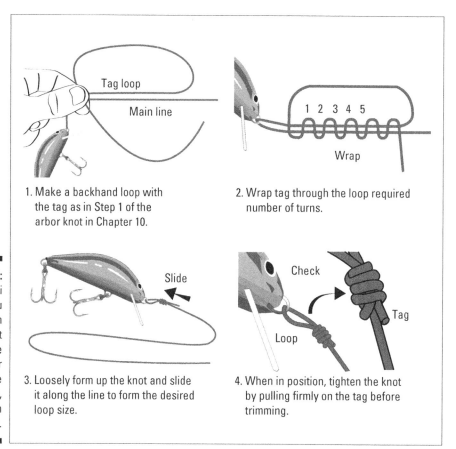

Figure 11-5: Tying a uni knot. You can tighten a uni knot short of the hook, lure or fly to leave a small loop, as shown here.

1. Make a backhand loop with the tag as in Step 1 of the arbor knot in Chapter 10.

2. Wrap tag through the loop required number of turns.

3. Loosely form up the knot and slide it along the line to form the desired loop size.

4. When in position, tighten the knot by pulling firmly on the tag before trimming.

5. **Either slide the uni knot down snugly against the hook eye or ring, or tighten the knot in place to leave a small loop of line at the eyelet.**

    Leaving a small loop at the eyelet is extremely useful when rigging light lures and flies because the loop greatly enhances the fish-attracting action of the lure.

6. **Test the knot with several strong, firm tugs.**

7. **Trim the tag end to half a centimetre or less.**

    Uni knots can handle shorter tag ends than the full blood knot family because uni knots rarely slip when properly tied and securely tightened.

Double uni knot

Anglers who take to the standard uni knot and can tie the knot easily and quickly in most conditions are sure to find the *double uni knot* to be a superb connection for joining together two lines with roughly the same strength and thickness.

The double uni knot is at least as strong as the full blood knot and — as a bonus — you can trim the tag ends much shorter than usual without any risk of the knot slipping, which makes the knot extremely compact, ensuring that it doesn't catch on, for example, rod guides.

To tie a double uni knot:

1. **Lay the two ends to be joined alongside each other with an overlap of at least 20–30 centimetres (see Figure 11-6).**

2. **Tie one tag end around the other main line using a standard uni knot.**

3. **Repeat Step 2 with the other line's tag end.**

4. **Partially tighten both uni knots in place.**

5. **Lubricate the two individual uni knots with saliva and lick or wet the strands of line between the two knots.**

6. **Tighten each of the uni knots and then slide the two knots together and tighten the two main lines.**

7. **Test the finished connection with several firm, steady pulls.**

8. **Trim the tag ends to a couple of millimetres or less.**

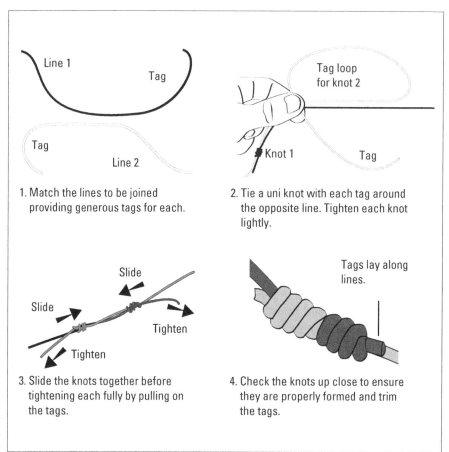

Figure 11-6:
Tying the double uni knot to join two lengths of line.

1. Match the lines to be joined providing generous tags for each.

2. Tie a uni knot with each tag around the opposite line. Tighten each knot lightly.

3. Slide the knots together before tightening each fully by pulling on the tags.

4. Check the knots up close to ensure they are properly formed and trim the tags.

Looking at Exotic Knots

The blood knot and the uni knot (refer to previous sections) can take care of the vast majority of your angling needs, particularly in freshwater, estuary, beach, rock and inshore fishing scenarios. However, as your level of angling sophistication increases, you may occasionally require additional knots and connections — or you can nonchalantly tie a couple of the following exotic creatures just to impress your friends!

✔ **Doubles:** Three of the advanced knots I explain in this section are used to form *doubles*. A double is a doubled-over length of line at the working end of your rig that you use to improve the strength of the line and increase the line's resistance to abrasion where it matters most. A double is particularly useful in demanding situations such as offshore game fishing. A double is also good for use as a loop for quickly connecting items of terminal tackle to your line without tying any additional knots. The three advanced double knots are

- Surgeon's loop

- Spider hitch

- Bimini twist

✔ **Homer Rhodes loop:** Another fancy knot, which I describe in this section (see 'Looping the loop'), is used to form a smaller loop when attaching a hook, lure or fly to your line or leader. Connecting items of tackle via a small loop can be handy for improving the swimming action and fish-appeal of a natural or artificial bait, especially when using thick lines and leaders.

✔ **Shock leader knot:** The penultimate fancy knot, which I show you in this chapter (see 'Shock leader knot'), is for joining a thick, strong length of line to the end of your thinner main line without using a swivel or ring. This trick is useful when you want to construct a long leader or trace that you can then retrieve smoothly through the rod runners and then cast out again (such as when surf fishing with heavy sinkers or lure casting for big fish with teeth or sharp gill covers).

✔ **Slim beauty knot:** The final knot I show is for the same purpose as just described — joining a relatively thin, main line to a much thicker leader — but is a stronger, neater connection better suited to really demanding situations (see the section 'Slim and beautiful').

Double knots

You can use double knots for forming a doubled length of line at the end of your main line to add strength and durability to the line, or to form long loops.

Doubles can be long or short, depending on the reason the knot is being used. When tying a double knot, remember that the knot takes up a fair bit of line, so you need to allow for this or your finished double may be too short for the job!

To explain how to make double knots, I have two easy double knots (the surgeon's loop and the spider hitch) and a more complex double knot (the Bimini twist) to show you. Try tying all three knots to see which one you prefer.

Surgeon's loop

The *surgeon's loop*, or a variation of it, is also referred to as the blood bite or blood bite dropper in some books. This knot is a quick, easy method for forming loops or doubles in a line and is especially popular for making the short dropper loops used to attach sinkers or other items of terminal tackle to the paternoster rigs described in Chapter 12.

To create a surgeon's loop:

1. **Form the required length of doubled line, then make an overhand loop with it, as shown in Figure 11-7.**

2. **Thread the end of the doubled line through this loop, as indicated in Figure 11-7.**

3. **Repeat this process from 2 to 4 times.**

   Two or three turns are enough in thick, strong nylon lines with breaking strains over around 10 kilos, while three or four turns are better in lighter nylon lines, and even more turns should be used when tying this knot in GSP lines.

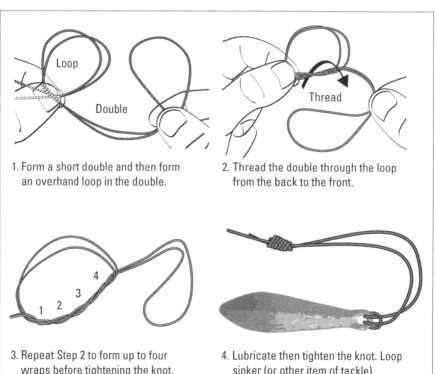

Figure 11-7:
Tying the surgeon's loop.

1. Form a short double and then form an overhand loop in the double.

2. Thread the double through the loop from the back to the front.

3. Repeat Step 2 to form up to four wraps before tightening the knot.

4. Lubricate then tighten the knot. Loop sinker (or other item of tackle) on to the double as shown.

4. **Lubricate the turns of line with saliva, then draw the knot tight and test it with steady pressure before trimming the tag end.**

5. **To quickly and easily attach a sinker, hook or similar item of terminal tackle to a surgeon's loop or any other double, pass the end of the doubled line through the eyelet and take the loop over the end of the item of tackle before pulling the resulting hitch tight.**

The surgeon's loop is a reasonably strong knot, but it isn't especially suited to very light lines.

Spider hitch

The *spider hitch* (also known as the *Cairns quickie*) is another simple knot to use when forming a doubled length of line, but the spider hitch is nowhere near as strong or as reliable as the Bimini twist (see the next section).

In particular, the spider hitch isn't well suited for use with the new generation of slippery GSP lines.

The following explains how to tie a spider hitch:

1. **Double the desired length of line, and form a backhand loop at the top of the double, holding the loop between your thumb and forefinger (see Figure 11-8).**

2. **Take the doubled length of line and wrap it 5–6 times around the end of your thumb, working from the back towards the front or tip of your thumb.**

3. **Take the end of the doubled length of line, pass it through the loop and pull the double completely through the loop.**

4. **Lubricate all of the turns of line on your thumb with saliva or water and slowly tighten the knot, allowing the turns of line to slip off your thumb one at a time.**

5. **Draw the knot tight, test it with several firm pulls and trim the tag end to just a few millimetres.**

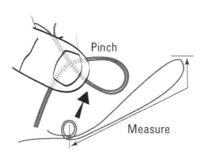

1. Measure the required length of double and pinch a loop in it near the tag.

2. Neatly wrap the double around both your thumb and the pinched loop.

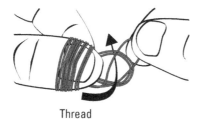

3. Make six wraps before before threading end of the double through the loop.

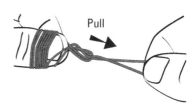

4. Pull on the double, slowly drawing the paired wraps off your thumb.

5. Lubricate and form the knot by pulling evenly from both ends.

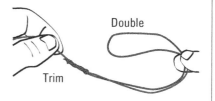

6. Fully tighten by pulling on each strand before trimming the tag.

Figure 11-8:
Tying the spider hitch double.

Bimini twist

The *Bimini twist* — named after an island in the Bahamas — is an extremely strong double knot. However, the knot is rather cumbersome to tie single-handed, especially when you need the double line to be longer than a metre.

To tie a Bimini twist:

1. **Double the desired length of line and twist it 25–50 times (see Figure 11-9).**

   In general, use fewer twists (25–30) for thicker line and more twists (40–50) for fine nylon line or GSP.

2. **Widen the loop between the double strands to force or compact the twisted area down on itself.**

   You can widen the loop by putting your legs through the loop of doubled line and forcing your knees apart to spread the strands.

3. **As you continue to spread the two strands, pull the tag end out at 90 degrees to the twists until the tag end begins to wrap back in tight spirals over the twisted line. Maintain the pressure until the spiral wrap reaches the end of the twists.**

4. **Grasp the knot at the point shown in Figure 11-9 to stop the twist unravelling, then take a half hitch around one leg of the double, then around both strands of the double together.**

5. **Make several more half hitches around both strands, lubricating the line as you tighten each hitch.**

6. **After you make at least half a dozen hitches, trim the tag end to around a millimetre.**

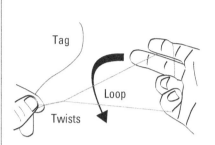

1. Form a loop and tag. Rotate your hand in the loop to twist its two strands together 25–50 times.

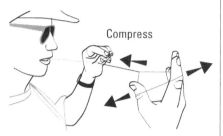

2. Grab the tag between your teeth. Spread your fingers and pull on the tag to compress the twists.

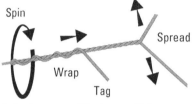

3. Further spread the loop until the twists start to spin, then wrap the tag up to the apex of the loop.

4. Pinch the base of the loop while you make a half hitch in the tag around one leg only of the double.

5. Make at least three half hitches around both strands of the double to lock the knot.

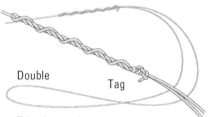

6. Trim the tag, inspect the knot up close and test with a firm pull before fishing.

Figure 11-9: The Bimini twist double knot is an extremely strong knot, but is relatively tricky to tie.

Looping the loop

A range of fishing applications require the use of a small loop at the end of the line to allow an item of terminal tackle a certain amount of free-swinging mobility. This is particularly important when tying lures or flies to fairly stiff lines or to thick leaders that may otherwise restrict the swimming action of the lure.

The *Homer Rhodes loop* — named after an American angler who lived in the mid-twentieth century pioneering days of sportfishing — is a quick, easy loop for attaching hooks, sinkers, lures and flies to the end of your line. The loop can be tied in both nylon monofilament and multi-strand wire.

Because the Homer Rhodes loop incorporates granny knots (refer to the 'Knot good enough!' sidebar), the line's strength is reduced by about a half, so the loop is best reserved for leaders and traces made of wire or heavy nylon that are at least twice as strong as your main line. Because the loop reduces line strength so radically, don't use the Homer Rhodes loop in light line.

The following explains how to tie the Homer Rhodes loop:

1. **Form a loose overhand loop or granny knot in the wire or heavy monofilament leader.**

2. **Pass the tag end through the hook, ring or swivel, then back through the overhand knot (see Figure 11-10).**

3. **Take the tag end and tie another overhand knot around the main strand of the leader above the first overhand knot.**

4. **Lubricate and tighten the knot, locking the two overhand knots against each other.**

5. **Test the knot with several firm pulls.**

6. **Trim the tag end to half a centimetre.**

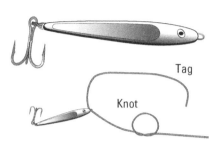

1. Tie an overhand knot in the line then thread the tag through the lure eye.

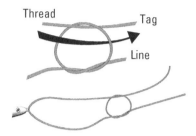

2. Pass the tag through the loop so that it emerges from the same side as the line.

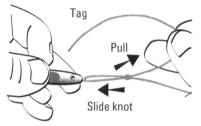

3. Tighten the knot around the tag slide it up towards the eye of the lure.

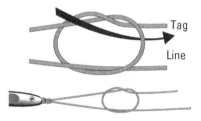

4. Now tie an underhand loop knot in the tag around the main line.

Figure 11-10: The Homer Rhodes loop is useful for connecting hooks, lures or flies to very thick, strong leaders or traces.

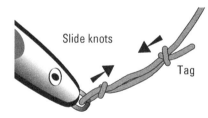

5. Pull on the tag to slide the two knots together along the line.

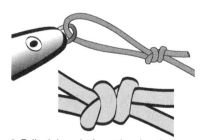

6. Fully tighten before trimming the tag. Check the knots fit properly together.

Shock leader knot

Occasionally, you need to connect a relatively light, fine line or a doubled length of fine line directly to a heavy leader made of nylon monofilament or even to a trace of nylon-coated wire. The advantage of using a *shock leader knot* over a swivel or ring is that you're still able to crank the line through the rod runners and you're able to cast with minimal bumping and snagging of the knot on the rod runners.

Here's how to tie a shock leader knot:

1. **Form an overhand knot (granny knot) in the heavy leader material (see Figure 11-11).**

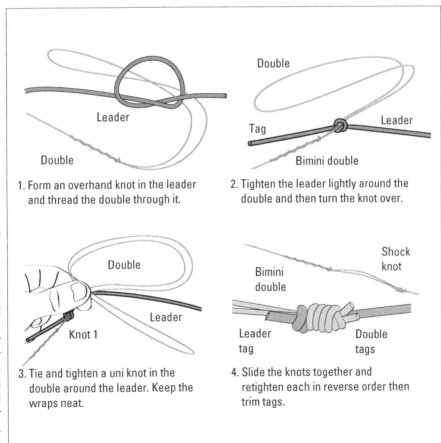

1. Form an overhand knot in the leader and thread the double through it.

2. Tighten the leader lightly around the double and then turn the knot over.

3. Tie and tighten a uni knot in the double around the leader. Keep the wraps neat.

4. Slide the knots together and retighten each in reverse order then trim tags.

Figure 11-11: Use the shock leader knot to connect a length of heavy nylon or even nylon-coated multi-strand wire to your main line.

2. **Pass the lighter main line (either single or doubled) through the overhand knot and tighten the overhand knot with firm, steady pressure.**

3. **Tie a uni knot (refer to the 'Uni knot' section, earlier in the chapter) around the heavy leader with the lighter line.**

4. **Lubricate the uni knot with saliva.**

5. **Tighten the uni knot and slide it hard up against the overhand knot.**

6. **Pull the overhand knot closed again as tightly as you can.**

   If necessary, you can use pliers for this step, but only pull on the tag end because the jaws of the pliers can damage the line.

7. **Trim both tag ends to just a few millimetres in length.**

As the name indicates, this knot is particularly useful when using a *shock leader* (a section of line that is much stronger than the main line). The shock leader prevents the line from breaking when casting extremely heavy sinkers or fighting big, strong fish with sharp teeth or gill covers. A shock leader, in this application, is essentially a leader or trace (refer to Chapter 7), which is long enough to be retrieved through the rod runners and onto the reel.

Slim and beautiful

The *slim beauty* is a relatively new knot — created specifically to cater to the needs of anglers joining slippery, thin-but-strong GSP main lines to thick monofilament leaders. Choose the slim beauty knot when fishing for big, powerful target species such as barramundi, Murray cod or yellowtail kingfish. This knot effectively replaces the once-popular Albright knot (credited to 1960s American fishing guide, Jimmy Albright, and not shown here) and is, in my opinion, superior to that older knot.

Once, at an angling seminar, while espousing the benefits of this slick new connection, I suggested that anyone wishing to learn how to tie the knot should simply search **slim beauty** on the internet. However (and as one joker in the audience quickly pointed out), fishing connections are likely to be well down the list of possibilities when you type **slim beauty** into a search engine! I had to admit he had a point. Fortunately, you don't need to wade through the search list because I show you how to prepare the slim beauty knot right here:

1. **Form a double overhand (double granny knot) in the heavy leader material and draw it partially tight, until it rolls into a small figure-of-eight (see Figure 11-12).**

2. **Take the end of the finer main line and pass it through both holes or loops in the figure-of-eight.**

3. **Pull on the end of the leader and its tag to fully tighten the double overhand knot around the main line.**

4. **Take the main line and make seven neat turns or wraps along the heavy leader, snugging each turn neatly against the previous one.**

5. **After the seventh wrap or turn, start wrapping back down towards the tightened double overhand knot, making seven more neat turns over the top of the first seven.**

6. **Pass the tag end of the main line through the small opening shown (Figure 11-12), just above the double overhand knot.**

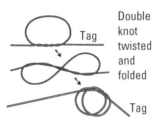

1. Double-knot the tag end of the leader and tighten to twist into a figure of eight before folding the halves over onto themselves.

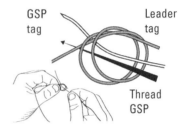

2. Pinch the folded knot and thread the tag of the GSP though it, in the path shown, before tightening the knot around the braid main line.

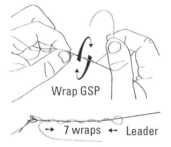

3. Partly tighten the leader knot around the GSP and then turn the knot over and make seven wraps of the GSP tag up along the leader and then back down.

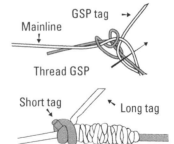

4. Thread the tag of GSP through the gap above the leader knot. Moisten knot and tighten carefully. Trim the leader tag close, and the GSP to 1cm for security.

Figure 11-12:
Use the slim beauty knot to connect slippery, thin-but-strong GSP main lines to thick mono-filament leaders.

7. Lubricate the knot with water or saliva and pull firmly on the tag end of the main line and the main line itself so that the turns pull up really tightly and bed down neatly.

8. Apply firm, steady pressure to both tag ends, the main line and the leader, and then trim the tags. If using GSP main line, leave around a one-centimetre tag.

Chapter 12

Rigs That Really Work

. . . .

. . . .

*M*any people put together the rig before leaving home, only to reach the fishing spot and discover that the water is deeper than expected, that a strong current is flowing and that the wind is on the rise. Additionally, according to other anglers in the vicinity, an unexpected species of fish is on the bite, rendering the carefully constructed rig ineffective.

The best time and place to make decisions about rigging is when you arrive at the fishing spot, so that you can accurately judge the conditions.

For many styles of fishing, the simplest rigs are the most successful and, fortunately, are the easiest to create. This chapter describes a range of relatively simple rigs that satisfy the majority of angling requirements in Australia's most popular fishing environments.

Choosing from Five Basic Rigs

A *rig* is any assembly of terminal tackle such as hooks, sinkers, swivels, floats, leaders and lures (refer to Chapter 7) tied or connected to your fishing line.

A rig can be just a hook knotted to the end of the line or a complex arrangement of fancy bits and pieces restricted only by your imagination. Remember, however, that fish are rarely impressed by finding everything but the kitchen sink dangling off a fishing line! In fact, the approach of throwing a tonne of tricks onto your line is more likely to scare the fish away than induce the critters to bite.

Of all the possible rig combinations, you only need to know five basic rigs to be able to fish in virtually any situation. The only trick is to learn how to construct each of the rigs using a range of terminal tackle (refer to Chapter 7) and knots (refer to Chapter 11). Set your rig up in one of the following ways and that first delicious feast of self-caught seafood is yours! I promise!

No-sinker rig

Often, the simplest approach is the most effective of all, and you can't get much simpler than a hook tied to the end of a line.

- ✔ **Basic requirements:** Line and hook.
- ✔ **Most positive feature:** Simple to put together.

The easiest of all fishing rigs, the *no-sinker rig* consists of a sharp hook tied directly to the end of your main line. Now that's what I call simple!

The only weight on a no-sinker rig comes from the hook and any bait attached to the hook. As a result, the no-sinker rig is only suitable in areas where short casts are sufficient to reach the fish and where the water is fairly shallow with minimal current or tidal flow. Fortunately, this type of environment is easy to find at freshwater lakes and quiet estuary backwaters out of the main current.

The no-sinker rig is effective for catching a range of common species such as trout, bream, snapper and school mulloway in shallow, still water. You can bait this simplest of all rigs with earthworms, blood worms, yabbies, whole prawns, fish flesh strips or small, live fish such as mullet.

No-sinker rig with swivel

One step beyond the no-sinker rig involves the addition of a swivel to prevent or reduce line twist and the tangles that twisting can cause.

- ✔ **Basic requirements:** Line, hook, swivel and hook link (also called a leader).
- ✔ **Most positive aspect:** Simple to put together and reduces line twist.

A swivel added to the no-sinker rig (see Figure 12-1) helps to stop your line from twisting if the bait spins when being retrieved. This rig is particularly useful if you're using a sidecast reel or spinning (threadline) reel — both of which can induce additional line twist because of their design (refer to Chapter 6).

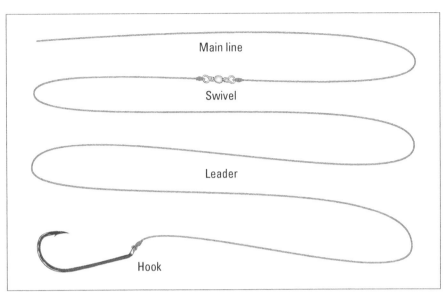

Figure 12-1:
The
no-sinker
rig, with
or without
a swivel,
is deadly
in shallow
water with
little or no
current.

Tie the swivel into the line anywhere from 10 centimetres to 1 metre from the hook. If you add the swivel any further than a metre or so from the hook, casting and retrieving becomes difficult because the swivel can end up caught in the tip of your rod.

As well as reducing or eliminating line twist, a swivel adds a tiny amount of additional weight to the rig and helps you cast the bait a bit further out and then hold the bait down under the water in slight currents or tidal flows.

As a bonus, the no-sinker rig with a swivel (which involves tying just three knots) allows you to use a length of line either thicker or thinner than your main line between the swivel and the hook. The added section of line is called a leader or *hook link*. The strength of the hook link depends on the species of fish you're after:

- ✔ **A hook link that's lighter (finer) than the main line:** Handy when pursuing small, finicky species such as whiting, trout and bream.

- ✔ **A hook link that's heavier (thicker) than the main line:** Useful for reducing *bite-offs* from toothy fish such as flathead, tailor and leatherjackets.

Running sinker rig

A *running sinker rig* with the sinker sliding all the way down to the hook is deadly in many fishing situations, especially where your hook is likely to get *snagged* or caught up on underwater obstructions.

✔ **Basic requirements:** Line, hook and one or two sinkers.

✔ **Most positive aspect:** Is simple to construct, allows finicky fish to swim off with the bait without feeling the weight of the sinker and is also more easily jiggled or bounced off a snag than most other rigs.

Adding weight to your line helps you to cast the hook further out and helps carry the bait down through the water in a tidal flow or current. The simplest method of attaching weight is to slip one or more sinkers onto the line before tying on the hook, leaving the sinkers to slide freely on the line. This system is known as a running sinker rig.

Ball, bean, barrel or bug style sinkers are best for making a running sinker rig. Always choose the smallest size of sinker that you can use in the prevailing conditions (refer to Chapter 7) and, generally, two small sinkers are more effective than a single, larger sinker.

When you cast using the running sinker rig (see Figure 12-2), the sinker sits right on top of the knot connecting the line to the hook. However, as soon as the rig enters the water, the sinker usually slides away from the hook as the lead weight descends through the water faster than the baited hook, giving the set up a natural appearance.

Figure 12-2:
A running sinker rig is ideal for many styles of fishing in both freshwater and saltwater.

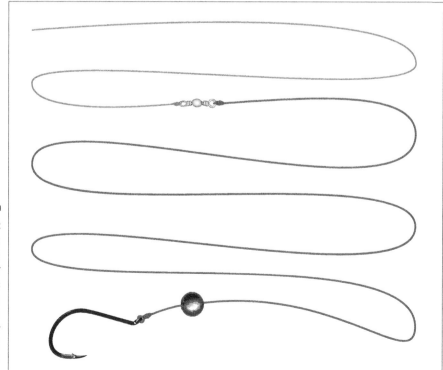

You can use the running sinker rig with a sidecast reel, but as this type of reel tends to make the line twist, you need to add a swivel into the line above the sinker, at least 50 centimetres–1 metre back from the hook.

The best aspect about running sinker rigs — apart from being easy to construct — is that a biting fish can pick up the bait and swim away without dragging the sinker along and becoming alarmed by the sinker's weight. *Note:* If you place a swivel above the running sinker, the line slides freely through the sinker only until the swivel reaches the sinker.

Running sinker and swivel rig

The running sinker and swivel rig is without doubt the most popular and successful rig used in Australasian angling today.

- ✔ **Basic requirements:** Line, hook, one or more sinkers, swivel and hook link (also known as a leader).

- ✔ **Most positive aspect:** Makes the best use of a sinker and swivel, keeps the sinker away from the bait where its position is less likely to alarm shy fish and allows different strengths of leader or hook link to be used.

The running sinker and swivel rig (see Figure 12-3) incorporates the best of the features used to create the previous three rigs. The rig includes the use of a fairly short hook link (usually 20–60 centimetres, but sometimes longer) below a swivel, with one or more sinkers running freely on the main line above the swivel. Many anglers regard the running sinker and swivel rig as the most effective of all rigs and rarely use any other rig.

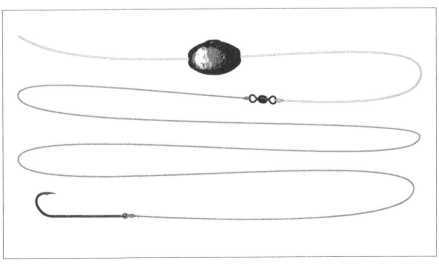

Figure 12-3: A running sinker and swivel rig is one of the best and most versatile set-ups for many styles of Australasian fishing.

One of the best features of the running sinker and swivel rig is that you can easily use a hook link of a different strength or thickness to your main line (refer to the section 'No-sinker rig with swivel').

Paternoster rig

Sometimes, you can gain an advantage from suspending your baited hook or hooks above the sea bed, or by having the sinker fixed at the end of the line rather than sliding on the line itself. A good way of achieving this result is to use a paternoster rig.

- ✔ **Basic requirements:** Line, hook, sinker and droppers (formed by using knots or adding three-way swivels).

- ✔ **Most positive aspect:** Opportunity to add a number of hooks and corresponding baits, ability to suspend the hooks above the sea bed and improved casting performance through having the sinker at the end of the line.

Paternoster is a rather old-fashioned British name for a rig that has the sinker located at the end of the line and the hook or hooks on short *droppers* or lengths of line above the sinker (see Figure 12-4).

You can form the droppers by tying knots in the main line or by adding special three-way swivels to the rig and tying short lengths of line to the middle (side) eyelets of the swivels.

Figure 12-4:
The paternoster or dropper rig is well suited to keeping baits clear of the bottom.

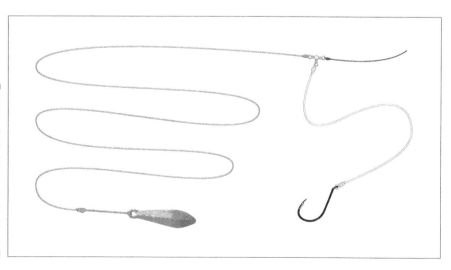

Taking care of the details

You need to tie every rig you construct — simple or complex — as if the rig is going to catch the fish of a lifetime!

All too often a really big fish grabs a rig intended for much smaller fare. This commonly happens when fishing for bait and a large predator grabs either the hook or one of the hooked and struggling baits. Equally, big mulloway or jewfish are known to grab tiny bait originally intended for whiting, or hefty Murray cod are tempted by small trout lures.

If you're haphazard in your preparations, the big fish is sure to end up as another 'one that got away' story. On the other hand, if you tie each knot carefully and check the working end of the line regularly for damage or weak spots, you're bound to have at least a fighting chance of success.

Over the years, anglers land a range of incredibly big fish on ultra-light line and tiny hooks because the individual incorporates the right combination of a carefully made rig, cool-headed patience, skill and luck.

Although primarily used when casting from the ocean rocks and surf beaches or when deep-sea fishing from a boat, paternoster rigs (also known as *dropper rigs*) can also be used in estuaries, bays, harbours and even in freshwater. Paternoster rigs are especially handy when you want to use more than one hook and bait, either to increase your chances of hooking a fish, or to try out different baits in order to discover which offering is the most popular on the fishy menu that day. The paternoster or dropper rig also works well if you want to keep a bait or baits clear of the bottom to reduce snagging. Snagging easily occurs when drifting about in a boat or when fishing over soft, muddy bottom strata or beds of short sea grass and other weeds, which might foul the hook or hide your bait from fish.

Mastering Five Fancier Rigs

While the five basic rigs that I describe in the previous section are sure to catch plenty of fish under an incredibly wide range of conditions, certain situations can force you to be slightly more inventive.

The five rigs in this section are relatively complex and use a few additional items of terminal tackle, but the rigs are still quite easy to construct — assuming that you master a few of the basic knots necessary for fishing (refer to Chapter 11).

Fixed float rig

A float is very useful for suspending your bait at a pre-determined depth beneath the surface of the water, and also acts as a visual bite indicator. The fixed float rig is simple to construct and ideal for setting baits close to the surface.

- ✔ **Basic requirements:** Line, hook, split shot or sinkers and a stemmed float or bobby cork (swivels are optional).

- ✔ **Most positive aspect:** Easy to construct and ideal for applications where the bait needs to be suspended close to the surface.

You can create the *fixed float rig* (see Figure 12-5) by attaching a quill, pencil or stemmed float, or a bobby cork to your line anywhere from a couple of centimetres to a rod length above the hook. Add split shot or sinkers between the float and the hook to correctly ballast the float (refer to Chapter 7). You can also add swivels to the rig to reduce line twist or stop sinkers from sliding right down to the hook — but adding swivels isn't essential.

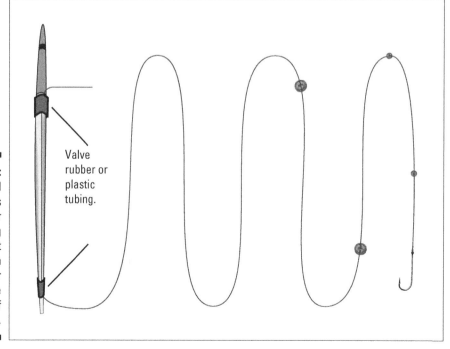

Figure 12-5:
A fixed float rig is perfect for suspending a bait at any depth shallower than the length of your rod.

Valve rubber or plastic tubing.

The following describe the main types of floats and how to use the floats to create a fixed float rig:

- **Floats with metal or plastic eyelets:** Fix in place by passing the line through each eyelet 2–3 times.

- **Floats fitted with plastic or rubber sleeves:** Attach by pulling the sleeves off the float stem, passing the line through the tubing, then pushing the tubing firmly into place on the float stem, trapping the line between the sleeve and the float.

- **Floats with pegs:** Fix in place by pushing the peg into the central line channel to jam the float in place on the line and stop it sliding up and down.

Pencil, stemmed and quill floats need to be weighted or ballasted so that only the brightly coloured tip protrudes above the water. Bobby corks should be weighted so that they are at least three-quarters submerged. Correctly weighted, the float sinks under the surface when a fish nibbles the bait, instantly telegraphing the bite to you visually.

However, like all rules, these have exceptions, and this exception relates to occasions when you present very shallow bait. In this case, you often don't need to weight the float, allowing the float to lie flat on the surface of the water, and standing or tipping up to indicate a bite.

Fixed float rigs are especially useful for catching trout, garfish (piper), mullet, luderick (blackfish), small bait fish species and even bream in certain scenarios.

Running float rig

A running float rig is ideal when you wish to present a bait at a depth beneath the surface of the water greater than the length of your rod.

- **Basic requirements:** Line, hook, stopper (such as a swivel or knot), split shot or sinkers and a float.

- **Most positive aspect:** Allows you to set a bait deeper in the water than the length of your rod and still easily cast the rig.

You can rig running floats to run freely on the line below a *stopper* such as a swivel, ring, split shot, piece of wool or a knot. The positioning of the stopper determines the depth at which the bait is presented. Without a stopper, the hook sinks to the bottom, making the float rather superfluous in its role as a device to suspend the bait at a pre-determined depth.

Running floats (see Figure 12-6) are especially handy when you want to set a bait deeper in the water than the length of your rod. Casting a fixed float rig of this length is extremely hard, but with a running float, you can easily wind the small stopper through the rod tip and guides or runners — even back onto the reel itself — and then make a normal cast.

To make this useful rig, first attach the stopper to the line. The stopper can be a short length of nylon line or wool tied around the main line, a rubber band twisted in place or a very small split shot. Or, best of all, a special rubber stopper on a little wire loop bought from a tackle shop (the wire loops make it easy to slide the stopper onto the line — just follow the instructions on the back of the packet).

In the case that the float has a rather wide channel, you may need to run a small plastic bead onto your line between the top of the float and the stopper to prevent the stopper from either becoming stuck or travelling right through the float's line channel.

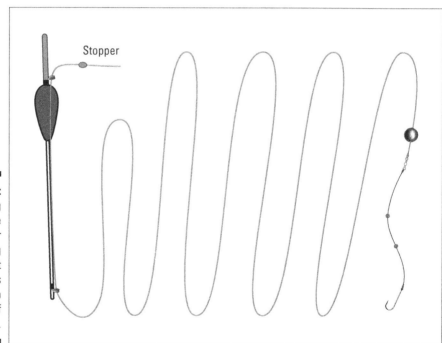

Figure 12-6:
Running floats are excellent for suspending baits at depths greater than the length of your rod.

You can construct all sorts of terminal rigs beneath the float — regardless of whether you rig the float fixed or running. This type of rig can range from a single hook tied to the line to various combinations of swivels, sinkers, single hooks or ganged hooks. Whichever combination you choose, you need to ballast the float with weight in the form of sinkers or shot until the float is at least three-quarters submerged, with just the float's top showing above the water.

Bubble float rig

Unlike most other floats, you can use the *bubble float* not only to suspend a bait in mid water, but also to provide additional casting weight without resorting to extra sinkers and split shot.

- ✔ **Basic requirements:** Line, hook, swivel, hook link and a bubble float.

- ✔ **Most positive aspect:** Allows you to partially fill the float with water to provide extra casting weight.

Bubble floats are much favoured by trout anglers casting mudeyes (dragonfly larvae) and similar natural baits into freshwater lakes, dams and rivers. Also, you can use these special floats (refer to Chapter 7) with artificial flies without the need to use special fly-casting equipment (refer to Chapters 5, 6 and 7).

The greatest advantage of the bubble float is that the float can be partially filled with water (via a built-in slit or a hole with a plug), giving the line extra casting weight without the need for sinkers.

One of the best and most popular bubble float rigs for delicately presenting natural baits involves passing the main line through one eyelet of the float and allowing the bubble float to run freely on the line, without a stopper of any kind above the float. The line below the float eyelet is then tied to a swivel, which is in turn attached to a short hook link down to the baited hook or fly.

With this rig, the float acts solely as a casting weight and the bait ultimately sinks through the water column towards the lake or stream bottom. You can add split shot between the swivel and float to help take the bait down in a current.

An extremely effective variation on the basic bubble float rig involves the use of a small sliver or block of cork or Styrofoam attached to the line between the swivel and the bubble (see Figure 12-7). The small object acts as a tiny float, suspending the bait at a pre-determined depth, but offering minimal resistance to timid fish.

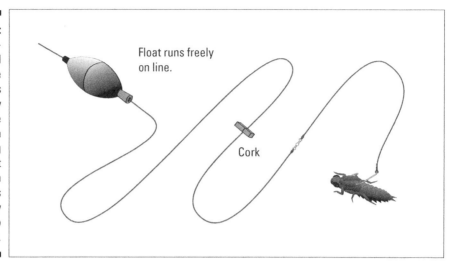

Figure 12-7: A sophisticated bubble float rig is extremely effective when presenting tiny, soft baits such as mudeyes (dragonfly larvae) to timid trout.

Float runs freely on line.

Cork

You can easily attach the sliver of cork or foam to the line by cutting a slice in the material with a sharp knife and then wrapping the line once or twice around the little float, making sure the line pulls down into the slice. Greasing the line between the reel and float with a petroleum jelly type product or another type of *floatant* also improves the effectiveness of this deadly set-up.

Ganged-hook rigs

Ganged or linked hooks seem to be a uniquely Australian invention, which developed immediately after World War II among surf fishers casting whole garfish baits for tailor. Ganged hooks have gone on to become an important part of the Aussie saltwater fishing scene. Gangs have been slower to take off in New Zealand, but do see some use there nowadays.

- ✔ **Basic requirements:** Line and 2–6 hooks (sinkers and swivels are optional).

- ✔ **Most positive aspect:** Holds and presents longer baits very nicely and effectively hooks tail-biting fish, as well as reducing the incidence of bite-offs from sharp-toothed critters.

Ganged-hook rigs (also called *linked hooks*) are extremely popular in many parts of Australia, especially among anglers targeting tailor and salmon using whole pilchards (mulies) or garfish as bait (see Chapter 2). You can also use ganged hooks for catching flathead, snapper, kingfish, mackerel, mulloway and many other popular species.

A *gang* or *flight* of hooks consists of 2–6 hooks (but usually four), linked together by passing the point of one hook through the eye of the next. Many keen anglers construct gangs themselves, but sets are available at most tackle stores.

The major advantage of ganged hooks lies in the way the set-up can carry and present a bait such as a whole pilchard, whitebait, garfish, fish flesh strip or squid tentacle (see Figure 12-8). As a bonus, ganged hooks effectively catch tail-biting fish and help to prevent bite-offs from sharp-toothed species such as tailor and mackerel, even without the use of a wire leader or trace.

The most useful and popular ganged-hook rig involves simply tying a flight of ganged hooks directly to the end of the line and relying on the bait itself to provide the necessary casting weight. However, you can also use gangs with any of the running sinker rigs (already described in this chapter), or suspended under a fixed or running float rig (also described in this chapter).

When using a sidecast reel, you're best to incorporate at least one swivel in a ganged-hook rig, preferably between the reel and any other items of terminal tackle such as sinkers or floats. The swivel helps enormously in reducing line twist and tangles.

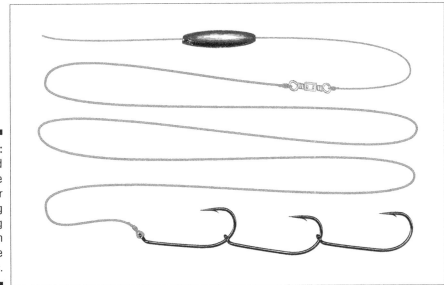

Figure 12-8: Ganged hooks are useful for presenting big, long baits such as whole pilchards.

Lure fishing rig

Lure fishing is one of the fastest growing facets of angling, and many people enjoy the added challenge and constant activity of lure fishing. As with other forms of angling, the simplest rigs are usually best when lure fishing.

- ✔ **Basic requirements:** Line, hook and a lure (swivels are optional).
- ✔ **Most positive aspect:** Lures, unlike natural bait, stay fresh forever.

You can tie a lure directly to the end of your main line to catch many different sorts of predatory fish, whether you're casting and retrieving or trolling the line behind a moving boat. One of the major benefits of using lures is that the artificial bait stays fresh forever!

If the lure is likely to spin in the water, or if you're using a sidecast reel, always add a small, strong swivel 30–60 centimetres ahead of the lure to reduce line twist and the resulting tangles the twisting can cause.

A range of predatory fish — for example, tailor, Spanish mackerel and barracuda — are equipped with sharp teeth or other line-damaging bits of anatomy. When targeting fish of this nature, add a swivel and a short leader (see Figure 12-9) or a trace of heavy nylon line or light wire to the basic lure fishing rig (refer to Chapter 7).

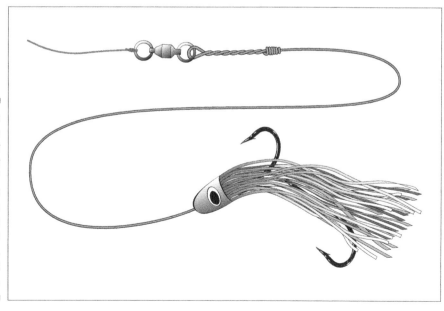

Figure 12-9: When lure fishing for 'toothy critters' such as tailor, barracuda and Spanish mackerel, use a short wire trace.

Chapter 13

Cast Away

. . . .

. . . .

*U*nless you're fishing from a boat, a jetty or a bridge, where you can simply drop your baited hook and line straight into the water, you need to be able to cast your rig a certain distance to reach the fish.

Casting is an important part of fishing, but perfecting the art gives many people headaches. Forget the aspirin and take it from me that casting is easily mastered as long as you remember two critical points:

✔ Distance is less important than accuracy.

✔ Practice makes perfect.

To use a golfing analogy, anyone can hit a golf ball with a golf club (even me!) and with practice the ability to belt that little white pill down the fairway improves. Although not many people can ever hope to drive the ball as far and as straight as Tiger Woods, with practice the amount of time spent hacking about in the rough becomes considerably less. Learning how to cast is very much the same as learning how to play golf (with the notable difference that, in casting, placing the hook in the water is actually desirable!).

The Mechanics of Casting

When casting with a fishing rod and reel, the idea is to use the mechanical advantages of the equipment to propel a baited hook, sinker, lure or fly much further than you can ever hope to throw the same items of terminal tackle by hand.

The most important tool in casting is the rod. The fishing rod is your club, bat or racquet, providing reach, power and directional control. Chances are, for example, that you can probably throw an apple a distance of 30–40 metres (or maybe 60 metres if you have a strong arm from regularly playing cricket or baseball). If you take that same apple, ram it on the end of a broom stick, swing the stick briskly through the air and flick the apple off, you're probably able to propel the apple 70, 80 or even 100 metres. The mechanics of this process are very similar to casting with a fishing rod.

The actual casting stroke — the swing of the rod through the air — is basically the same in all forms of tackle, with the exception of fly gear (which I look at separately in the section 'Casting with Fly Gear', later in the chapter). The idea is to use the swing of the rod to generate speed and momentum, then release the line at the optimum moment in the casting stroke and allow the sinker, bait or lure to fly out through the air towards the intended target. Whatever the type of rig you have, this action is the same, with only slight variations in how you hold the outfit, prepare to make the cast, and release the line depending on the type of reel you own. (I describe the various reels in Chapter 6.)

Casting with a Threadline Outfit

Fortunately, the most popular style of fishing reel — the threadline reel — is also one of the easiest reels to cast.

As I explain in Chapters 5 and 6, threadline reels (also known as spinning reels or eggbeaters) and the rods that match them are available in single-handed and double-handed forms, but the operation of both outfits during the casting process is exactly the same.

Regardless of whether you're using a single- or double-handed threadline outfit, your dominant hand (for example, your right hand if you're right-handed) wraps around the handle of the rod. The reel's stem protrudes either between the index and middle finger or the middle and ring finger of that hand (whichever is more comfortable).

When holding a threadline outfit this way, you can easily pick up the line with the index finger of your dominant hand or trap the line against the spool rim, then reach across and open the bail arm with the other hand (see Figure 13-1).

Most people learn to cast a threadline outfit with the line held in the crook of the first joint of the dominant hand's index finger. However, accomplished casters (the Tiger Woods of the fishing game) prefer to trap the line against the spool rim with the tip or pad of their index finger, rightly claiming that this method gives greater control at the point of release and improves accuracy. As the latter method is a little more difficult, I recommend you learn to cast using the method shown in Figure 13-1 and try the more advanced spool rim method later (after 40-plus years of casting, I still use the crook of my index finger!).

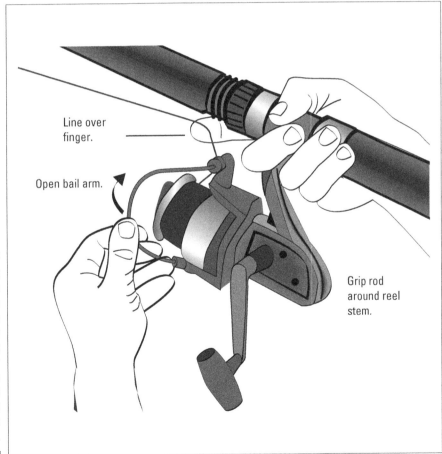

Line over finger.

Open bail arm.

Grip rod around reel stem.

Figure 13-1:
To cast a threadline reel, pick up the line on your index finger or trap the line against the spool lip and open the bail arm.

Holding the line in this manner, you move the rod behind you (see Figure 13-2) and then sweep the rod smoothly forwards, straightening your finger at the optimum moment to release the line and send the sinker or lure on its way. At the completion of the cast, turn the handle of the reel and the bail arm automatically snaps shut and you can begin to recover the line.

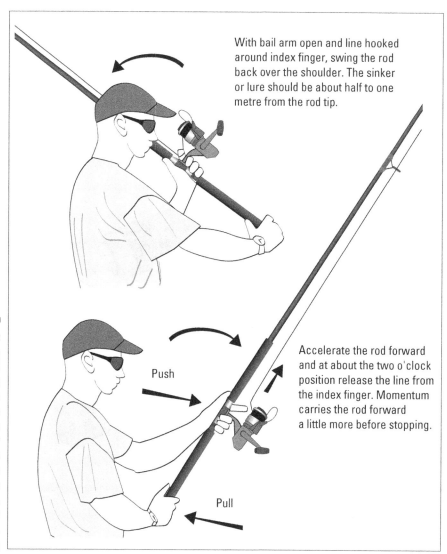

With bail arm open and line hooked around index finger, swing the rod back over the shoulder. The sinker or lure should be about half to one metre from the rod tip.

Push

Pull

Accelerate the rod forward and at about the two o'clock position release the line from the index finger. Momentum carries the rod forward a little more before stopping.

Figure 13-2: The casting stroke and optimum release point are the same whatever the type of tackle you're using, except fly gear.

Before accelerating into the casting stroke, always take the time to glance behind you to make sure you're not going to hook anyone or anything. Hitting someone with a fast moving sinker, hook or lure can cause nasty injuries!

Working out when to release the line

Learning when to release the line at the optimum moment takes practice. Don't be dismayed if your first few casts go straight up in the air (indicating that you released the line too early in the casting stroke) or slam into the water at your feet (indicating that you released the line too late).

When casting, your aim is to release the line so that the rig travels on a trajectory beginning about 45 degrees above the horizon and has the optimum casting distance.

Restricting the length of your cast

Accuracy in casting is at least as important as distance. You not only need to be able to drop the hook into a particular piece of water, you also need to avoid hazards such as trees, bridge pylons, passing boats, seagulls, innocent bystanders and the opposite bank of the river.

To achieve accuracy, you need to control not only the line and direction of your cast, but also the length of your cast. In golf, your *short game* is often more important than distance off the tee — 'drive for show, putt for dough' — and fishing is no different.

Target practice

In most forms of fishing, casting accuracy is far more important than distance. For example, when fishing from a surf beach or ocean rock platform, you often need to be able to deliver your rig into a specific gutter, hole or gap between areas of shallow reef, rather than sending the rig over the horizon.

If you learn the habit of aiming every cast at a particular spot, your accuracy is bound to improve. For example, even when I'm casting into open water, I aim at a floating leaf or a patch of foam rather than just firing blindly into the blue yonder. If you want to practise casting, but have limited access to water, you can practise casting accurately by setting up a target such as a plastic bucket in your backyard or in a park and casting at the target from varying distances.

You can control or limit the length of a cast by either reducing the amount of power and speed of the casting stroke or by slowing the sinker or lure in flight by restricting the flow of the line off the reel with your fingers. Experienced casters use a combination of both techniques to hone their short game.

Casting with a Sidecast Outfit

Casting with a sidecast reel is a little different to casting with a threadline outfit. As I explain in Chapter 6, the spool on a sidecast reel is actually twisted or turned through 90 degrees in order to achieve a cast. To turn the spool, you depress a lever at the base of the reel near the foot and rotate the whole assembly on the turntable. At the same time, the thumb or fingers of the lower casting hand (usually the left hand of a right-handed caster) trap the line against the lip of the spool, as Figure 13-3 shows.

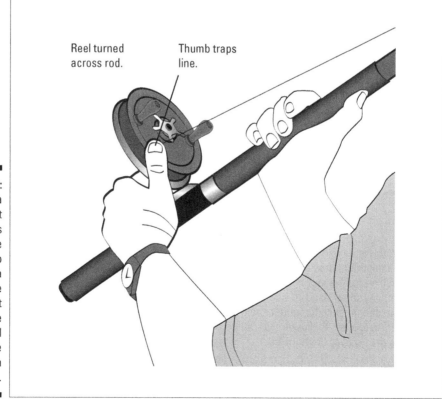

Reel turned across rod.

Thumb traps line.

Figure 13-3: Casting a sidecast reel is a little different to casting a threadline outfit because the spool must first be twisted on its turntable.

Learning how to cast with a sidecast outfit is relatively simple and, before long, you can become adept at being able to depress the turntable lever, trap the line with your thumb and swing back in preparation for the casting stroke — all in one fluid movement.

To release the line and deliver the cast at the optimum point in the forward stroke, simply straighten or lift your thumb off the spool lip to free the trapped line.

At the completion of the cast, you rotate the spool back to the in-line position on the rod and turn the handle to recover slack. At this point in the fishing process, you need to lightly trap the line between the thumb and forefinger of the non-winding hand in order to tension and control the line.

Casting with an Overhead Outfit

Unlike threadline outfits and sidecast reels, which hang underneath the rod, spincasters or closed-face reels, baitcasters and overhead reels are designed to sit on top of the rod when casting and fishing.

Closed-face reels have a button on the back of the housing that is depressed with the thumb of the casting hand to free the line from the internal pick-up pins and trap the line against the inside of the conical housing over the spool. Release the button to free the line and send the sinker or lure on its way at the optimum point in the casting stroke. Recover the line after a cast by turning the handle to re-engage the pick-up pins.

Overhead reels other than close-faced reels are quite different, in that the reels have revolving drums that spin on an axle to yield line during a cast. This set-up makes overhead reels a little trickier to master than the other fixed-spool reels already described in this chapter.

To cast a revolving drum overhead reel (see Figure 13-4), first disengage the gears by depressing the free-spool lever, button or thumb bar. At the same time, you trap the spool under your thumb and hold until the release point in the casting stroke, at which point you lift your thumb to release the spool and send the sinker or lure on its way.

You can control the rotation of the spool during the cast by gently *feathering* or *thumbing* the spinning spool rim or line load with your thumb and then clamping down to stop the spool spinning when the sinker or lure hits the water. By turning the handle, you can then engage the reel's gears.

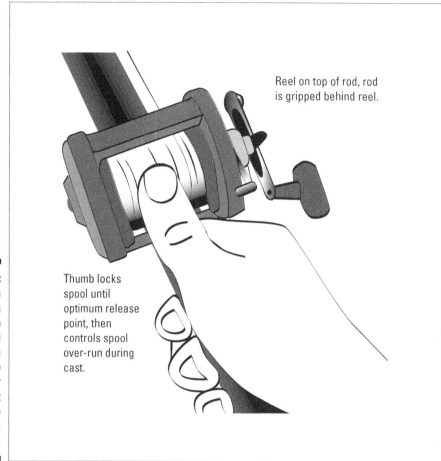

Reel on top of rod, rod is gripped behind reel.

Figure 13-4:
To cast a revolving drum overhead reel, use the thumb on your dominant hand to control the spool.

Thumb locks spool until optimum release point, then controls spool over-run during cast.

Banishing backlash

When you make a cast, the spool of a baitcaster reel or overhead reel spins at high speed, which means you can easily lose control of the line, especially when the sinker or lure slows in flight towards the end of the cast. If the spool continues to spin faster than the line pulls out through the rod runners, loose loops of line form at the reel. In extreme cases, the loops turn into over-runs or backlashes — nasty tangles of line that bring everything to a crunching halt, spoiling a day's fishing.

Happily, most modern overhead casting reels, especially the smaller baitcaster models, are fitted with various forms of anti-backlash devices. The devices use either friction or magnetic field force to slow the spool near the end of the cast and greatly reduce the incidence of over-runs and backlashes.

When learning to cast overhead reels, turn the anti-backlash control to the highest setting. Although this setting results in cutting down on casting distance, you're bound to have fewer frustrating tangles in the line. Later, as your confidence increases, you can begin to back off the controls and develop what experienced casters call an *educated thumb*.

Practising makes perfect sense

Casting overhead reels takes more concentration and practice than mastering the other reel styles that I describe earlier in this chapter, but the effort is worthwhile in many forms of angling because the reels offer excellent casting accuracy and control when fighting strong, active fish.

Unfortunately, however, overhead reels aren't suited to all forms of fishing, especially when casting light baits, sinkers or lures. (For more information on overhead reels, refer to Chapter 6.)

Casting with Fly Gear

As I mention in Chapters 4, 6 and 8, fly-fishing relies on different casting principles to all other styles of angling because the weight of the line, rather than the weight of the sinker or lure, allows you to deliver a lightweight fly to the target point.

Fly casting involves moving a specially designed rod back and forth through the air to generate travelling waves or loops of line (called *false casting*) before finally laying that line out on the water to present the fly (see Figure 13-5).

Fly casting is difficult to learn from a book and, although videos and computer graphics certainly help, in the long run the best way to learn fly casting is to spend a few hours with a competent caster. As a result, I strongly recommend that if you want to take up fly-fishing, you should enrol in a course or have professional tuition from a qualified fishing instructor.

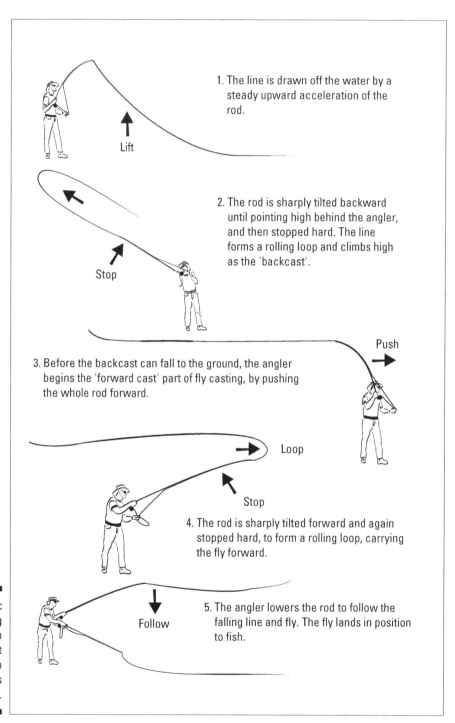

1. The line is drawn off the water by a steady upward acceleration of the rod.

Lift

2. The rod is sharply tilted backward until pointing high behind the angler, and then stopped hard. The line forms a rolling loop and climbs high as the 'backcast'.

Stop

Push

3. Before the backcast can fall to the ground, the angler begins the 'forward cast' part of fly casting, by pushing the whole rod forward.

Loop

Stop

4. The rod is sharply tilted forward and again stopped hard, to form a rolling loop, carrying the fly forward.

Follow

5. The angler lowers the rod to follow the falling line and fly. The fly lands in position to fish.

Figure 13-5: Fly casting relies on different principles to other forms of casting.

Chapter 14

Hooking, Playing and Landing Fish

*L*earning about tackle, rigs, knots and casting techniques is all well and good, but don't forget that the ultimate goal of this entire recreational angling game is to actually catch a few fish.

Assuming you buy and assemble your gear (using the information provided in the preceding chapters) and master the casting process, chances are you're eventually going to feel a nibble from an interested fishy customer. What you do next can spell the difference between a prize catch flopping in the bucket and another boring yarn about the 'one that got away'.

Fish or Wish?

When a hungry fish takes a chomp at your baited hook, lure or fly, you can usually tell immediately that this exciting event has occurred. The feeling you get ranges from a tiny pluck on the line, to a dip of the rod tip, to a quiver of the float (if you're using one), to a full-blooded wrench that threatens to rip the outfit clean out of your hands.

Indications of a bite take two forms — tactile and visual.

  ✔ **Tactile:** You feel anything from a tenuous nibble to a lusty pull.

  ✔ **Visual:** You see a movement of the line, rod tip or float.

Your chances of detecting a bite by both means — sight and feel — dramatically improve if you're holding the outfit in your hands and concentrating on your rig. Sitting back with the rod propped up on a stick and your hat pulled down over your eyes is a sure way to lessen the odds.

Controlling the line

Detecting a bite is easier if you minimise the amount of slack in the line. You can reduce slack by slowly retrieving excess line, by moving the rod to reduce the *belly* of loose line between the rod tip and the water or by using a combination of both actions. Exercising *line control* so that you stay in touch with your bait or lure is one of the important skills that characterises a successful angler and is an art you can only master by spending lots of time fishing.

Maintaining hand or finger contact with the line also helps you to feel when a fish is nibbling. To do this, use the fingertips of the hand not holding the rod to pick up the line between the reel and the first runner or stripping guide (see Figure 14-1).

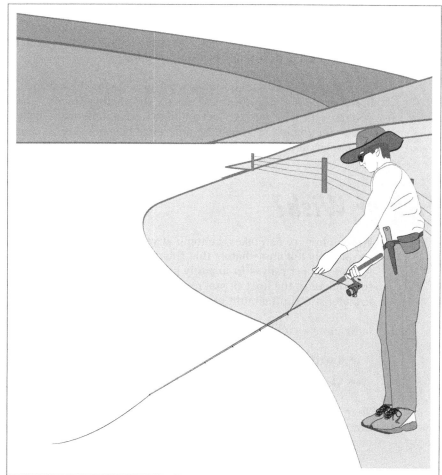

Figure 14-1: Whenever possible, keep your outfit in your hands and hold the line between the reel and the first runner to feel for bites with your fingertips.

The flip side of the control story is that if the line is too tight, your bait behaves unnaturally, and if you take too much slack out of the line, you risk dragging your rig away from the fish and in towards the shore or boat.

Constantly reeling in and checking the bait to see if a fish has been by for a snack — even if no bites have been detected — is a common trait amongst new chums to the sport and is to be avoided. Remember that you can't catch a fish if your line's not in the water.

Again, the flip side is that if you do register a strong bite or series of bites, but don't hook the fish, you do need to reel in and check your bait (replacing the bait if necessary) and then cast straight back out to the same spot.

Striking and setting the hook

How you react to a nibble or bite can mean the difference between hooking a fish and losing your bait. In most cases, when you feel a fish on the hook you need to strike in response.

To *strike* is to raise the rod tip or crank the reel handle (or both) in order to pull on the line and *set* the hook (make sure the hook is firmly planted) in the fish's mouth.

Two common mistakes in this area are to strike too hard or to strike too late:

- **Striking too hard:** You don't need to rip the fish's head off when striking! Fish hooks are wickedly sharp and only a modest pull is required to bury the point and barb, especially if the fish is also pulling in the opposite direction. Too much gusto can also be counterproductive because you can rip the hook clear off the fish's gob or, in extreme cases, break the line.

- **Striking too late:** If you're going to set the hook, you're best to make the strike while the bait or lure is actually in the fish's mouth — not after the bait has been thoroughly chewed up or nibbled at and spat out or stolen.

Rather than strike too hard or too late, try the following steps:

1. **Concentrate on reacting quickly, smoothly and with the minimum of excess force to a movement in the line.**

2. **Briskly, but smoothly, raise the rod tip 30–40 centimetres or quickly turn the reel handle 2–3 times.**

   This response is usually all the effort you need to securely set a hook.

3. **If you can feel by the lack of extra weight that your restrained striking action has missed the mark, gently lower the rod to the original position and stop winding the reel.**

By doing this, the bait stays near the fish and chances are that the critter may come back for a second bite at the cherry.

Countless exceptions exist to the general rules of dealing with a strike, but with practice it becomes obvious when striking needs to be significantly delayed, when no strike is necessary or when an opportunity warrants a much harder, more aggressive hook-set. To begin with, however, try maintaining a high level of line control and reacting quickly but smoothly to biting fish. In most instances, this strategy offers the greatest chance of success, and only if you consistently fail to have results should you experiment with different strategies.

Play Time

Hooking a fish is surely one of the most thrilling moments in angling. You lift the rod tip or crank the reel and suddenly the line springs taut and an urgent, electric energy pulses through the previously inanimate outfit in your hands. You're instantly connected to another life force by a gossamer thread of line and the excitement is palpable — you can virtually taste it! But what happens in the next few seconds or minutes is the key to landing the fish.

If the fish is relatively small, you can simply raise the rod to around 45 degrees above the horizontal and crank the reel handle to land the catch. Bigger, stronger fish require a little more finesse, as I explain in the next section.

Playing the fish

If you hook a fish of a reasonable size, and the fish is heavy and strong in relation to the strength of your tackle, thickness of your line and size of your hook, attempting to use sheer muscle to haul the beast in is likely to result in disaster for the following reasons:

- ✔ The hook may tear free of the fish.
- ✔ The hook may straighten out, releasing the fish.
- ✔ The line may snap.
- ✔ The rod may break (fortunately, rods don't break easily unless already damaged, so this last scenario is unlikely to happen).

Note that particularly active fish, such as tailor, salmon, trout or tuna, are capable of breaking a line with a rated strength greater than the fish's own weight. Many anglers are surprised and dismayed to learn that a fish weighing 2 kilos can snap a 4-kilo line in a direct pull, which is why larger, more active fish need to be *played*.

The term *playing a fish* means taking your time and bringing the fish in slowly and smoothly while using the flex of the rod as a shock absorber. If necessary, allow the hooked fish to *run* or take line against the reel's pre-set drag or slipping clutch (refer to Chapter 6 for more information on reels and drag).

A big, strong fish can pull the rod down and rip line off against the resistance of the reel's drag and if the drag has been tightened too much, the line can easily snap. On the other hand, if the drag is too loose, the fish may be impossible to bring in or may strip all the line from your spool.

To stop the fish from having the upper hand, the drag needs to be set firmly enough to tire the fish and allow you to ultimately gain control, but not so tightly that the line snaps. Playing a fish is a form of piscatorial karate, where you use your opponent's own strength to wear down the fish. Brute force is rarely the answer.

Ordinarily, you're best to set the resistance of the drag at just less than one-third the rated breaking strain of the line, as measured in a direct pull from the reel. In other words, if you're using 3-kilo breaking strain line, the pre-set drag pressure should be around 1 kilo or a little less at the reel.

In reality, few people carry spring balances or weights around to test the drag level. Instead, with practice you develop a feel for the right drag setting and learn a keen sense of when the drag level is too great. Basically, however, if the rod bends too deeply or the line whistles and sings in the breeze when the fish strikes, chances are the drag's too tight. If in doubt, err on the lighter side.

Your rod also has a vital role in playing a fish. For the most part, you need to hold the rod so that the angle of the lower part of the rod sits at around 45 degrees to the horizontal. By doing this, the rod is high enough that it has a good working bend for fighting against the hooked fish, but isn't so high that the rod is in risk of snapping. You need to avoid:

- **Pointing the rod directly at your opponent:** This angle negates the strength and shock-absorbing flexibility of the rod.

- **Pointing the rod straight up at the sky:** This angle adds to the line's friction as it passes over the rod runners, with the result that the line may snap. This angle also gives you less control over the fish and increases the chances of a powerful opponent snapping the rod.

Pumping and winding

As soon as the fish stops running and pulling line from your reel against the drag, you need to begin recovering lost line and bringing in the fish.

The best way to recover the line is to use a process called *pumping and winding*, which means lifting the rod without cranking the reel and then lowering the rod while turning the reel handle. The pump-and-wind routine is efficient, effective and saves your tackle from excessive wear and tear.

When a fish takes the hook, chances are the rod tip is pulled down towards the horizon. To pump and wind, begin by smoothly lifting the rod from just above the horizontal until the butt or lower portion is angled up at least 45 degrees above the horizon (see Figure 14-2). Don't crank the reel as you perform the lift or pump part of the process because this action puts extra and unnecessary strain on the rod and the gears of the reel. When the lower portion of the rod reaches the 45-degree angle, begin turning the reel handle as you lower the rod back towards the horizontal. Repeat the process of lifting the rod without winding the reel and then cranking the reel as you lower the rod.

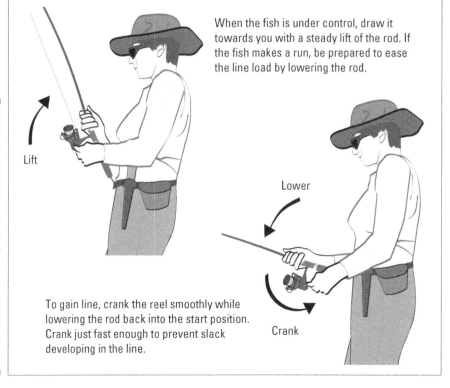

Figure 14-2: To play a fish, the angler uses the flex of the rod and the reel's drag to wear down her opponent, then recovers line by pumping and winding.

When the fish is under control, draw it towards you with a steady lift of the rod. If the fish makes a run, be prepared to ease the line load by lowering the rod.

Lift

Lower

To gain line, crank the reel smoothly while lowering the rod back into the start position. Crank just fast enough to prevent slack developing in the line.

Crank

The physics of fishing

Without needing to be overly scientific, being aware that physics plays an important part in fighting and landing a hooked fish can help you get that result.

Think of the rod as a lever, with the fulcrum or balance point located where your hands grasp the rod near the reel. In many ways, the angler is at the wrong end of the lever and forces are increased at the butt end of the rod, which is one reason why a fish can feel bigger and stronger than it is in reality. This is especially true with particularly long rods.

Physics also comes into play when a hooked fish runs and pulls line from the reel against the drag or slipping clutch. Friction over the rod runners greatly increases the actual strain imposed on the line and, if you hold the rod too high in the air, the line can snap — even if the drag is set within safe parameters. If in doubt, lower the rod tip a little to reduce runner friction.

Finally, if a hooked fish pulls a great deal of line from the spool of a reel and significantly decreases the diameter of the line load on the reel, pressure on the line increases dramatically. One reason for the increased pressure is that the spool has to turn faster and more often to yield the same amount of line. Bear this in mind if you lose a lot of line during a struggle with a hooked fish because you can easily reduce drag pressure at the reel and lower the rod tip to prevent the line from breaking.

Be extremely careful to keep a certain amount of tension in the line during the winding of the reel because loose line can easily wrap around the rod tip or allow the fish to shake free of the hook. The best way to avoid slack line is to start turning the reel a split second before you begin to lower the rod and to maintain enough pressure to keep a slight bend in the rod even on the down stroke. I find that focusing first on winding the reel and second on lowering the rod is helpful in achieving constant line tension.

A smooth action is absolutely vital when fighting or playing a fish. Your aim is to keep steady pressure on the fish at all times without generating any sudden jerks or slack line. If the hooked fish finds another reserve of strength and runs again, simply lower the rod tip slightly, stop winding and allow your adversary to pull line against the drag. Always remember that time is on your side.

Catch Me if You Can

Most fish that escape are lost in the first or last few seconds of the encounter. Of the two, the riskiest moment is when that big fish finally swims into view after a drawn out battle. At this point, feeling a surge of excitement and an overwhelming desire to haul that prized catch to safety as quickly as possible is natural. This approach can be disastrous!

How you actually land and secure your catch depends on where you're fishing, the tackle you're using and the size of the hooked fish. Having a game plan of how you're going to land the fish, however, means the battle is half won. The following are the basic methods used to land fish:

- **Lifting the fish from the water:** You can lift or swing smaller fish from the water by using the rod rather like the derrick of a crane.

  The risk of using the rod to lift the fish is that hooks can pull free at this stage and even relatively light fish can snap finer lines (or even your rod tip) if the fish kicks or twists violently in the air.

- **Dragging the fish ashore:** When fishing on a beach, river bank or sloping, rocky shoreline, dragging the fish towards you along the ground rather than lifting or swinging it through the air is safer. When possible, use an incoming wave or surge of water to help bring in the fish.

- **Picking up the fish with your hands:** In many cases, you or an assistant may be able to physically pick the fish up from the water, grasping the fish by the wrist of the tail, jaw or gills or by simply placing one or both hands underneath the fish. However, don't attempt to pick up a fish, even with gloves, unless you're absolutely sure of the species you've hooked and know about the fish's physiology. A number of species of fish have either venomous spines, sharp gill covers, spiky scales or sharp teeth that can inflict nasty injuries on the unwary.

- **Using a net or gaff:** With unknown species, larger catches or when fishing from a boat, jetty, pier or high rock ledge, the safe method of bringing in the fish is to use a net or gaff, as I explain in the following sections.

Using a landing net

A landing net is the most common tool used to land a fish, but many people make a mess of netting (and the next trophy fish to be knocked from the hook by an overly enthusiastic net wielder certainly isn't going to be the last).

The most important aspect of netting a fish is to remember that landing a fish with a net has absolutely nothing in common with catching butterflies! Forget about swooshing, swooping, dipping and scooping at a flailing fish. Instead, take the following steps:

1. **Place the net in the water.**

   Set the net so that the front of the hoop is submerged and the back of the hoop (where the handle is connected) is flush with the surface.

2. **Using the rod, bring the hooked fish to the net and swim the fish into the net head first.**

   If you're fishing on your own, you need to perform these actions yourself, holding the net handle in one hand and the rod in the other. If you need to reel in line during this process, tuck the net handle under your arm.

3. **Relax the pressure on the line as you lift the net from the water.**

   This relaxation of pressure induces the fish to dive deeper into the net, making sure you securely restrain the fish.

Are you set with nets? This is such an important part of fishing, I'm going to run through the instructions one more time: Submerge the net, bring the fish to the net, swim the catch into the net head first, reduce pressure on the line, lift the net (see Figure 14-3).

Up to a point, a large net with a wide hoop is easier to use and is more efficient than a smaller net. A landing net stops being useful when dealing with fish over 15–20 kilos. You can best land fish of this size using a gaff, especially if you intend to kill and keep the fish, as I explain in the next section.

Never, ever chase a swimming fish with a net or attempt to net the fish tail first. Such efforts usually result in disaster because the fish can swim much faster than you can move the submerged net through the water. The fish almost always evades capture in this situation, often breaking the line or shedding the hook in the process.

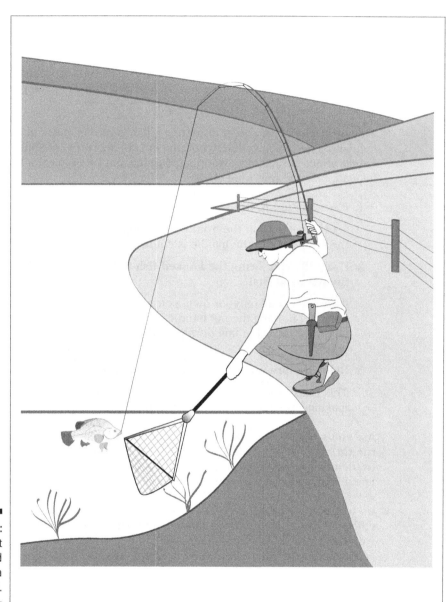

Figure 14-3:
The correct
way to land
a fish with a
landing net.

Using a gaff

A *gaff* is a big, strong hook on a pole or rope. Gaffs are a useful choice for securing large, active fish and especially heavyweight targets such as tuna, mulloway, Spanish mackerel, sharks and marlin.

Gaffing is a little trickier than netting and requires a bit more practice to master. Unfortunately, most anglers don't have the opportunity to catch large fish very often, so practice can be hard to come by. Therefore, being clear on the steps you need to take to gaff a fish is important.

Before thinking about using a gaff, consider whether you want to keep or release (see Chapter 15) the fish because gaffing usually kills or badly injures the fish. Also, gaffs aren't permitted by law in some freshwater fisheries, so check the rules first (see Chapter 26).

As with netting fish, the greatest chance of success occurs when the gaff operator keeps a cool head and acts smoothly but decisively at exactly the right moment. The following steps describe how to use a gaff in most situations:

1. **Just before the fish breaks the surface, place the gaff handle over the fish's back behind the head with the hook facing down.**

2. **Pull back smoothly on the gaff, using the weight and resistance of the fish to bury the hook of the gaff in the fish's flesh.**

3. **Smoothly continue the hook-setting stroke to lift the fish from the water and into the boat or onto the rocks or pier.**

   Sounds easy, but in practice, this last step is often easier said than done.

When dealing with each aspect of hooking, playing and landing a fish, you need to try to think coolly and act smoothly. Although staying calm isn't always easy when the adrenaline starts pumping, keeping a lid on your emotions brings rewards in the shape of more fish for dinner! The time to go wild and start jumping up and down with unbridled excitement is *after* you land that fish-of-a-lifetime or haul in a record-breaking catch!

Part IV

The New Age of Fishing

'Before we take this any further,
I need to know where you stand
on the issue of catch-and-release.'

Part IV

The New Age
Of Fishing

In this part ...

The primary motivation for going fishing — despite all
the philosophical talk about finding your way back
to nature and escaping the rat race — is to try to catch
a fish or two! This part of the book is all about how best
to catch, release or kill, and prepare your catch, while at
the same time being mindful of the sustainable nature of
this recreational sport.

Chapter 15 deals with deciding to release or kill the fish
and doing a professional job of either task (making it,
in my book, a must-read for all anglers). And, when you
decide to take home a meal, Chapter 16 looks at the
nitty gritty of cleaning, preparing and cooking the catch.
Chapter 17 deals with the even larger issue of fishing
sustainably and protecting our aquatic resources so that
our children and their children may continue to enjoy the
thrill of angling, far into the future.

Chapter 15

Kiss or Kill?

*F*ishing is unique among the hunting sports. Anglers can enjoy the full experience of finding and stalking the prey, hooking the fish and playing and landing the beast. Yet, anglers can still exercise the option of returning the catch to the water alive, with a high expectation that the fish is going to survive.

Catch-and-release has become increasingly popular in Australia and New Zealand over the past decade (thanks largely to the fine example set by high profile television anglers such as Rex Hunt). However, fishing is still a form of hunting; so, one of the most important motivating forces for many participants is the promise of a meal of seafood at the end of the day.

Keeping a feed of fresh fish is absolutely fine, as long as you abide by the rules and regulations in the area where you're fishing. I do think that catch-and-release is a positive trend, and one practice to be encouraged in many, many fisheries, but I also believe that great pleasure can be found in providing fresh fish for the family table.

Every angler must abide by fishing rules and regulations by taking only 'legal' fish and by taking a limited number of fish. For ethical and moral reasons, the next obligation for an angler is to kill a fish destined for the dinner table promptly and humanely, which I also cover in the following sections.

Fortunately, plenty of room exists in Australasian recreational angling for a mix of both styles of fishing — catch-and-release and catch-and-kill. The trick lies in identifying the more appropriate approach under a given set of circumstances.

Let 'em Go, Let 'em Grow

In a range of circumstances, the only option open to you is to catch and release a fish, particularly when keeping the fish may place you on the wrong side of the law and leave you liable to being prosecuted, having your gear confiscated or paying a hefty fine.

The most obvious examples of instances when you must release your catch include

- Fish that are shorter than the minimum legal length in force for that species in the area where you're fishing
- Fish that are longer than the maximum legal length where such *slot size* limits exist
- Fish in excess of the per angler or boat bag limit for a particular species
- Fish you unintentionally take during the closed season for that species
- Protected or endangered species you hook accidentally when targeting other types of fish
- Fish you catch in designated *no kill* waters

Other circumstances under which catch-and-release makes good sense include

- When you catch unwanted, surplus, undesirable or potentially poisonous fish
- When you catch a species of fish that can't be accurately identified (and may therefore be toxic or protected by law)
- When you don't have the facilities or equipment to store and maintain the catch in a good enough condition for eating
- When competing in designated live-release or catch-and-release competitions, tournaments or other organised events

Deciding how many fish to keep

Beyond the previous legally binding and commonsense scenarios, the decision of whether to release or keep a fish becomes a matter of personal choice, ethics and peer pressure.

Today, keeping any fish that you don't intend to eat or give to someone else to eat is increasingly difficult to justify. Killing a fish purely for a photo, trophy, competition or record claim is an unpopular move and is likely to invite criticism from other anglers and the general public.

Similarly, keeping fish beyond your needs is neither smart nor particularly justifiable. By this, I mean that catching and killing fish purely to give away to others or bury in the freezer for a rainy day doesn't make a lot of sense. Why not let the extra fish go and catch fresh ones when you're ready for another meal of fish?

Many fish populations are under increasing pressure to survive and, as a result, society places a growing emphasis on preserving the *brood stock* of certain species by carefully releasing larger adults, especially females. (***Note:*** The extremely large specimens of a number of species, for example, flathead, bass and barramundi, are usually females.) Therefore, keeping a couple of smaller fish for the table and letting the big breeders go to continue spawning and thereby maintaining the population makes sense.

Equally sensible is releasing bigger examples of the slow growing species such as Murray cod, bream and snapper, where exceptionally large individuals may be 20, 30 or even 40 years old. A long time passes before this type of fish is replaced naturally in a population, so anglers are increasingly opting to release the bigger, older specimens and keep a couple of younger fish for the table instead (while still abiding by minimum size restrictions).

Finally, when fishing in waterways with strictly limited fish populations, using a catch-and-release system makes sense. For example, many tiny trout or bass streams are only capable of sustaining a small number of adult fish and man-made lakes must be constantly restocked. In limited waters, killing too many fish is counterproductive and unpopular. Instead, let the fish go and take a meal from a larger, more open and sustainable system.

Releasing fish to ensure survival

When releasing a fish for compulsory or personal reasons, you can optimise the fish's chance of survival.

The best way to release a fish so that the critter survives is to keep the fish in the water (see Figure 15-1). Bring the hooked fish to the boat or bank and use a pair of long-nosed pliers, forceps or a similar device to grasp the hook shank and twist it free of the fish's mouth, allowing the fish to swim away — without even touching the catch, when possible.

Figure 15-1:
To ensure survival, remove the hook from the fish without taking the fish from the water. If you must lift the fish, wet your hands first.

Using *barbless* hooks greatly facilitates fast and easy catch-and-release; however, few hook models are sold without barbs. You can easily remove the barb from a hook by using a pair of pliers to crush the barb flat (see Figure 15-2). As a bonus, barbless hooks are much safer to use and if one happens to become stuck in your own skin, the hook slips out far more easily than a barbed hook. (I talk more about barbless hooks in Chapter 4.)

Handling the fish with care

Occasionally, you may find that releasing a fish without touching it is impossible. Instead, you may have to lift the catch from the water by hand or with a landing net and then remove the hook, lure or fly — at which point, try to make an effort to minimise the time the fish spends out of the water and to touch the fish as little as possible, thereby maintaining the fish's slime protective coating. If you must touch the fish, make sure your hands are wet and try to avoid contact between the fish and hard, metal objects and surfaces. Even better, use a damp towel or wet gloves to handle the fish.

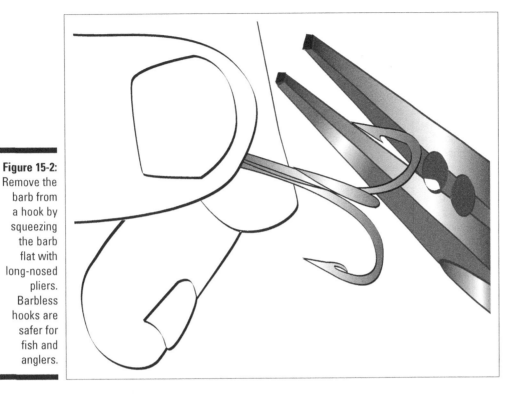

Figure 15-2:
Remove the barb from a hook by squeezing the barb flat with long-nosed pliers. Barbless hooks are safer for fish and anglers.

As you remove the hook, avoid placing the fish on hot, dry surfaces such as aluminium or steel boat decks and, after removing the hook, gently place the fish back into the water.

If the hook is right down the throat of the fish, don't attempt surgery to recover the hook or yank on the line in an effort to tear the hook free! Instead, use a knife, clippers or scissors to cut the line as close as possible to the fish's mouth and return the catch immediately to the water, with the hook left in place.

Often, the fish regurgitates the hook or passes it through the intestines and out into the water. On other occasions, the catch's stomach acids eventually break down the hook. Either way, any deeply hooked fish stands a much better chance of survival if you return it to the water as quickly as possible with the hook left in place.

Knotless nets

If you need to employ a landing net to secure your catch prior to unhooking and releasing the fish, consider using a specialised net that doesn't use a knotted mesh construction (see Figure 15-3).

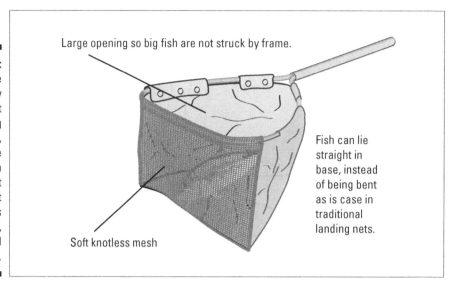

Large opening so big fish are not struck by frame.

Figure 15-3:
Be gentle on any catch that you're going to release, and choose to use a knotless net to protect the fish's slime coat, eyes and fins.

Fish can lie straight in base, instead of being bent as is case in traditional landing nets.

Soft knotless mesh

So-called knotless nets are made from flat mesh or rubber and are much kinder to fish than the more traditional style of knotted mesh net. Knotted mesh can cause serious injuries to fish by scraping off the fish's protective slime coating, scratching eyes or splitting the membranes between fin rays. Scientific research has consistently proven that the use of knotless nets results in much higher survival rates for released fish.

Reviving the catch

From time to time, you may need to revive a fish after capture — more commonly with large, fast swimming species such as tuna, trevally, queenfish, sharks, sailfish and marlin. Big bass, barramundi, snapper and trout that you take on relatively light tackle and battle for a long time before being landed may also require revival.

To revive a tired fish, support its body horizontally in the water, facing the fish into any current or flow. Use a gloved hand or wet towel wrapped around the wrist of the tail and another placed under the forward part of the fish's belly to hold the fish. If no significant current exists, you can walk or wade forwards or have the boat move slowly ahead to create water flow in through the fish's mouth and out through the gills.

Most fish revive quickly when subjected to flowing water, and begin to 'kick' strongly in your grasp. As well, the fish's fins and eyes move and swivel, indicating a rapid return of strength. When the fish's movements indicate an ability to swim, release your grasp and allow the fish to move ahead into the current. If the fish rolls onto its side or turns belly up, grab the fish again and continue the revival process. Be prepared to spend 10–15 minutes, if necessary, reviving a really tired fish before setting the fish free.

Grip a lip

These days, lip-gripping devices (sometimes generically called Boga Grips, because of the brand name of one popular form of lip gripper) are popular with many anglers. These spring-loaded devices allow an angler to secure the catch by engaging the metal or plastic jaws of the gripper around the fish's jaw bone.

Used correctly, lip grippers can be handy for preventing injury to both fish and angler. *Warning:* Incorrect use of lip-gripping devices can be very injurious to fish intended for live release.

The most important thing to remember is that fish restrained with a lip-gripping device should either not be removed from the water or, if removed, be cradled with another hand under the fish's belly to support the catch's weight and prevent injury (see diagram).

Some lip-gripping devices are also fitted with a spring balance or weighing scales so that the catch may be weighed. However, anglers should never weigh a live fish intended for release by hanging it vertically from the lip-gripping device, because this action can cause fatal injuries to the catch. Only weigh fish you intend to keep in this manner.

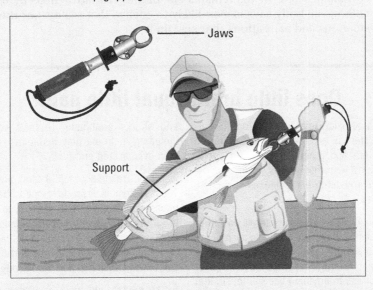

Jaws

Support

Kill 'em and Grill 'em

Whether you use a catch-and-release or catch-and-kill system when fishing (or a mixture of both), you can't avoid the fact that fishing is a form of hunting.

Although a number of anglers regard themselves as purist catch-and-release advocates and voice disdain at the killing of any fish by recreational anglers, fishing remains first and foremost a blood sport. On that basis, people who object to such activities on religious, cultural, moral or ethical grounds really shouldn't fish, because even catch-and-release anglers who adopt the most careful methods simply can't guarantee a 100 per cent survival rate. In other words, if you go fishing, a number of fish are bound to die.

I believe that too often in this modern age, this blood sport aspect of fishing is ignored or glossed over. Instead, every angler must realise that fishing is a type of hunting and gathering, and that this aspect is clearly part of the sport's attraction for many fans. In an age when people are increasingly insulated from nature and from the processes involved in providing food for the table, fishing provides a refreshingly hands-on link to the past — to an age when we hunted and gathered successfully, or went hungry.

Few people in Australia and New Zealand (if any) are likely to starve if fishing isn't an option. However, the ability to provide fresh seafood for our families and friends remains one of the great attractions of angling and nothing anybody says is ever likely to change that reality, nor the human emotions and aspirations that sustain it.

Does little brain equal little pain?

The vexing question related to the catch-and-release system is whether fish feel pain and stress — are fish traumatised by the act of being caught? In other words, is angling — and particularly catch-and-release fishing — a cruel sport?

At this point, no-one truly knows whether fish feel pain and stress, but a large amount of anecdotal and semi-scientific evidence does appear to show that fish don't register pain and stress to anything like the levels that humans or other mammals suffer from these sensations.

For example, you may hook, land and release the same fish several times in quick succession, indicating that any pain felt by the fish didn't last long in the critter's memory banks! Equally, tales abound of mortally injured fish and sharks continuing to feed voraciously, including — in extreme instances — on their own eviscerated entrails!

Fish have relatively small brains and the nervous system is less developed than that of mammals. However, this attribute in itself isn't proof that fish don't register pain, nor that fish don't panic when hooked. In fact, the reactions of many hooked fish indicate that fish have a very strong desire to flee the vicinity!

As an angler, you have an ethical obligation to minimise the amount a hooked fish suffers, be this suffering real or perceived. To this end, you need either to land or release any hooked fish as quickly as possible. Equally, you must promptly and humanely kill any fish destined for the dinner table.

Killing Your Catch with Care

Killing your catch quickly and humanely isn't only a moral imperative, a quick kill makes sense from a purely practical perspective — dead fish don't normally jump off jetties or out of boats and escape.

You can kill a fish quickly and efficiently in a number of ways, including knocking the fish on the head or bleeding the fish to death.

The last rites

In ye olden days, trout and salmon fishers used a small club called a *billy club* for killing fish. As the club was used to administer the last rites, over time the little cosh or baton became known as a *priest*.

Many trout anglers still carry a priest in the shape of a heavy wooden or metal club 15–20 centimetres in length. The priest usually has a tapered handle and a wrist lanyard at one end and a broader, rounded head at the other end (many fish priests look extremely similar to miniature baseball bats).

You can kill a fish using priests or billy clubs by striking the fish firmly on top of the head, directly between the eyes. One or two strong blows are usually sufficient to kill smaller fish.

As fish bigger than 2 kilos may be too strong to kill using a priest, a more substantial club, called a fish billy or *donger* (no giggling, please), is used. A donger often takes the form of a wooden or aluminium baseball bat, although a section of water pipe or even rubber tubing with a bit of lead in the business end is also highly effective.

Whereas killing fish with a hard blow to the head is fast and efficient, the method fails to drain the blood from the carcass, which is an important part of ensuring optimum eating quality in many species. As a result, if you do use the knockout system to kill a fish, you still need to bleed the fish (see the next section).

A bloody business

One of the most popular methods for killing a fish is to use a sharp knife to slice quickly through the *throat latch* area (under the head and between the gills). You then bend the fish's head back sharply to snap the backbone and spinal cord just behind the head (see Figure 15-4).

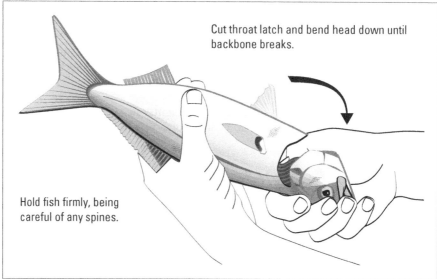

Cut throat latch and bend head down until backbone breaks.

Hold fish firmly, being careful of any spines.

Figure 15-4:
You can quickly kill and bleed most fish by severing the throat latch with a knife and bending the head back.

This method not only kills the fish, but also causes the fish to bleed profusely, draining blood from the meat and greatly improving both the flavour and continued freshness of the flesh.

The disadvantages of using the previous bleeding method is that the process is messy and the fish don't look appealing in photos or when dished up whole on a platter. Who, after all, wants to dig into a beast with its head skewed back at an odd angle and locked in place through rigor mortis?

You can also bleed the fish by reaching inside the gill cavity (under the gill covers or gill plates) with the blade of a knife. You then sever two or three of the bright red, feathery gill arches on either side, ideally where the arches join at the throat latch. Using this method, you avoid cutting through the throat latch and breaking the spinal cord, but, as a result, the fish may take a few seconds to die, occasionally thrashing violently in the process.

Sharks need to be thoroughly bled and as much fluid drained from the bodies as quickly as possible to avoid the occurrence of an unpleasant smell or taste of ammonia in the flesh (caused by the shark's blood chemistry). The best method of draining a shark is to cut off the head and tail and then remove the internal organs and allow the carcass to drain completely before washing the catch in plenty of clean saltwater.

Because of the mess involved in bleeding fish, the job is best done over the side of a boat or pier, or in a bucket or plastic fish tub that is easy to wash out later.

Good point!

Over the last few decades, a traditional Japanese method for killing fish has become extremely popular around the world — first among commercial fishers and more recently among recreational anglers.

Called *iki jimi*, the process involves the use of a sharp, metal spike to destroy the fish's brain. Special *iki jimi* spikes are available, but a sharpened screwdriver, metal skewer or stout knife can be just as efficient.

The precise location for inserting the *iki jimi* spike varies slightly from species to species, but ordinarily is around an eye's width behind the eye and slightly higher than the mid-line of the eye. The spike needs to be inserted firmly into the centre of the fish's head and then twisted slightly (see Figure 15-5). This action results in immediate death and is usually accompanied by a rapid twitching of the fish's eyes, a flickering of the fins and occasionally slight muscle spasms along the body, indicating destruction of the central nervous system.

Blood doesn't drain from a fish when killed using an *iki jimi* spike. Instead, the blood accumulates in the fish's kidney, along the top of the stomach cavity, and is easily removed when the fish is cleaned, as described in Chapter 16.

Spike the fish one `eye width' to the rear, and slightly above the eye.

Figure 15-5: The *iki jimi* spiking method is a fast, effective way to kill most fish.

To recap, the three key advantages of using an *iki jimi* spike over other forms of fish killing and bleeding are

- Death is virtually instantaneous.
- The amount of external bleeding is limited because the blood coagulates in the fish's kidney, along the roof of the stomach cavity.
- The amount of external damage is limited and the fish's colours tend to remain bright and clear.

The combined use of *iki jimi* and an *ice slurry* (that I describe in the section 'Slurry with a fringe benefit on top', later in this chapter) is today recognised as the best method for killing and caring for most species of white-fleshed fish, with the exception of sharks, which are best bled out thoroughly, as I describe in the section 'A bloody business', earlier in this chapter.

Many of the tunas and other *blood fish*, such as tailor, tommy rough (herring) and Australian salmon (kahawai), also benefit from a more thorough external bleeding, although the *iki jimi* method does work.

Alive and kicking

A number of anglers prefer to keep fish alive in a *keeper net* or a submerged cage, in which they can live well until the end of a fishing session. The fish are then killed and cleaned or a number of the fish are returned to the water.

The approach of keeping fish alive offers the benefit of allowing you to release unwanted fish if you catch larger or more desirable specimens later in the day. However, remember that by the letter of the law, live fish in a holding tank are the same as kept fish. If you exceed your bag limit or hold specimens outside of the legal length limits, you risk prosecution, even if you had intended on releasing the extra fish later in the day.

You need to avoid using small or overcrowded keeper nets and cages, which place unnecessary stress on captive fish. If you're relying on a live well in a boat to keep the fish alive, make sure the well has a circulating capacity to regularly refresh and replace the water, thereby keeping the fish in good health.

Keeping Your Catch Cool

From the moment a fish dies, bacteria both from within the fish's body and introduced through openings made from injuries begin to degrade the quality of the flesh (I describe this process in detail in Chapter 16).

High temperatures greatly accelerate bacterial growth and decay of fish flesh. Conversely, lowering the temperature of the carcass can significantly slow the growth of bacteria.

In the absence of anything better, you're best to cover dead fish with a wet towel or hessian bag and place it in the shade. If you don't have a bag or towel, use a few leafy branches or ferns to cover the fish, being careful to avoid contact with any potentially toxic plants.

Ideally, don't keep dead fish in water unless the water is appreciably colder than the air. Even then, leaving a dead fish for more than an hour or two in water without any ice tends to degrade most fish, gradually softening the flesh and leaching out the colour and flavour.

Ice is nice

The best way to keep fish for the table so that the fish presents in the optimum condition, is to make a habit of carrying an insulated cooler containing crushed or cubed ice. If you're on foot, carrying a cooler can pose problems, but is easy for people fishing from a boat or from a spot close to a vehicle.

Chilling fish on ice rapidly lowers the body temperature and dramatically slows the growth of bacteria. When chilling fish, avoid placing the catch directly onto the ice (especially if the individual ice pieces are large) because chunks of ice can burn and bruise the flesh. Instead, support the catch just above the ice or separate the fish from the ice with a few sheets of newspaper or a wet cloth. Direct contact with crushed or flake ice is fine, however, and you can even pack shaved ice into the internal cavities of gutted fish.

So as not to degrade the flesh, be careful not to leave a fish lying in pools of melted ice water.

Slurry with a fringe benefit on top

Placing dead fish in an icy cool environment is the best option when caring for fish in the field or out on the water. This step is especially necessary if you don't have time to immediately clean your catch.

The best way is to make up an *ice slurry* — a mixture of cube or chunk ice and saltwater (ideally ordinary seawater). And the ultimate form of ice slurry is when the ice itself is also made from seawater.

Making and using an ice slurry is easy, as the following shows:

1. **Half fill a cooler with small chunks of ice.**

2. **Add small quantities of seawater, stirring the mixture as you go, until the ice turns to a thick, sludgy consistency.**

3. **After killing and bleeding the fish, drop the fish into the slurry.**

4. **Push the fish well beneath the surface of the slurry.**

An ice slurry keeps fish extremely cold and maintains the fish's colour and eye clarity, greatly enhancing both the fish's appearance and keeping qualities. However, avoid leaving fish in a slurry for longer than 6–8 hours, and, if the slurry is heavily tainted with blood and slime or all the ice has melted, remove the fish from the slurry as soon as possible.

Ice boxes are cooler

You need to clean and process fish as soon as possible (see Chapter 16). If you must keep the fish in a whole state for several hours or the better part of a day, make sure you have access to plenty of ice and a high quality, insulated cooler or ice box (known as a 'chilly bin' in New Zealand).

A high quality cooler and the occasional bag of ice is a valuable investment in the sport of fishing — just have a look at the cost of fresh seafood in the fish shop and you're bound to see what I mean.

Fish that you thoroughly chill in an ice slurry or on ice in a cooler are generally much easier to handle, clean and prepare for the table than fish that you simply keep in the shade under a wet bag or a few leafy branches.

Chapter 16

Cleaning, Preparing and Cooking Your Catch

*T*he job of cleaning the catch has a reputation for being the least enjoyable, most tedious and messiest part of the entire recreational fishing process. Fish cleaning is a chore many anglers dread and try to avoid.

But, given that providing meals of freshly caught seafood is one of the primary motivations for going fishing in the first place, preparing the catch for the table is as inevitable as death and taxes. In most cases, no one else is going to do the work for you and, as the old saying aptly states: 'You caught 'em, you clean 'em!'

This chapter looks at the whole clean, gut, scale, fillet process so that when the time comes to cook your catch, the wonderful satisfaction you get from producing fish for the table touches a deeply instinctive part of your psyche by fulfilling the hunter and gatherer role.

Getting 'em Clean and Prepared for Chef

The best piece of advice I can give you about cleaning fish is to roll up your sleeves and go to work! Don't be shy and don't hang back. If you can peel an orange, carve a roast, slice a cake or cut the rind off a rasher of bacon, you can certainly clean a fish.

As a general rule, the sooner you clean the catch after you kill and bleed the fish (refer to Chapter 15), the better, because the fish is easier to handle and the end product is tastier. You can include in this time frame an hour or two for chilling the fish on ice or in an ice slurry (refer to Chapter 15 for how to prepare this important chiller) because chilling makes the flesh firmer and easier to handle.

A number of states and territories ban the filleting, skinning or other dismembering of fish carcasses while you're still out on the water. The reason for this is that an official inspection has difficulty identifying, measuring and counting your catch accurately if the fish are already cut into bite-size pieces. (For more information about where to find out about the rules and regulations that surround fishing, see Chapter 26.)

On the other hand, you're certainly allowed to bleed and gut your catch immediately, as long as the inspector can still identify the type of fish and measure the overall length of the fish.

The main steps in the process of cleaning fish are gutting and gilling, scaling, filleting, skinning and steaking, as I describe in the following sections.

Cleanliness is next to fishiness

To make the job of cleaning your catch a little easier, the following are a few tricks of the trade:

✔ **Limit your kill, rather than kill your limit:** Keep only as many fish as you require for your immediate needs and stay well within any bag and size limits for the species involved.

All my memories of horror fish-cleaning sessions that stretched far into the night arose from excessive catches. You may feel like a hero when you're hauling the fish in one after another, but if you keep every fish, someone is going to have to gut, gill, scale and fillet the catch — and that someone is likely to be you.

✔ **Clean the catch promptly:** Fish cleaned soon after landing are easier to handle and smell less than fish cleaned hours (or even days!) later. Clean the fish before you tidy up and have a shower yourself (it's amazing how much messier and smellier a pile of dead fish seems to be when you're all pink-skinned, freshly-scrubbed and anointed with sweet-smelling toiletries).

✔ **Use the right tools for the job:** Set yourself up with the right tools in a suitable working area and have a set procedure for handling the catch. As with most things in life, a little preparation and planning go a long way towards breaking the back of even the most daunting task.

Gutting and gilling fish

The easiest and most common way to clean a fish is to use a sharp knife and make one long cut from the fish's *vent* or anus all the way forwards along the fish's belly and through the throat latch area under the gills (see Figure 16-1). For safety's sake, make sure you slide the knife away from yourself. After slitting the fish open, remove the internal organs and gill arches.

When opening the stomach cavity of a fish, try to limit the depth of the cut so that you avoid slicing into the internal organs of the fish, allowing the contents to spill out. Remember that the stomach wall is usually only a few millimetres thick (even in reasonably large fish) so don't hack too deeply into the stomach region.

If you take the time to study the physiology of the first few fish you open, you can learn how to remove the internal organs and the gill structure in one or two large pieces with the minimum of fuss and mess.

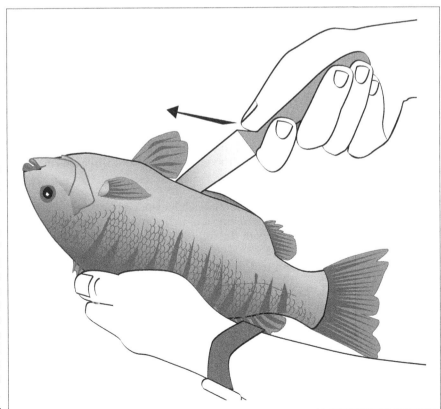

Figure 16-1: To clean a fish, open the stomach cavity by slicing forwards from the anus between the pelvic fins to the gill latch area and the fish's throat.

Removing the kidney

Most fish have a dark red, blood-rich organ running along the top of the stomach cavity, separated from the other internal organs by a membrane. This organ is the fish's kidney and although the kidney can be tricky to remove, doing so greatly improves the keeping qualities of most fish.

You can use the following tools to remove the kidney:

- ✔ Blade of a knife
- ✔ Brush with stiff bristles
- ✔ Teaspoon
- ✔ Toothbrush

Of the various tools you can use to remove the kidney, an old teaspoon or toothbrush are two of the best. (Beware, however, mixing up your toothbrushes when camping because kidney paste is likely to leave a rather unpleasant taste in your mouth!)

Thorough gutting and gilling (including the removal of the kidney) significantly slows the deterioration of the catch and is advisable if you intend to keep the fish in top condition for a day or more or serve the fish whole.

Disposing of fish scraps

After removing the guts and gills from the fish, you can drop the waste overboard if you're fishing a fair distance away from the shore. If you're in an estuary, on the beach, rocks or a jetty, or by the banks of a freshwater lake or stream, you need to work out a way of disposing of the fish scraps so that you don't pollute the environment and threaten the wellbeing of other people using the area.

Popular fishing spots sometimes have special bins in designated fish cleaning areas for the disposal of fish scraps. If not, you can dispose of or use the guts and gills in the following ways:

- ✔ Add the chopped or minced scraps to your berley (refer to Chapter 8).
- ✔ Bury the fish scraps in a deep hole.
- ✔ Take the scraps home and dump the lot in your household garbage.

Never leave fish guts lying around because the scraps attract flies and other pests and ultimately become a health hazard.

Battling live bacteria in dead fish

Bacteria multiply in the internal organs and flesh of a fish from the moment the critter dies. Many of the bacterial organisms are naturally present in the fish; whereas, others are introduced from outside sources. If the level of bacteria becomes concentrated, the flavour and nutritional value of the fish can seriously degrade and can ultimately pose a health risk to anyone eating the fish.

The greatest concentrations of bacteria occur in the stomach cavity and intestines, particularly if the organs contain partially-digested food. You can dramatically reduce the growth and spread of bacteria by removing the fish's innards and washing out the stomach cavity.

Bacteria multiply much faster at higher temperatures than in cooler conditions, which is why chilling the fish or cleaning the fish promptly is a vital part of the process of preparing fish for the table.

Scaling fish

Many anglers prefer to scale the fish during the cleaning process, particularly if the plan is to cook and serve it whole or prepared with the skin intact. You can't scale all fish because a number of species such as catfish, eels, sharks and leatherjackets don't have scales! Equally, other species such as redfin perch, groper and sergeant baker have tough scales that are difficult to remove. Instead, you can skin the fish (see the section 'Skinning fish', later in this chapter).

A number of fish species, including trout, trevally, mackerel and some tuna species, have tiny scales that you can leave in place because the itty-bitty scales don't detract significantly from the quality of the meal.

Scaling is best done with a specially designed, serrated plastic or metal tool called (surprise, surprise!) a *fish scaler*, or a knife with a stiff blade (an old metal butter knife does the job admirably). Avoid using the cutting edge of your filleting knife to scale fish because the action dulls the blade. If you must use your best knife to scale a fish, turn the knife over and use the back edge of the blade.

To scale the catch, use your fish scaler or knife back to scrape forwards from the tail towards the head of the fish, catching the back edge of each scale and removing each as you go. Pay particular attention to the tricky little areas between and under fins, along the belly and back and around the gills and throat. If you fail to remove scales that are hard to reach, the result can be an unpleasant mouthful of crunchy bits instead of a taste of heaven!

Scaling is by nature a messy process because the dislodged scales fly every which way and stick firmly to smooth surfaces. Dried scales are virtually impossible to remove, so nobody is likely to be happy about the result if you scale fish in the kitchen, laundry or bathroom! Instead, do the job outside, preferably by the water.

 If you have to scale the catch indoors or on board a boat, partially fill a basin, sink or similar container with water and scale the fish while submerged. Scaling underwater greatly reduces the number of flying scales and makes cleaning up an easier task.

Filleting fish

Filleting is a popular method of preparing many fish species for the table because the resulting pieces of fish flesh contain relatively few bones or no bones at all and are easy to handle and quick to cook.

 You don't need to gut and gill fish that you're going to fillet within a few hours of capture because you're going to be throwing out the organs with the carcass after the filleting process.

Usually, if you fillet a fish, you skin the fish at the same time. This method is an increasingly popular fish-handling option and is one that doesn't require the removal of scales. For example, I fillet and skin at least three-quarters of the fish I keep for the table. (Because fish filleting and skinning are two different operations, I describe how to fillet the fish in this section and then how to skin the fillets in the following section.)

Fish filleting is a knack that definitely requires a little practice — and if you ever start to think you're becoming pretty skilled at the job, slip down to the local fish market and watch a few professional filleters at work (a humbling experience for most mere mortals!).

Thankfully, few anglers need (or want!) to fillet several hundred fish in a day or produce a pair of boneless fillets from a big, slippery fish inside one minute. Instead, you can take your time to make sure you do the job as neatly as possible — and still count to ten on your fingers after you finish the job.

For most newcomers, the axiom 'haste makes waste' is particularly applicable to fish filleting.

 The approved method for filleting a fish is to begin just behind the head and cut downwards until your knife blade strikes the backbone (see Figure 16-2). You then lay the knife over and carefully cut along the backbone and ribs, separating as much meat as possible from the structure known as the fish's *frame* (basically, the fish's head, skeleton and tail).

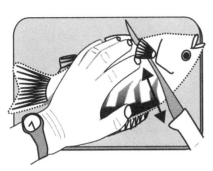

1. Lift the pectoral fin and make a cut close behind the head, down to the backbone.

2. Use just the point of your knife to make a shallow cut down along the dorsal fin, towards the tail.

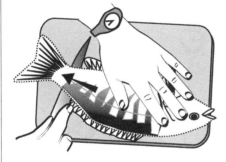

3. At the end of the dorsal fin, push the point of the knife through the fish and cut down to the tail.

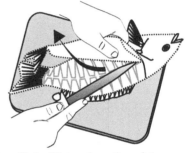

4. Now lift the fillet, and use the point of the knife to `peel´ it away from the vertebrae and ribs.

Figure 16-2:
The recommended method for filleting most fish.

Keep your hands well clear of the knife blade as you work, and never, ever, cut towards yourself.

When filleting, use a specially designed filleting knife and make sure the knife is sharp (I describe the perfect fish-filleting knife in Chapter 9).

Every angler ultimately develops his or her own little personal touches and flourishes when filleting fish, which is fine as long as the techniques used are safe. For example, I fillet fish by starting at the tail wrist and working forward whereas many anglers work the other way around. Another trick that helps you to avoid personal injury is to keep the hand not holding the knife flat on top of the fish, rather than wrapping it around or slipping it inside the gills.

Watch other filleters at work and then try a few different styles of filleting to find out which method or combination of methods works best for you. Remember that there's more than one way to skin a cat — or fillet a catfish.

Skinning fish

Tough-skinned species that don't have scales (such as sharks, leatherjackets, eels and catfish) need skinning before cooking. *Note:* Even when skinning isn't necessary because of the type of fish you're dealing with, the end result can be greatly improved by skinning. Skinning is a relatively simple process (see Figure 16-3) and, as I mention in the previous section, I fillet and skin the majority of my catch without gutting, gilling or scaling the fish first because the end product is so appealing to eat.

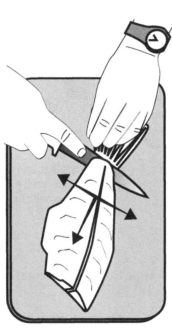
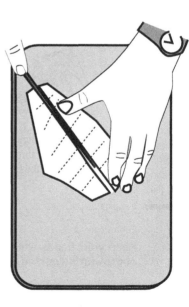

Figure 16-3: Skinning fish fillets saves the mess and fuss of scaling the catch.

1. Lay the fillet `skin side down´ on the cutting board and hold it in place at the tail. Then slice the fillet away from the skin by running the knife flat along the board.

2. Score the skin side of the fillet lightly with your knife to prevent `curling´ when cooked, and halve it lengthwise to remove the blood line if desired.

Skinned, boneless fillets are an especially big hit with kids and older folk, who often don't like fiddling about with bones and skin when eating fish.

The following method is the easiest way to skin a fish:

1. **Place the fillet on a hard, clean surface with the skin facing downwards.**

2. **Working from the narrow tail end of the fillet, slide your knife blade between the meat and skin and carefully begin to separate the two sections.**

3. **After sliding your knife a few centimetres between the fillet and the skin, firmly grasp the little tag of skin at the tail of the fillet.**

4. **Hold the knife steady and angle the blade a few degrees down towards the table or cutting board.**

5. **While pulling on the skin, saw or drag the fillet back and forth across the blade until you reach the end of the fillet. In other words, the knife remains virtually stationary and the fillet is pulled back and forth across it to separate meat and skin.**

Leaving the fish's scales on makes skinning much easier and reduces the chance of the knife cutting through the skin midway through the process. If you find the tag of skin at the tail difficult to grasp, either cut a small hole to slip your index finger through, or sprinkle some coarse salt on the flap of skin to provide a better grip.

After skinning the fillets, you can easily trim unwanted flesh and remove any obvious *blood line* (dark meat). You can also cut away any remaining bones or pull the bones out using a pair of tweezers (look for miniscule bones by running your fingertips carefully over the flesh). The end result is a neat, clean and perfectly boneless piece of fish flesh ready for preparation in any number of delicious ways (see the section 'Cooking Your Catch', later in this chapter).

Making steaks

You can cut large fish, such as mulloway, tuna, Spanish mackerel, Murray cod and big snapper, into cutlets by repeatedly slicing straight through the fish at right angles to the backbone after removing the gills and guts. To sever the backbone of fish, use a sturdy knife with a serrated blade, a hand saw, a professional meat saw or a power driven band saw. Alternatively, you can make your life easier by seeking out a friendly butcher or fishmonger willing to do the job for you at a reasonable price.

Be aware that some people don't enjoy the taste of the marrow and fluids that often leak from a fish's spinal column in the process of making cutlets.

Although making cutlets is certainly an acceptable way of dealing with fish, cutting large fillets into smaller steaks, scallops or medallions is generally easier.

Cooking Your Catch

Fresh fish is a delicious and highly nutritious food and every year bespectacled experts in white lab coats report another link between seafood and a healthy lifestyle.

For example, the omega-3 fatty acids found under the skin of some ocean dwelling species can lower cholesterol levels and reduce the risk of having a heart attack. Recent research also proves that if a pregnant woman eats seafood on a regular basis, the child is less likely to suffer from asthma. A number of pundits even claim that fish is a 'brain food' and that regularly eating fish makes you smarter!

Medical and intellectual benefits aside, cooking and serving up the fish you catch yourself is wonderfully satisfying because, in this modern era of fast food, it helps you to re-engage with the process of providing the food that you eat.

Recreational anglers can also have the perverse pleasure of checking current market prices and working out exactly what that latest meal of self-caught flathead, snapper, barramundi or trout was worth in an age when seafood is clearly moving into the luxury food category.

I say 'perverse' because you can't truly save money by catching rather than buying fish. Based on the value of my own boat and fishing tackle, combined with the amount I spend each year on fuel, accommodation, line, lures, hooks, sinkers, bait, licences and so on, the fish I bring home to eat are worth at least $250 a kilo.

Instead, I prefer to think of self-caught meals of seafood as a bonus rather than a primary justification for going fishing. By thinking of the fish you catch as a bonus, you're less likely to feel lousy when you do the sums and figure how much those 'free' fish really cost you! As I often explain to people, fishing and golf cost around the same — but you can't eat golf balls!

Dining In Is Simply Delicious

By following the killing and cleaning methods in Chapter 15, you can have a product of superior quality to most of the seafood available in the best fish shops and most expensive restaurants because the fish gets to your table faster.

Top-quality fish deserve equal care at the cooking stage and the best way to finish up with a delicious meal is to keep things as simple as possible in the kitchen.

Most types of fish are best cooked quickly and served with a minimum of fancy accompaniments. Crisply grilled fish fillets served with a garden salad, steamed vegetables, fried potato chips or rice make a superb, healthy meal. The only condiments this type of dish needs are a pinch of salt and pepper, and a squeeze of lemon juice or a splash of vinegar.

Novice fish chefs often make the mistake of over-cooking seafood and of masking the fresh, delicate flavours with heavy sauces, thick coatings and complex side dishes. To truly appreciate the subtle flavours of a fresh bream, snapper, flathead, perch or trout, try steaming or grilling the fish with a splash of oil or a dab of butter. Alternatively, dust the boneless fillets lightly in flour and fry the fillets quickly in a tablespoon or so of hot, high-quality vegetable oil.

Adopting a Recipe for Success

You don't need a lot of fancy equipment to prepare and cook delicious fish dishes, as the following basic list shows:

- ✔ **Clean, non-porous cutting board:** For a hygienic start.
- ✔ **Fork:** For testing the flesh or turning small fish.
- ✔ **Non-stick or heavy-based frying pan:** For an even cooking temperature.
- ✔ **Slotted spoon:** For working with garnishes (such as chopped onions) in the pan.
- ✔ **Spatula or egg slice:** For lifting and flipping the fish.
- ✔ **Tongs:** For lifting and turning the fish.

Cooking in the raw

The simplest way to cook seafood is to negate the heat!

Twenty or 30 years ago, most Aussies and Kiwis went pale at the notion of eating uncooked fish. The positive influences of multiculturalism have now opened minds to culinary traditions from Asia, Oceania, South America, Europe and Africa, where seafood comes raw, pickled, dried, smoked and preserved.

The Japanese dishes of sushi (raw fish wrapped in rice and dried sheets of seaweed) and sashimi (bite-sized pieces of fish served with a hot sauce of soy and wasabi) are now regularly seen in Australasian restaurants and on family tables. You can also find pickled and marinated recipes such as kakonda (raw fish marinated in coconut milk), ceviche (raw fish marinated in lime or lemon juice) and numus (raw fish marinated in a mix of vinegar, oil and citrus juices).

You can eat most fish raw and the fish is best if chilled before being thinly sliced and then eaten by dipping the fish in various sauces. Alternatively, you can pickle the fish pieces in vinegar, lemon juice, lime juice, coconut milk or a combination of the above marinades.

The basic list of ingredients you need is equally simple, as the following shows:

- Butter (or margarine)
- Flour
- Lemon
- Oil
- Pepper
- Salt
- Vinegar
- Oh! And fish.

As time goes by and your skill at cooking fish improves, your list of basic ingredients is bound to grow, but the preceding group is enough to start you off (see Figure 16-4).

Your aim when cooking and serving fish and other seafood should always be to retain the natural flavour and nutritional value of the catch. Because many fish have subtle, delicate flavours that are easily lost through poor handling or over-cooking, you're best to treat the fish well, cook it as quickly and in as simple a manner as practical, and before long you can be sure to appreciate the true delights of freshly caught seafood.

Figure 16-4:
The fish
chef's
kitchen
needs are
simple.

If you choose not to cook your fish, instead eating it raw (see the sidebar 'Cooking in the raw'), be aware that fish sometimes have potentially harmful parasites in the flesh. For example, barracouta often have parasites, as do other species of fish. You can avoid ingesting parasites if you avoid eating the raw flesh of known parasite carriers and by closely examining any thinly sliced fish for obvious infestations. If in doubt, cook or discard the fish.

Freezing Points

You can freeze fish for consumption at a later date but, like all seafood, fish are best when eaten fresh — within 12–48 hours of capture.

You can store fish in the refrigerator or on ice for several days without significant deterioration, as long as the temperature stays below 5 degrees Celsius and any melted water can drain away. If you want to keep fish for longer than a couple of days, you must freeze the fish as soon as possible after capture.

To freeze fish or fish pieces, wrap the flesh tightly in cling wrap or aluminium foil to exclude all air and bring the temperature down as rapidly as possible.

The colder the temperature, the longer frozen fish maintain a high quality (commercial operators aim at temperatures between minus 20 and minus 30 degrees Celsius). Most household freezers run at about minus 10 degrees Celsius, which is sufficient to keep most fish for a maximum of three months. Species with high oil or fat contents, such as trout, salmon, tuna, mullet and so on, are best used within a month or two of being frozen.

Chapter 17

Fishing for the Future

*I*ncreasingly, anglers are accepting that the future of their passionate pastime depends on each person who drops in a line adopting a stewardship role. Such a role can go a long way towards limiting the impact of the sport on the resource, working wherever possible to enhance fish stocks and protect aquatic environments, and spreading this positive message to the new chums and juniors who are attracted to the sport.

This chapter looks at the acknowledgement of the issues at hand and the willingness to take proactive steps towards a solution as the true meaning behind the concept of 'fishing for the future'.

Thinking About Yesteryear

Recreational fishing in Australia and New Zealand has changed dramatically in my half-century on the planet. In the middle of the 1900s, amateur fishers were virtually unregulated and, within very loose bounds, were catching and keeping whatever they wished, using any technique or equipment (short of dynamite and hand grenades) they chose, simply because they could. Over the second half of that century, this attitude of free-for-all and fish-for-all changed. That change was driven by necessity, and the recognition that Australasian fish stocks represent a finite and potentially fragile resource.

Today, recreational anglers on both sides of the Tasman Sea operate under an increasingly complex and restrictive set of state-, territory- or district-specific rules and regulations that the governing authorities review and update on a regular basis (often, but not always, with input from anglers). As a result, most of the fisheries and fish stocks that recreational anglers target are now managed via a raft of size limits, bag limits, closed seasons and gear or tackle restrictions. More importantly, the vast majority of responsible, modern anglers willingly embrace these rules, and many (me included) actually go further by imposing personal codes of conduct that are even more stringent than the existing legislation governing the areas where you cast a line. (For more information about these kinds of rule, see Chapter 26.)

Thinking About Tomorrow

The sheer effectiveness of modern fishing tackle, marine electronics (especially depth sounders and global positioning systems or GPS), along with lures such as the latest generations of super-realistic soft plastics, can be a double-edged sword when it comes to managing fisheries resources. While these marvellous innovations enhance your (and my) angling pleasure, they can also place increased pressure on fish stocks.

At the end of 2003, fisheries managers in Victoria introduced new size and bag limits for dusky flathead in the east of that state. In doing so, they specifically cited the impact that recreational anglers armed with modern soft plastics were having on resident populations of these important fish in popular Gippsland waterways such as Mallacoota Inlet.

This forward-thinking approach was the first time in Australian angling history that a specific fishing technique was singled out and clearly identified as the primary catalyst for a change to amateur catch regulations. The fact speaks volumes for the sheer effectiveness of using soft plastics fishing tackle, particularly for flathead, but also on a range of other species, including both saltwater and freshwater fish.

And in New Zealand, a similar thinking is now being applied to snapper fishing regulations, because of concerns about the effectiveness of soft plastic lures in that fishery.

Limit your kill

Interestingly, the advent of modern soft plastics, and the rise of 'finesse' tackle for presenting them, carried the same potential threat to flathead and snapper stocks that the evolution of ganged-hook rigs (as described in Chapter 4) posed for tailor populations through the 1960s. Fortunately, you live in a more enlightened era today and increasing numbers of anglers are recognising the potential impact of their activities on the resource. More and more anglers are choosing to fish not just for today, but also for the future. While this trend is also being reflected in increasingly tight legal limitations on fish sizes, bags and angling methods, the positive fact is that many anglers are already ahead of the game, voluntarily imposing tighter restrictions on themselves than those written as laws on the state, territory and regional statute books.

The days of open slather and a deeply entrenched freezer-filling mentality are thankfully waning, particularly among the younger generation of anglers. But all anglers need to remind themselves that modern tackle and techniques are incredibly effective fish-catching tools, and, as a result, to moderate their activities accordingly. In other words: Limit your kill, don't kill your limit!

Toxic tackle?

Pollution and contamination are areas of concern for those who value the aquatic environments and have fears for the long-term future of the sport of fishing. Questions are regularly being asked by marine environmentalists about the environmental impacts of lost and discarded tackle, and PVC-based soft plastics are high on the list of potential contaminants that are now being closely examined.

Tackling lead

Manufacturers are slowly beginning to respond to the issue of replacing lead in sinkers and weights with other materials, including steel, brass and tungsten, although none of these alternatives are without their problems:

- Steel weights can rust badly in tackle boxes.
- Brass is considerably lighter for its bulk than lead.
- Tungsten, while dense, remains prohibitively expensive.

However, breakthroughs in this important area of phasing out toxic lead are sure to occur in coming years.

Focusing on PVC

In some ways, the intense focus on soft plastics is somewhat misguided, especially when you stop to consider the impacts of lead, nylon line, gel-spun polyethylene fibres, spilt fuel or lubricants and various non-lure-making plastics (especially bait packaging and plastic bags) that consumer communities lose or discard every year (not to mention the many past decades). All the same, PVC lure tails *are* now part of the bigger, global picture and, in some Japanese and American bass lakes, they're fast becoming a serious concern, with deep drifts of old and damaged soft plastics building up along lee shorelines under certain weather conditions. Apart from being unsightly, these build-ups beg questions about potential impacts on animals (particularly fish, birds, reptiles and mammals) that might unwittingly ingest these plastics.

In response to marine environmental issues, and as a part of the drive to create lures that are even more attractive to fish, some manufacturers are moving towards developing and, in some instances, providing so-called 'biodegradable' or 'edible' artificial baits (see the sidebar 'Fishing for biodegradability').

While the concept of biodegradable plastics is appealing, other issues are emerging regarding their long-term use including:

- ✔ Concerns about the chemicals and residues produced by the breaking down of starch-based materials and biodegradable plastics

- ✔ Possible adverse health effects on animals that may eat these products before the plastics can completely decompose

The most popular varieties of biodegradable fishing lures currently on the market are made from polyvinyl alcohol (PVOH), and contain a high percentage of water (which is why they dry out, shrivel up and go hard when exposed to air). Higher grade PVOH, of the sort best used in lures, doesn't dissolve readily in water unless temperatures are high (reportedly over 60 degrees Celsius), so it seems unlikely they're going to degrade all that quickly at normal water temperatures. However, just like standard PVC-based soft plastics, PVOH lures are subject to another process known as *bioerosion*, meaning they're actually worn down or abraded by constant contact with the river or ocean bed and suspended sediment in the water. This process takes years rather than months and, ultimately, affects both standard PVC and PVOH tails.

The bottom line is that if anglers want to use biodegradable soft plastic lures that truly do break down into largely harmless residues within six months or so, then they're still waiting for most manufacturers to offer such products in their ranges. The sooner they come, the better.

Fishing for biodegradability

Biodegradable plastics are based on either natural or synthetic resins and polymers. The actual 'biodegradability' of these materials depends on their chemical structure and the shape and size of the end product. (So, for the fishing scientists: Biodegradation incorporates biological activity, via enzymes, that leads to actual changes in the chemical structure of the material in question. The plastics ought to break down cleanly, and in a defined time frame, to molecules (such as water and carbon dioxide) that are found in the environment.

As far as materials that so far are being used in fishing lures go, very few truly meet the strict science behind biodegradability — especially when applying a standard decomposition time of say six months.

Ultimately, how important is this issue of true biodegradability in soft plastic lures going to be? Potentially, very important. Lead sinkers, split shot and shotgun pellets are already banned in some countries. Eventually, they may come under the spotlight here in Australia and New Zealand, too, along with products such as PVC-based soft plastic lures. As with most product development, the industry is best to try to stay ahead of the game rather than play catch-up after the event. Major lure makers are already well and truly on the case.

Fish for your kids and their kids, too

Many who are passionate about recreational angling would love nothing more than to see their children, and their children's' children, go on enjoying this wonderful pastime for generations to come. Theoretically, this option should be possible, despite the stresses that growing populations, climate change and a host of other environmental pressures impose.

Only by thinking about issues of sustainability and resource management every single time you fish, by discussing these matters intelligently with your peers, and by actively promoting the philosophy of fishing for the future to fellow anglers and non-anglers alike — through personal interaction, on-line chat rooms and social networking sites, for example — can you hope to achieve that noble goal of leaving a healthy recreational fishing legacy for future generations.

Reservations about marine reserves

One particularly contentious issue in modern times, not just here in Australia and New Zealand, but right around the globe, is the creation of a growing network of marine reserves, protected areas and sanctuary zones within which recreational angling (and many other activities such as spear fishing and water skiing) either is banned completely or strictly controlled and limited.

While marine protected areas at first appear to make excellent sense and to mirror the national parks and nature reserves willingly embraced by most people on land, some sportsmen believe that the creation of many of these no-fishing zones in public waterways is often based more on political expediency than cool, rational science. These groups believe some politicians view aquatic reserves as both vote winners and as powerful bargaining chips in negotiations with minority or single-issue parties and candidates.

So far, solid science backing the many claims made in support of marine reserves is either non-existent or based on very limited studies. In particular, the assertion that marine reserves enhance fisheries in surrounding waters through recruitment of juvenile fish and the 'overflow' of fish stocks currently remains unsupported by any credible, long-term research.

What is known, however, is that the creation of no-fishing zones has a tendency to increase fishing pressure in adjacent areas, often with detrimental impacts on fish numbers in those places.

While few thinking, recreational fishers are opposed outright to the notion of protected areas for good sense, anglers are best to become actively involved in the public consultation processes that typically accompany the creation or expansion of these zones, and to have their say on what they do and don't want to see happen. The bottom line is that as soon as an area has been placed off-limits to fishing, it is unlikely to ever be reinstated as an angling destination. That situation is something worth thinking about as human populations continue to grow, and the waterways left open to fishing continue to shrink and to be exposed to greater and greater pressures.

Part V

What Kind of Angler Are You?

'I guess I'll always be a jetty gal.'

Part V

What Kind of
Angler Are You?

In this part ...

The sport of fishing includes many specialist areas and, so, this part describes the various directions you can take in your fishing life. Chapter 18 looks at the difference between a specialist angler and a casual angler; whereas chapters 19 through 25 look at a range of fishing environments and types of angling.

Your interest level in the chapters is sure to depend on a number of personal factors; for example, if you become nauseous sitting in the bath, you're unlikely to be interested in reading about deep-sea angling and boat fishing. Remember, as you read through this part, that your angling aspirations are almost definitely going to change over time, so this part is useful as a future reference tool, which you can use to branch out in the wonderful sport of fishing.

Chapter 18

Specialise or Speculate?

*A*ustralasian anglers are blessed with having access to a wide array of fishing styles, species and locations. The sunburnt continent of Australia and those beautiful, mountainous islands across the Tasman to its east offer everything from alpine trout streams to tropical mangrove-lined estuaries to rugged rocky headlands and the wide horizons of the deep blue sea beyond, with dozens of permutations between the extremes. Talk about being spoilt!

As your interest in recreational fishing grows, you're bound to face choices regarding your career path in the sport. Many devotees are happy to be casual weekend or holiday danglers (as I call people who enjoy fishing, but aren't devoted to the chase). Other people go on to become keen and dedicated anglers, spending every spare moment planning the next fishy outing.

So, if fishing becomes an important part of your leisure time, you need to decide on the form of angling you enjoy most, which fish species you want to target and the environments in which you want to track down your prey, which is where this chapter comes in.

Anglers versus Danglers

Popular wisdom has it that just 10 per cent of the recreational fishing fraternity accounts for at least 90 per cent of the non-commercial catch taken in Australia and New Zealand each year. People who are deeply involved in the sport — such as myself — believe the figures may be even more skewed in favour of the so-called 'expert'. In other words, 5 per cent of anglers probably catch 95 per cent or more of the recreational catch!

Despite this fact, a vast army of occasional anglers and hopeful danglers appear to be reasonably content soaking baited lines with only the slimmest chance of actually catching a critter. Hmmm ... Are the unsuccessful danglers really happy? Is unwinding on a peaceful riverbank or by the sparkling sea enough to forget the clamour of daily life going by?

Certainly, for some people, the answer is yes. For the casual dangler, fishing provides the ideal escape hatch from the hassles and stresses of modern life. To others, angling is a passion to pursue with vigour and determination, as if the sport is a noble quest or calling. Perhaps this aspect of fishing is the pastime's greatest virtue — that is, the art of fishing is capable of representing many things to many different people, while providing a true recreation (in the purest sense of the word) for each type of angler.

The All-Rounder

In my opinion, one of the biggest mistakes you can make as an angler is to be haphazard in your approach to the sport. Remember, for example, that the 'all-round' fishing rod doesn't exist (refer to Chapter 5). Equally, precious few 'all-round' anglers exist (precious few successful ones, anyway!).

Ask a weekend dangler what he or she is likely to catch and the answer is bound to be 'Whatever comes along' or 'I'm not fussy — whatever's biting'. You can attach more than coincidence to the fact that the vast majority of weekend danglers catch a limited number of fish and therefore belong to the 90 per cent of anglers who account for 10 per cent (or less) of the fish caught.

You may well be happy enough to remain a member of this all-round majority, but I suspect that if you take the trouble to read this far, you're eager to catch a few fish from time to time! One of the best ways to ensure you do bring home the barramundi, so to speak, is to specialise.

The Specialist

Specialisation in fishing takes many forms:

- ✔ **Environment:** You can specialise in one or two fishing environment types, such as beaches, rocks, estuaries and so on.

- ✔ **Species:** You can specialise in the pursuit of a particular fish species or a small group of species.

- ✔ **Style of fishing:** You can specialise in using one style of fishing gear, such as fly tackle or lures.

- ✔ **Style, species and location:** You can even take specialisation to the ultimate conclusion and select a single location, a single species and a single form of tackle, and learn as much as you possibly can about that place, fish and gear.

True specialists tend to become extremely skilful. The person who only targets luderick (blackfish or parore) from a particular rock ledge, or casts lures for bass or trout in a specific river system, invariably learns lots of little tricks. Specialists also frequently develop into highly successful fishing 'experts' — members of the elite 10 per cent.

By telling this tale, I'm not advocating that you need to devote your entire angling life to fishing one location using one type of gear or that you aim for just a single species of fish (a very boring scenario!). However, a degree of specialisation, especially early in your fishing career, is sure to make you a more successful angler in the long run, even when you move on to other types of places, other species and different styles of tackle.

The Serial Specialist

A useful approach to fishing is to become what I like to call a 'serial specialist', that is, an angler who concentrates on a particular form of fishing or angling environment until reaching a level of proficiency. At that point the angler moves on to add another string to the piscatorial bow.

In this way, you can constantly broaden your horizons and set new personal goals, returning from time to time to those areas you've already partially mastered, but always finding untravelled avenues to explore. This method keeps fishing fresh in your mind and the sport is bound to continue to offer up exciting challenges and surprises.

In the following chapters (chapters 19 through 25), I examine the most popular angling environments and styles found in Australia and New Zealand, and offer tips and pointers for each. Try a few of the styles to see which you enjoy the most and then specialise to some extent in just one or two until you become moderately proficient.

Clubbing together

Four million Australians list fishing as a primary leisure-time activity, yet less than 2 per cent belong to an angling club or association. The proportions are similarly skewed in New Zealand.

The main reason that so few anglers join clubs is that fishing — rather like surfboard riding or bushwalking — tends to be an individualistic activity that doesn't lend itself particularly well to the sort of structural organisation inherent in the club scene.

Nonetheless, successful fishing clubs do exist, in the same way that successful surfing and hiking organisations exist. Clearly, clubs and associations suit a number of people — and the clubs certainly offer benefits.

Clubs can be especially useful for the keen newcomer to recreational fishing because:

✔ You can meet like-minded individuals.

✔ You can benefit from the knowledge of more experienced members.

That said, not all fishing clubs are of equal value and before joining a club, it pays to find out what sort of activities the club offers, especially for newer and less experienced members.

To find a listing of clubs, enter **Fishing Clubs** into your search engine. Try to find a club that runs regular seminars and workshops or organises trips away, so that you have a chance to cast a line with more experienced anglers and try out different environments. Steer clear of the clubs that are little more than old boys' drinking networks (unless you're into drinking with the old boys)!

Chapter 19

Surf Casters and Rock Hoppers

. . . .

. . . .

*T*he powdery crunch of clean sand underfoot, the thump and hiss of ocean swells breaking on an empty beach — aaah! What a way to soothe your mind and ease a work-weary body. Carry a fishing rod in this delightful scene and you have an extra purpose to be strolling by the sea!

Not surprisingly, surf or beach fishing is an immensely popular pastime, especially around the more populated southern and eastern sides of the Australian mainland and on New Zealand's North Island and, to a lesser extent, parts of its South Island. Along thousands of kilometres of shoreline, each year tens of thousands of anglers cast a line into the surf in the hope of making a catch.

Casting a line into the sea from rocky shorelines, headlands and ledges is also popular throughout the southern half of Australia and in a number of tropical areas, as well as around much of the New Zealand coastline, especially on the North Island. Devotees of this branch of fishing are widely known as rock hoppers.

This chapter examines both of these specialist areas of fishing — covering how to read your environment, targeting your potential catch with the correct rig, as well as staying safe.

Finding Fish off the Beach

By world standards, many of our beaches are large and range in length from a kilometre or so up to giants, such as Victoria's aptly named Ninety Mile Beach and the seemingly endless strands of the Great Australian Bight and New Zealand's Northland. Finding and catching fish in all that foaming surf can seem a daunting task; but, read the tips in this chapter and your fishing life becomes a little easier.

Desirable fish species — for sport or the table — are typically scattered in the water alongside beaches, but the overall densities of the fish are often light. The rock band America's song *Horse with No Name* included the line 'The ocean is a desert with its life underground'. The sentiment is apt when describing beaches because plenty of life is swimming about out there, but the critters are thinly spread and are often well concealed.

Common target species on Australasia's beaches include

- ✔ Australian salmon (kahawai)
- ✔ Bream
- ✔ Flathead
- ✔ Mullet
- ✔ Tailor
- ✔ Trevally
- ✔ Whiting

Anglers with an ambitious streak may set their sights higher and pray for the fish gods to send them a gleaming 20-kilo mulloway, a big snapper or a man-sized shark to test the tackle. (You can read more about most of the preceding species, including each species' habits, in Chapter 2.)

As in a land desert, the trick to finding concentrations of activity off our beaches lies in locating an oasis. On an ocean surf beach, an oasis takes the form of a hole, a gutter, a reef or a rock outcrop. This is especially true if the formations lie close to shallow flats and sandbars where burrowing worms, cockles, pipis and other piscatorial taste tempters are on tap in generous quantities.

Reading the waves from the beach

To experienced surf casters, the water alongside beaches is an open book. By watching how waves travel and break, the casters can glean an accurate picture of the underwater topography. If you spend a few hours sitting high on a sand dune or headland watching a surf beach, especially at low tide, you can sharpen your water-reading skills (see Figure 19-1).

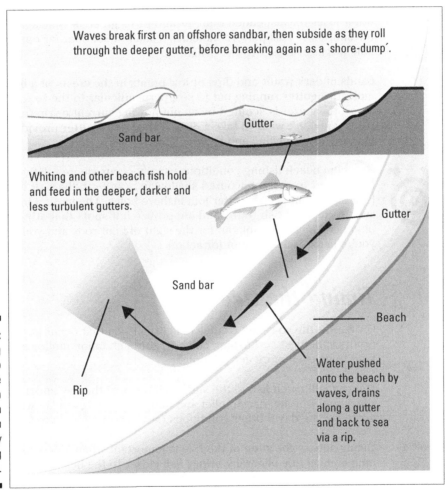

Waves break first on an offshore sandbar, then subside as they roll through the deeper gutter, before breaking again as a `shore-dump'.

Gutter

Sand bar

Whiting and other beach fish hold and feed in the deeper, darker and less turbulent gutters.

Gutter

Sand bar

Beach

Water pushed onto the beach by waves, drains along a gutter and back to sea via a rip.

Rip

Figure 19-1: Learning how to 'read' the water off a beach can help you to identify fish-holding formations.

The colour of the water tells you a great deal about the depth of the water. As a general rule, darker water is deeper than lighter water. Wave patterns reinforce this theory because waves peaking and breaking far offshore and rolling in as foamy, aerated white-water indicate a shallow, shelving seabed. By contrast, lower, fast-moving swells that run almost to the beach before standing up abruptly and dumping on the shore signify deeper, steeper drop-offs (refer to Figure 19-1).

Often you can see a combination of the preceding surf patterns on a beach that includes waves breaking well offshore and then reforming so that the water loses its suspended bubbles and turns green or blue again closer to the shoreline. This pattern indicates a shallow sandbar far out with a deeper hole or gutter closer to the beach.

Bands of dark water and dips or low points in the crests of a line of breakers indicate a gutter running out to sea, perpendicular to the beach. In many cases, the gutter is scoured by an out-flowing current or rip (exactly the place you don't want to take a dip!). This type of gutter provides a natural highway for travelling and feeding fish.

Optimum beach fishing conditions usually occur where relatively deep holes lie adjacent to current-scoured shallow flats and sandbars or where gutters leading in from deeper water join inshore holes. The natural intersections see the heaviest fish traffic and are proven hot spots that attract groups of hopeful anglers. Look out for the sight of bent rods and you can be sure you're in an excellent spot for action.

Timing the tide

Ordinarily, the so-called change of light periods that occur at dawn and dusk produce the best surf fishing catches, although tailor, mulloway and sharks tend to be even more active at night.

You can still catch fish in the surf at all times of the day and a number of species — whiting, dart, mullet and flathead — are even known to bite in the middle of the day if other conditions (such as the tides) are favourable.

Taking note of the state of the tide is important when fishing from a beach. An incoming tide generally brings fish closer to the beach and into holes near the shore. By contrast, an outgoing tide, or the *ebbing* flow of a tide concentrates activity around the seaward ends of gutters, especially towards the time that the tide reaches its lowest point.

Novice surf casters can fall into the trap of casting too far out from the beach, even at dead low tide. Hurling the bait far over the horizon is tempting, but this enthusiasm can be a big mistake because many fish swim close to the edge of the shore, where the wave action constantly exposes food.

Baiting Your Beach Fishing Rig

The bait you attach to your rig can be even more important than when and where you fish on the beach, or how far you cast your bait.

Big, desirable fish generally prefer fresh, natural offerings such as live beach worms, pipis and cockles. Other prime beach baits include

- Crabs
- Fresh prawns
- Pieces of flesh cut from oily species such as mullet, bonito and tuna
- Small live fish such as yellowtail and mullet (particularly for larger predators such as mulloway and sharks)

For more detail on the best baits, refer to Chapter 8.

True grit

Sand can be so annoying. The gritty stuff finds its way into your bathers, sticks to skin and makes sandwiches inedible. Sand can also wreck your fishing gear — especially reels (refer to Chapter 6).

Geared reels and sand don't go together, so be careful not to drop or lay your gear in the sand. If sand does find a way onto your reel, brush or blow as much of the sand away as possible, then rinse the reel under gently running fresh water before wiping the reel dry and spraying the vital gear with an aerosol lubricant. If sand does work its way into the reel's internal workings, you may need to have the reel stripped, cleaned and serviced by a reputable dealer.

You can limit the amount of sand getting onto your rods and reels by carrying a short length of PVC pipe (costing next to nothing) or a commercially made rod holder for each outfit (a stainless steel model can set you back around $100). Push the base of the tube firmly into the sand and insert the butt of your outfit for rigging, baiting up or leaving your rod unattended.

Introducing Rock Hopping

Rock fishing locations cover a broad range of geographic forms from sheltered sandstone platforms in large bays and estuary mouths to rugged granite ridges and basalt razor-backs plunging into the deep, open ocean. Each environment offers a variety of different target species and the tackle you use needs to take into account both your surroundings and the type of fish you're trying to catch.

Fishing off the rocks requires skill and courage, but the drawcard is the incredible diversity of fish to target. In fact, a staggering array of saltwater fish species are available to the Australian and New Zealand rock hopper, from mullet to marlin — few other places on Earth offer shore-bound anglers such a choice.

The only factor that most styles of rock fishing have in common is that an element of potential danger exists for the rock hopper (see the section 'Rock fishing safety first — staying alive' and the sidebar 'The ten golden rules of rock fishing safety', later in this chapter). Before delving into the dangerous aspects of the sport, the first part of this chapter looks at the various types of areas where you're likely to catch a few critters.

Locking into Rock Fishing Locations

Australasian environments that are best for rock fishing can be broadly divided into three categories (see Figure 19-2):

✔ Shallow reefs

✔ Mixed-depth locations

✔ Deep-water ledges

Fishing on shallow reefs

Areas with shallow reefs made of rocks are especially common inside ocean bays and harbours, but are also found along ocean shorelines at the bases of cliffs and at the foot of sloping rock formations. This type of reef is mostly found in the southern parts of Australia; whereas, further north, in tropical regions, reefs of live and dead coral are found off a similar range of shorelines, as well as along some beaches. These rock formations are also quite common in New Zealand.

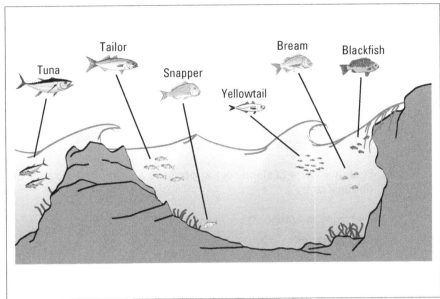

Figure 19-2:
Rock fishing
locations
can include
a mix of
a shallow
'wash',
deeper
areas,
islands and
bomboras.

The locations for working shallow reef areas typically feature low rock
ledges or platforms that are often awash at high tide. The depth of water
within casting range of the reef usually measures from half a metre to 3 or
4 metres and the seabed usually consists of broken rock, boulders, rock
shelves, kelp beds and occasional patches of gravel or sand (or, further
north in Australia, coral).

Any sort of wave action over a shallow reef results in the formation of a
wash zone — heavily-aerated white water.

Marine life is prolific in shallow, wave-washed areas and, usually, you can
find an abundance of crabs, shellfish, cunjevoi (sea squirts) and other rock-
dwelling organisms, as well as various types of algae and seaweed. Fish are
also abundant in shallow reef areas, although during most times of the day
the fish you do find are relatively small or of a type not often targeted by
anglers. You can find the bigger, more desirable fish in shallow reef locations
when the tide is rising, at night or during and immediately after a storm that
whips up the sea.

In latitudes south of the tropics (in other words, south of around Shark Bay
in Western Australia and Gladstone in Queensland), fish you can commonly
catch in shallower reef locations include

  ✔ Australian salmon

  ✔ Black and silver drummer

- Bream
- Groper
- Luderick (blackfish or parore)
- Sweep
- Trevally

Snapper and tailor occasionally enter shallow areas, particularly after heavy seas or under the cover of darkness.

Shallower New Zealand rock spots have a more limited range of species, dominated by

- Blue mao mao
- Kahawai
- Snapper
- Trevally

Rock fishing in mixed-depth locations

The geographic category I classify as 'mixed depth' covers the vast majority of Australasian rock fishing locations. Mixed-depth areas consist of ledges, platforms or sloping headlands that front water with an average depth of 2 to 10 metres within your casting range. This type of location often includes deeper holes and shallower areas of reef, bomboras or small islands.

In the south of Australia and around much of New Zealand, the seabed adjacent to a mixed-depth location for rock fishing may be composed of flat rocks, reef ledges, boulders, gravel or even sand. In tropical seas, both hard and soft corals can also be found at a mixed-depth location.

Often, mixed-depth locations are adjacent to or are sandwiched between shallow reef areas. Equally, mixed-depth locations may lie in close proximity to deep-water ledges (see the following section). Demarcation zones between the three topographic forms are often fishing hot spots and have an interesting mix of target species.

The huge majority of rock hoppers prefer mixed-depth locations because the areas contain a large range of species. Common target species in mixed-depth areas include

- Australian salmon (kahawai)
- Bonito

- Bream
- Drummer
- Groper
- Kingfish
- Luderick (blackfish or parore)
- Mackerel
- Mulloway
- Pike
- Smaller tunas
- Snapper
- Tailor
- Trevally
- Wrasse

Most of the fish in the preceding list bite best in mixed-depth areas:

- Around dawn and dusk
- On rising tides
- When enough wave action exists to produce a zone of foamy, aerated white water

Rock fishing from deep-water ledges

True deep-water ledges are less common than shallow reef areas and mixed-depth locations (see preceding sections). Excellent for fishing for game species, a number of deep-water ledges are famous in the sport and include the following:

- **Beecroft Peninsula:** Jervis Bay, south of Wollongong, New South Wales.
- **Dirk Hartog Island:** Ocean side of Shark Bay, north of Kalbarri, Western Australia.
- **North and East Capes:** New Zealand.
- **Quobba Coast:** North of Carnarvon, Western Australia.
- **Steep Point:** Just south of Dirk Hartog Island.

The famous deep-water ledges have relatively flat rock ledges or platforms, often backed by cliffs, and the ledges themselves plunge into water with a depth ranging from 8 to 20 metres. The ledges range from being 1 or 2 metres up to 15 or 20 metres above the water.

You can catch a range of true deep-sea species at the famous hot spots, including

- Billfish such as marlin and sailfish
- Mackerel
- Sharks
- Tuna
- Yellowtail kingfish

Many of the locations listed are also excellent snapper fishing spots and the more northerly of the locations on the Australian mainland produce various emperor species, cod and large wrasse.

The total amount of marine life is less abundant along the relatively narrow inter-tidal zones of deep-ledge locations than in areas with shallower, more sloping rocks. The wave action is often heavy, resulting in less weed growth and fewer crabs or shellfish. Currents, water temperature and the presence of smaller forage or bait fish are important factors at deep-ledge locations and generally dictate the number of desirable target species. As a result, true deep-water ledges tend to have clearly defined seasons or cycles of activity.

Recognising the rock formations of overlap zones

Many overlaps occur between the three classifications of rock fishing environment — shallow reef fishing, mixed-depth locations and deep-water ledges (refer to previous sections).

A single headland may have all three geographic types within a 400-metre stretch and shallow reef can be found on the boundaries of many mixed-depth or deep-water locations.

Learning to recognise the distinct characteristics of each major class of rock formation and adapting your fishing techniques to the location helps to make you a more productive rock hopper, as the following section talks about.

Rock Fishing and Reading the Tides

As well as the physical structure of the rock formation, when rock hopping, you need to consider the water movement generated onto and along the rocks by tides, currents, wave wash and wind drift.

Most Australasian rock ledges and foreshores have four changes of tide in every 24 hours (for more detail about the tidal cycle, see Chapter 21). This section explains how to take advantage of the tide — and how to stay safe in this potentially dangerous environment.

Watching the ebb and flow

Tidal movement has a major influence on the positioning, behaviour and feeding schedule of fish that live among rocks and coral reefs. When fishing from rocks, the state of the tide also has a big part to play in your safety and comfort. For example, a dry and safe ledge during low tide can turn into a raging, wet nightmare at high tide.

Water movement around rock ledges offers fish varying degrees of access to food types. For example, luderick or blackfish may use a high tide to reach succulent beds of sea cabbage weed; whereas, blue groper like to take advantage of the same increase in water depth to grab red crabs from a wave-washed gutter. Conversely, kingfish or tailor may wait for a falling tide to force mullet or yellowtail out of the foamy shallows and into clearer, deeper water, when the predator's dinner is easier to see and catch.

To work out the best phase of the tide to pursue a particular species at your chosen rock fishing location, try fishing during various phases and learn from experience or ask the local experts for advice.

Rock fishing safety first — staying alive

Successfully reading the rocks and the water flow ultimately comes down to observation and the repetition of actions that give excellent results. Remember, too, that rock fishing is a potentially dangerous sport and that your level of safety increases with experience, so novice rock hoppers need to be especially vigilant.

Rock hopping claims dozens of lives and causes many serious injuries every year, particularly in New South Wales, Western Australia and in New Zealand's Northland where the sport is the most popular. Sadly, many victims are newcomers to the sport.

The majority of rock fishing injuries and fatalities occur when anglers are washed from ledges or platforms by heavy seas or large waves. A smaller number of deaths and injuries happen as a result of the angler falling from a cliff or steep slope, or being in the way of a landslide or rock fall.

You can avoid most rock fishing mishaps and tragedies by doing the following:

✔ Always watch the sea for at least 15 minutes before beginning to fish.

✔ Have a plan of action in case of an emergency.

✔ Never fish alone.

✔ Wear lightweight clothing that allows freedom of movement and secure footwear (never thongs!) with soles that give a solid grip on the rocks.

Bear the preceding precautions in mind (and see the sidebar 'The ten golden rules of rock fishing safety') and rock hopping can be a wonderful and highly productive form of angling.

The ten golden rules of rock fishing safety

You can greatly reduce the risks associated with rock fishing and enjoy a long and trouble-free career as a rock hopper if you stick to the following ten 'Golden Rules' of rock fishing safety:

1. Don't take part in rock fishing if you can't swim.

2. Never fish alone from ocean rocks.

3. Tell someone the details of your fishing location and the time that you expect to return.

4. Observe your chosen fishing spot from a safe distance for at least 15 minutes before venturing onto the rocks.

5. Wear appropriate footwear (with non-slip soles or cleats) and clothing.

6. Carry an approved throwable flotation device or wear a buoyancy vest (also called a personal flotation device — PFD).

7. Never climb ropes or ladders of uncertain age and strength.

8. Avoid turning your back on the sea, even for a brief moment.

9. Have a plan of action in case of an emergency.

10. Remember that your life is worth far more than any fish or piece of snagged tackle!

Chapter 20

Jetty Rats

In This Chapter
▶ Sitting on a dock on the bay
▶ Looking for the treasures beneath your feet
▶ Hauling in your jetty catch successfully every time

*A*s a youngster, I caught my first saltwater fish while dangling a baited line from a jetty and I suspect that many other anglers begin their fishing careers in exactly the same way.

Jetties, piers, wharves, docks and even bridges are wonderful fishing venues for the young at heart — whatever the age. Like American soul singer Otis Redding, who sang about sittin' on the dock of the bay (before he was sadly killed in a plane crash in 1967), one of my favourite activities is still doing just that: Sitting on a dock of a bay, watching the tide rolling away. Expectantly holding onto a fishing rod makes that sitting and watching an even more pleasurable experience.

Fishing is banned on some jetties and piers and is frowned at on most bridges that carry traffic, so make sure you don't fall foul of the law while wetting a line! (For more detail on this aspect of fishing, check out the sidebar 'Rod to bear'.)

Luckily, fishing is allowed (or at least tolerated) on many jetties and this chapter explains how the structures are a favourite environment for hordes of anglers, including the keen wharf fishing specialists affectionately known to the rest of the recreational fishing fraternity as 'jetty rats'.

Picking Prime Piscatorial Real Estate

Ask a real estate agent to nominate the three most important attributes of a property and chances are the answer is: 'Location, location, location'. The same answer is why wharves, piers, jetties and bridges are such prime pieces of fishing real estate, as the following shows:

- ✔ **Attractive to fish:** Wharves, jetties and bridges attract fish because the pylons and supports are encrusted with edible marine invertebrates and weed growth, while the shadow of the decking offers shelter from bright sunlight and predators. At night, lights on the jetty also attract squid and various bait fish species.

- ✔ **Deep water:** Wharves, jetties and bridges normally extend out over relatively deep water, offering access to fish that are otherwise impossible to reach by casting from the shoreline.

- ✔ **Room:** Jetties and wharves have plenty of space in which to spread out your tackle.

- ✔ **Safety:** Jetties provide safe, flat platforms for standing or sitting on while casting a line.

Having access to a jetty (see Figure 20-1) is the next best thing to owning a boat and, as a bonus, you don't have to winch a jetty back onto a trailer at the end of the day, tow a jetty home, hose a jetty down and refuel the tanks!

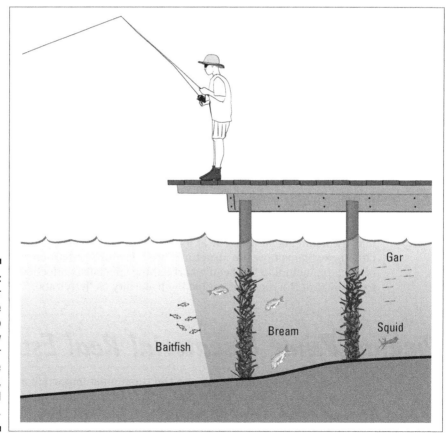

Figure 20-1: Jetties offer anglers safe access to relatively deep water and provide cover, shade and food for fish.

Finding Treasures at Your Feet

Jetties, piers, wharves and bridges actually attract and hold fish by offering the fish food, shelter and points of spatial reference in a watery, three-dimensional world.

Beware of casting your line far out and away from the jetty. In many cases, you can catch more and bigger fish by simply dropping your baited hook straight down beside a pylon or by flicking the hook back into the shadows underneath the structure.

Jetty pylons and supports also change the normal flow of the current, creating back eddies and pressure waves in the tidal flow, giving fish a sanctuary and a perfect lair from which to spring out and seize a passing morsel.

Often, the biggest, most active predators hold station on the up-current edges of a wharf or pier, using the pressure waves ahead of the structure to maintain position. Meanwhile, less dominant fish tend to tuck in behind the pilings and uprights. Large schools of bait fish — such as yellowtail, slimy mackerel, herring, anchovies and hardiheads — may form dense shoals in the shadows under the decking and between the pylons, or in pools of illumination cast by lights on the jetty at night.

Tuning in to the changing conditions

The fish move along a jetty according to changes in the tide (especially when the tide starts to fall) and the angle of the sun, which dictates exactly where the jetty's shadows fall throughout the day.

At night, the rules change again — small fish tend to cluster in pools of light spilling from the jetty, whereas big predators haunt the shadowy edges of the illuminated zones.

Just because the fish are biting at one corner of the wharf today, doesn't mean the critters are going to queue up at the same spot to take your bait tomorrow or next week. As a result, every time you turn up at the wharf, you need to check out what the various elements are doing and then pick your spot for fishing.

Casting out to cover all bases

As well as the fish that live directly under the jetty or visit the jetty's shadows to feed, a range of other fish hang off from the jetty — you can reach this group by a longer cast. As these structures usually extend out into relatively deep water, you can use the structures to plumb depths and reach fish that may otherwise be the sole province of people who have access to boats.

After deciding whether you want to cast out from the jetty or in close to the jetty, the following gives you an idea of what tackle to use and the type of fish you're likely to land:

✔ **Casting out from the jetty:** Use moderately heavy tackle with a reasonably large bait and you may end up enjoying a tangle with a real prize, such as:

- Kingfish

- Shark

- Snapper

✔ **Fishing close to the jetty:** Use relatively light tackle to drop smaller baits or lures down beside the pylons and under the decking and you may land a treat, such as:

- Bream

- Leatherjacket

- Luderick (blackfish or parore)

- Pike

- Trevally

By fishing close to or under the jetty you can also catch bait species such as yellowtail or mackerel.

Landing Fish from Jetties

Hooking a fish from a jetty or a pier and landing the fish on a jetty are two different kettles of ... er ... fish. Many big fish escape before you haul the beast up and onto the decking. Usually, the fish becomes free as the slippery creature swims around a pylon and tangles or cuts the line. The fish can also win freedom because the line breaks or the hook pulls out of the fish's mouth when you lift the critter from the water. The greater the distance that you need to lift the fish and the lighter your line or smaller your hook, the greater the chances are that the prize catch escapes.

For safely landing larger fish off a jetty or pier, you need a landing net or gaff with a long handle (for more information on how to use landing nets and gaffs, refer to Chapter 14).

If you hook a big fish and don't have access to a net or gaff, your best option is to play the fish until the critter tires (refer to Chapter 14). You then bring the fish to the surface and walk back along the jetty or bridge towards the shore, drawing the fish slowly along the surface without attempting to lift the fish clear of the water.

With luck, you may be able to lead the tired fish into shallow water and either beach the catch so that you can pop it into your bucket or have someone else go down to the shoreline and attempt to secure the prize for you. The exercise is fraught with risk and many big fish are lost before you can walk the fish to the shore and successfully beach the catch (especially on long jetties). However, the method is still a better alternative than attempting to winch a heavy, flapping fish several metres through the air and onto the jetty.

I bet that after you lose a couple of prize catches in this manner, your next purchase is a long-handled landing net or gaff to use every time you go fishing from a jetty!

Rod to bear

Jetties, wharves, piers and especially bridges are often out of bounds to anglers, mainly for safety and security reasons.

Working docks, private moorings and commercial or military port facilities are especially likely to be off limits to unauthorised personnel.

Ordinarily, you can tell whether fishing is banned in a particular spot if a sign announces the ban, or if fences surround the area.

Ignoring such warnings and entering this type of area without permission is regarded as trespassing and leaves you liable to prosecution. Don't risk it!

Luckily the authorities do allow fishing from many jetties, wharves and piers and if anglers treat the areas with respect by not leaving litter, old bait or fish offal behind, everyone is likely to be able to enjoy the facilities for many years to come.

Chapter 21

Estuary Anglers

In This Chapter

▶ Targeting estuary fish

▶ Recognising the rivers of life

▶ Putting the pieces together

*E*stuaries are stretches of coastal rivers, lakes, harbours and inlets that lie between the open sea and the upper limit of tidal movement, where brackish water gives way to fresh water.

This chapter explains why the moving waters of estuaries are important marine environments that provide a home, breeding ground, nursery and larder for many fish species. Not surprisingly, estuaries are also favourite stomping grounds for anglers. In fact, more hopefuls cast lines into Australasia's estuaries each year than into any other angling environment.

Taking a Look at Estuary Fish

You can fish estuaries from the shore and from boats or canoes. Many estuaries (see Figure 21-1) feature man-made structures such as bridges, jetties, breakwalls, *groynes* (small rock walls) and retaining walls that provide handy fishing platforms — as long as the dreaded 'No Fishing' sign isn't in evidence!

Target species in estuaries range from tasty tiddlers to heavyweights, including:

✔ **Small species:** Garfish (piper), mullet, tommy rough (herring) and silver biddies.

✔ **Medium species:** Bream, flathead, flounder, luderick (blackfish or parore), snapper, trevally and whiting.

✔ **Heavyweights:** Barramundi, sharks and mulloway.

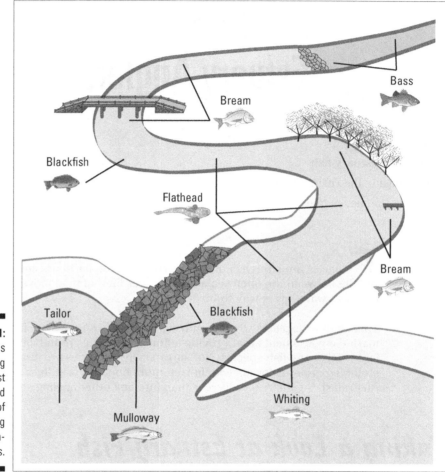

Figure 21-1:
Estuaries
are among
the most
diverse and
dynamic of
all fishing
environ-
ments.

Reading Estuaries

The dominant natural force acting on most estuaries is the tide, although a number of estuary systems — particularly smaller coastal lagoons and lakes — may be closed off from the sea by sandbars or mud bars for long periods. Such an estuary is harder to read than open tidal estuaries, although the environment can still produce worthwhile catches of fish.

Most Australian and New Zealand estuaries experience four changes in the direction of tidal flow every 24 hours. In other words, an estuary has two high tides and two low tides each day. Extreme variations between high and low water levels range from 8 to 9 metres in some tropical estuaries to less than a metre in more southern latitudes.

In addition, the size of the tides varies throughout the 28-day lunar calendar. The greatest variations (*spring tides*) occur on or just after the full and new moon, whereas the smallest variations (*neap tides*) take place around the first and last quarter of the moon.

 A period of virtually no tidal flow — called *slack water* — often occurs around each change of the tide. Slack tide can last from several minutes to an hour or more. At all other times, the water in an estuary open to the ocean flows in one direction or another — in from the sea on the rising or *making* tide and out towards the sea on the falling or *ebbing* tide.

Understanding tidal influences

The daily and monthly tidal movement and variation influences the location and behaviour of the estuarine fish species commonly pursued by anglers.

High water levels experienced during the last half of the incoming and first half of the outgoing tide give fish access to areas that are otherwise shallow or even completely dry. In tropical estuaries, the tide floods the root systems of dense mangrove forests; whereas, further south the inter-tidal areas are typically composed of expansive mud or sand flats, sometimes with weed beds around the edges.

Inter-tidal areas are typically rich with food life for fish, including:

✔ Algae

✔ Crabs

✔ Marine worms

✔ Prawns

✔ Yabbies (nippers)

The species that enjoy access to the flooded areas include

✔ Bream

✔ Flounder

✔ Garfish (piper)

✔ Juvenile snapper

✔ Mullet

✔ Whiting

The fishy opportunists are even more likely to take advantage of the access to the larder if the high tide occurs at night or in the reduced light of dawn or dusk.

Predators such as flathead, mulloway, barramundi and mangrove jacks also move up onto the food-rich flats during periods of high water. The predators come to feed on both the invertebrate life forms and the smaller forage fish. However, the best time to target predatory species in most estuary systems is during the run-out tide and around low water.

During the outgoing tide and at low water, forage fish are forced to spill back off the flats and shallows into deeper holes and gutters. At this point, predators such as flathead and barramundi lie in ambush for the smaller fish at gutter mouths, creek junctions and under the lips of drop-offs and shelves, intercepting the smaller fish as the tiddlers move with the falling water.

Tides of change

While tide charts and accurate predictions exist for almost all of the Australian and New Zealand coastlines, variations and anomalies do occur. The most common of these anomalies are locations that experience tides either earlier or later than the times given for a particular tidal station.

Estuaries typically exhibit a tidal lag or delay, and the further you move upstream, the longer this delay tends to be. For example, Kempsey, on the Macleay River in northern New South Wales, experiences tide changes approximately three and a half hours later than those given for the mouth of the Macleay and Fort Denison in Sydney Harbour.

At the opposite extreme, points and promontories may experience earlier tide changes than nearby bay or harbour locations. Cronulla tide changes, for example, run almost 40 minutes ahead of those in nearby Sydney Harbour. These lead and lag times are listed for major ports on most good tide charts and need to be factored in to your fishing equations. Similar 'leads' and 'lags' occur on many New Zealand estuaries, too.

Another phenomenon not widely acknowledged is the fact that, within many estuaries, the tidal current can sometimes continue to run seawards, at least on the surface, well after the actual water level has begun to rise. In other words, the tide still appears to be running out, but the water is getting deeper. This sounds impossible, but is actually quite common. In some cases, this can mean an estuary experiences 7–9 hours of outgoing flow and only 3–5 hours of in-flowing water.

Other forces acting to modify tides on a local basis include floods, strong wind, silted river bars and even fluctuations in barometric pressure. Tide forecasters aren't able to consider these factors when preparing predictions and tables, so switched-on anglers need to make a note of them and modify their fishing, bait-gathering and boating activities accordingly. In the final analysis, you can't beat your own powers of observation.

Low water levels also concentrate prey and predators into smaller areas as literally less water exists for the fish. The result is that low water can make it far easier to find and catch fish because the fish-to-water ratio is in the angler's favour.

Looking out for structural features

In addition to tidal movement, physical structures play a large part in influencing fish location and behaviour in estuaries (see Chapter 22 for detail on the concept of structure as it relates to fishing).

Prime fish-holding areas and structural elements within estuaries include

- **Man-made:** Breakwalls, wharves, jetties, oyster leases, bridge pylons and boat moorings.
- **Natural:** Current-scoured holes and depressions, river junctions, gutters running from shallow to deep water, the edges of weed beds, worm or yabby banks, mangrove roots, fallen trees and rock bars.

Less tangible structural elements are also important features to watch for when pursuing fish, including:

- Areas of high and low salinity
- Back eddies
- Lines of demarcation between fast- and slow-flowing currents
- Temperature changes
- Water colour

Over time and with practice, you can learn which types of fish prefer which form of structure in the estuaries where you fish.

Looking at the Big Picture

When looking for fish in estuaries, remember that moving water carries food and the level of food is greater if the moving water is flowing across flats rich in life.

Most fish looking for a feed don't like to hold position in the fastest flowing water, so look for sheltered, slower moving bodies of water and eddies or objects that break the current in close proximity to faster running currents.

In estuaries, as in most other angling environments, you're best to study the tides, use fresh, natural baits or lures and flies that imitate natural baits. Always be observant and look for areas with a concentration of food and feeders alike and try to eliminate the vast, unproductive stretches of relatively barren water common to so many estuaries.

Chapter 22

Deep-Sea Anglers

. . . .

In This Chapter

▶ Going fishing in private and charter boats

▶ Fishing over reef systems

▶ Drifting over sand and gravel grounds

▶ Going after game fish

. . . .

Slopping about in boats isn't everyone's cup of tea, but fishing in deep ocean waters certainly has its charms. Also, deep-sea fishing usually allows you to catch more fish and bigger fish than most other forms of angling.

Offshore or deep-sea fishing is divided into several different styles and this chapter looks at the most popular styles.

Boating Out to Deep Water

Fishing from a boat between the coast and the edge of the continental shelf (or even beyond the point that the ocean floor takes a sudden dive into the depths) is an extremely popular form of angling around the Australian and New Zealand coastlines (see Figure 22-1). In fact, statistics show that Aussies and Kiwis have some of the highest per capita levels of boat ownership in the world.

In addition to all of the privately owned craft, most major coastal ports and harbours around both countries are home to a number of charter vessels designed to take paying customers offshore for a day's fishing.

If you don't own a boat and the idea of offshore fishing attracts you, I recommend you make several trips out on both charter vessels and boats that belong to fishing friends before you outlay the considerable sums of money needed to buy and maintain an offshore fishing craft. (For more details on the pleasures and pitfalls of boat ownership, see Chapter 25.)

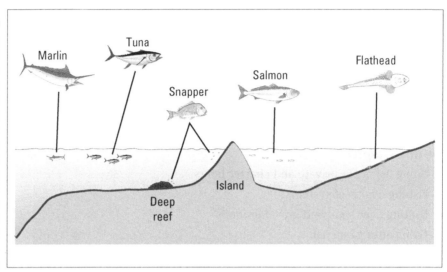

Figure 22-1:
Most deep-sea angling in Australasia is done between the shore and the edge of the continental shelf, where the ocean floor drops away.

Bouncing into Bottom Fishing

Bottom fishing over reef systems (in other words, dropping a weighted line and baited hook onto the seabed) is the most popular form of offshore angling in Australia and New Zealand. The method is successful for many species, of which the most common are

- Cod
- Coral trout
- Emperor
- Morwong
- Nannygai
- Pearl perch
- Snapper
- Sweetlip
- Teraglin
- Trevally
- Westralian dhufish

When offshore reef fishing, you can either anchor the boat or allow the boat to drift with the wind and current. Both approaches have advantages and disadvantages, although anchoring — and, more importantly, recovering the anchor — is extremely hard work in water deeper than 60–80 metres.

A number of offshore reef fishers use handlines or short boat rods fitted with centrepin, sidecast or overhead reels (refer to Chapter 6). Other deep-sea anglers use special devices called *deck winches* — large centrepin reels mounted directly to the boat's railing or *gunwale* (the upper edge of a boat's side). Deck winches are generally only seen on relatively large charter vessels (also known as *party boats*) that typically take groups of a dozen or more anglers out to sea for a day or more at a time.

Fishing lines for offshore reef fishing are normally 12–40 kilos in breaking strain (refer to Chapter 4) and a relatively heavy sinker (refer to Chapter 7) is used to take the baited hook or hooks to the seabed. Nylon lines are most commonly used, although recently many deep-sea anglers are discovering the advantages of braided or fused gel-spun polyethylene (GSP) lines for fishing in deeper water (refer to Chapter 4).

The weight of the sinker used to take your line to the seabed can range from 40 or 50 grams up to a kilogram or even more. The weight of the sinker you choose depends on the depth of the water and the speed of the current and, if you don't choose to anchor, the drift rate of the boat.

As a rule, choose the lightest sinker and the thinnest line (within reason) that coincides with the weather and water conditions to yield the best number and size of fish. By using a thinner line and a lighter sinker, you're more sensitive to bites and can hook more fish.

Another bonus of using lighter line is that when the rig becomes fouled or snagged on the bottom, you can more easily break the line. Becoming snagged is a reasonably common event in certain areas, especially when you're drifting rather than fishing at anchor.

The best baits for deep-water reef fishing are relatively tough so that the bait isn't torn from the hook by water pressure on the plunge to the bottom or picked away rapidly by small fish. Squid and pieces of fish flesh with the skin attached are popular choices among deep-sea anglers.

If you choose to use a soft bait such as prawns — which can be effective baits — make a bait cocktail by combining the prawn with a tough strip of squid or fish flesh on the same hook. Then, if the prawn is torn away, the fish flesh is still there to appeal to a passing fish!

Another approach to bottom fishing on or near reefs is to anchor the boat, make a trail of berley (refer to Chapter 8) and use lighter tackle to slowly waft baits on lightly-weighted lines, or lines with no weights at all, down through the water column. A double-handed threadline or spinning outfit is ideal for bottom fishing in this way, although a number of anglers prefer a sidecast or overhead combo (for more information about rods and reels, refer to Chapters 5 and 6).

Lightly-weighted lines and baits are called *floaters* by many anglers, even though the bait does sink, albeit in an extremely slow manner.

Dropping floaters through a berley trail is an especially effective technique for catching snapper, kingfish, trevally, tailor, mulloway and teraglin in temperate waters; whereas, target species further north in Australia include coral trout, emperor and mackerel.

Drifting the Sand and Gravel Beds

The second most popular style of fishing offshore (after bottom fishing on reefs, refer to the previous section) is to drift over sand, mud or gravel seabeds dragging baited lines held down with relatively heavy sinkers.

Many of the species encountered in sand, mud or gravel environments prefer to lie right on the seabed. For example, flathead, flounder, whiting, gurnard and various rays are bottom dwellers; whereas, trevally, snapper and morwong are known to feed a little higher off the bottom.

The tackle, rigs and baits to use when drifting over sand and gravel grounds are similar to the rigs used for reef fishing. The only real difference is that slightly lighter lines and smaller hooks are advisable because the target fish are generally smaller than the fish found on reefs.

Fishing for Game

In addition to the more sedentary, bottom-dwelling fish, Australasia's offshore waters offer a wide range of predatory, free-swimming pelagic and semi-pelagic species, including the following surface and mid-water feeders that are often called game or sport fish:

- Cobia
- Kingfish
- Mackerel
- Marlin
- Sailfish
- Salmon (kahawai)
- Sharks

✔ Tailor

✔ Tuna

✔ Wahoo

TIP

Saying goodbye to seasickness

Seasickness — known to the French by the deceptively romantic title of *mal de mer* — is the bane of deep-sea anglers and keeps many people from using boats to go fishing. The affliction can be extremely unpleasant, so an aversion to fishing at sea is understandable.

Many so-called experts insist that seasickness is 'all in your head', but believe me it's not — occasionally seasickness is all over your shoes and down the front of your shirt!

Seasickness is a form of motion sickness and is a genuine medical condition. The problem starts in the middle ear and leads to increased body temperature, lethargy and nausea. If you're susceptible to car or plane sickness and suffer vertigo in high buildings, chances are you're also prone to seasickness. Children, in particular, succumb easily to seasickness, but virtually no-one is totally immune.

All but a handful of particularly unlucky souls can beat seasickness most of the time. If you succumb to *mal de mer*, you can choose from a range of motion sickness drugs and experiment to find out which drug works best for you. The downside of the drugs is that many of the medicines cause side effects, including drowsiness and a dry mouth. I recommend that you set aside an afternoon at home to take your drug of choice the first time, so that you can test the drug in a safe environment.

Instead of taking drugs, you can try wearing a wristband that applies pressure to nausea-relieving acupuncture points or take a natural remedy for seasickness, such as ginger tablets.

If you're susceptible to seasickness, be sure to carry a few motion sickness pills in case the gentler remedies don't work.

The following are a few more tips on how to avoid seasickness:

✔ Avoid eating greasy foods for 24 hours before departing.

✔ Avoid drinking alcohol before going out on a boat (boozy beverages affect the function of the inner ear, making you sicker).

✔ Eat cereal and fruit on the morning of your voyage.

✔ Try to have a good night's sleep the night before the trip.

If you do succumb to nausea while out on the boat, the following may help:

✔ Nibble on crackers or bread.

✔ Drink plenty of non-alcoholic beverages.

✔ Pop a motion sickness pill if you feel really lousy.

✔ Stay active to keep your mind off the problem.

✔ Steer clear of fuel or bait fumes.

✔ Take off any clothing that may be keeping your temperature up (for example, a sweater or parka).

✔ Watch the horizon or land for a while.

Finally, if all the remedies fail, remember to throw up on the downwind side of the boat!

Learning from the experts

Fishing specifically for surface and mid-water hunters generally requires slightly more sophisticated tackle and techniques than bottom fishing. To learn a few of the basics needed for the sport before venturing out on your own, I recommend that you spend a day or two on board a professional sport and game fishing charter vessel with a trained crew.

For most forms of sport and game fishing, an overhead reel loaded with 10 to 40 kilo breaking strain line on a suitable game or jig rod is ideal (refer to Chapter 5 and 6).

Trolling offshore

Trolling means trailing or dragging a line behind a moving vessel. The technique is sometimes erroneously referred to as *trawling.* That term refers to the dragging of nets, not lines.

Lines trolled behind a moving boat are usually rigged with lures that come in a range of forms (refer to Chapter 8), including:

- Bibbed or bibless minnows and plugs
- Lead-headed feather jigs
- Plastic or rubber artificial squids
- Resin-headed skirted lures
- Saltwater flies
- Spoons

You can also troll using natural baits. Carefully rigged dead garfish (piper), mullet or pilchards are particularly popular choices, especially in tropical and sub-tropical waters when targeting mackerel, barracuda, wahoo, sailfish and marlin. Another effective method for targeting game and sport fish is to slowly troll live fish behind the boat.

Trolling is an excellent way of catching fish when travelling between point A and point B to pursue other styles of offshore angling, but the fishing style can also be an end in itself, with many experienced anglers turning it into a fine art.

Successful trollers don't just drag their lures or baited lines around blindly in the hope of crossing paths with a hungry fish. The experts search for the fish by looking for:

✔ Bait fish schools

✔ Concentrations of sea birds (indicating the presence of fish)

✔ Floating mats of weed or other items of flotsam and jetsam

✔ Lines of current

✔ Undersea pinnacles

As with all styles of fishing, keen observation and a little thought pay handsome dividends in offshore trolling.

TIP

Structuring your fishing

Again and again in specialist fishing literature, you're bound to come across the terms, 'structure' and 'structural elements'. The words stand for important concepts in successful angling. All fish gather close to significant structures at some time — and knowing this can make catching the fish relatively easy!

The relationship between fish and a structure is a trait known to zoologists as **thigmotaxis** or **thigmotropism**. This trait explains why, for example, the greatest number of ants on a footpath are observed near the edges of the concrete squares or in the cracks between the squares, rather than out in the middle of the squares. And, also, why cows gather in the corners of fields and why school children in a playground so often congregate around tables and benches or even close to garbage bins!

Motivated by the same force, fish gather under small items of flotsam, around a floating marker buoy and the accompanying mooring chain or over a submerged reef pinnacle.

The presence of food and shelter is also relevant to the phenomenon, but the trait goes

well beyond the basic necessities of life to include less tangible concepts such as living space and points of reference. The concepts help to explain why dozens (or even hundreds) of large tuna or dolphin fish (mahi-mahi) sometimes gather around a relatively small floating log or buoy in the middle of the ocean. They do this despite the fact that such an object offers very little in the way of additional food or shelter.

Remember that the open ocean is a vast, three-dimensional world with few obvious features, so points of reference such as drifting objects, current lines and undersea lumps and bumps become important signposts for fish. The features provide gathering stations and waypoints for migratory, pelagic species and longer-term homes for more sedentary types.

In almost all styles of angling, you're sure to catch more fish if you pay heed to this widespread trait and concentrate on identifying the major structural elements and present your baits, lures or flies as close as possible to the features.

Chapter 23

Freshwater Fanatics

*T*he challenge for Aussie freshwater anglers is to find the freshwater! Australia is the second driest continent on Earth (Antarctica is, surprisingly, the driest) and this fact tends to limit the freshwater fishing opportunities in Australia compared to the options available in places such as North America and Europe, or even just across the Tasman Sea, in New Zealand.

But it seems that freshwater anglers enjoy a challenge because the sport is extremely popular in Australia, with more people taking up the fishing style each year. Less surprisingly, freshwater fishing is also immensely popular in New Zealand, especially south from Auckland, all the way to the bottom of the South Island.

Australasia's freshwater habitats roughly divide into three distinct categories:

✔ Trout streams (some of which also contain other native and introduced species)

✔ Inland or outback rivers

✔ Lakes or man-made impoundments

Other environment types (such as coastal bass and barramundi rivers) share many of the features of trout streams and outback rivers. The features extend also to estuaries, which the rivers flow into (for more detail on estuary fishing, refer to Chapter 21). Because of the similarities between the coastal river and estuarine environments, this chapter focuses instead on the aforementioned three main freshwater categories.

Singing the Sweetwater Tune

Known rather poetically as the *sweetwater*, Australasia's freshwater environments are wonderful places to cast a line. These environments are incredibly diverse, ranging from snowy alpine and sub-alpine brooks to big outback rivers, sprawling lakes, deep, man-made reservoirs and tropical lagoons or billabongs.

The range of fish species available in the sweetwater is also considerable and, in Australia, includes a string of naturally-occurring native inhabitants such as:

- Barramundi
- Catfish
- Eels
- Golden and silver perch
- Jungle perch
- Murray cod
- Saratoga

Australian and New Zealand freshwater environments are also home to a range of introduced fish, such as:

- English perch or redfin
- European carp
- Goldfish
- Roach
- Salmon
- Tench
- Trout

Some of these exotic types of fish (especially members of the carp family) are less than welcome in our waters due to the ecological damage done by the species. Nonetheless, the fish do provide excellent sport for anglers.

Fishing Trout Streams

Australia's trout waters are primarily confined to the following areas:

- **Tasmania:** Everywhere.
- **Victoria:** In the higher, cooler areas.
- **New South Wales (and the Australian Capital Territory):** In the higher, cooler areas.
- **South Australia:** In a few rare pockets of the south-east.
- **Western Australia:** In the south-west corner.

Even in some of the preceding areas, the trout fishing is best described as being marginal, and needs regular restocking of hatchery-bred fish to maintain viable populations, especially after prolonged droughts.

By contrast, New Zealand seems to have been designed specifically to suit the needs of introduced trout and salmon. A plethora of wonderful trout waters lie between Auckland and Stewart Island and many well-travelled anglers rate The Land of the Long White Cloud as the finest trout fishing destination on earth! I tend to agree with them.

In many ways, trout streams are the easiest of all waterways for anglers to read. The currents are clearly defined, structural elements are often visible and the fish tend to adopt predictable *lies* or *holding stations*. In fact, many of the basic rules for reading trout streams form a valuable foundation for understanding all other waterways, be they freshwater or saltwater.

Trout streams range from tiny brooks and mountain creeks that energetic anglers can easily jump across to large, powerful rivers. Each environment is different, but a set of basic ground rules applies to all, as the following sections show.

Spotting pools and riffles

Most streams are composed of two alternating forms of topography called *pools* and *riffles* (see Figure 23-1). Other words for pools and riffles include

- *Holes* and *bars*
- *Pools* and *rapids*
- *Runs* and *riffles*

Regardless of the terminology, the pair of labels differentiates between the deeper, relatively slow-flowing areas of a stream (the pools, runs or holes) and the shallower, faster stretches (bars, riffles or rapids).

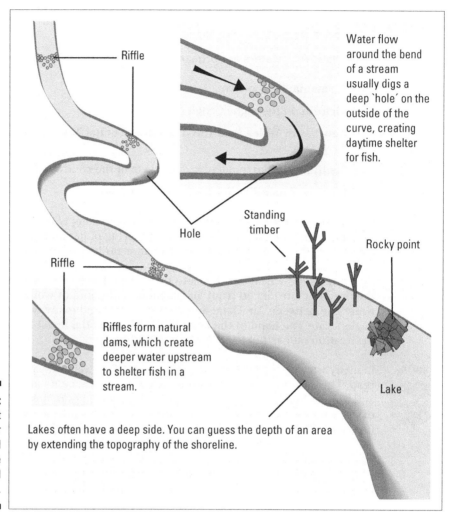

Water flow around the bend of a stream usually digs a deep `hole´ on the outside of the curve, creating daytime shelter for fish.

Riffle

Riffle

Hole

Standing timber

Rocky point

Riffles form natural dams, which create deeper water upstream to shelter fish in a stream.

Lake

Lakes often have a deep side. You can guess the depth of an area by extending the topography of the shoreline.

Figure 23-1:
Most freshwater streams and rivers have pools and riffles.

In a typical stream, pools and riffles alternate with a certain degree of pattern, although the length and depth of a pool and the speed of flow through a riffle can be significantly different in each case.

Generally speaking, the trout (and other fish) in a stream choose to lie facing into the current because this makes it easier for the fish to breathe and to see food drifting downstream. Most fish also seek cover of some sort, especially during daylight hours. The cover can take the form of aerated white water, depth, an undercut bank, fallen logs or the shadow of a tree, high bank or boulder.

Extremely shallow, fast-flowing rapids don't hold many big fish for long periods, except during times of hot weather or reduced stream flow, when stressed trout seek out the more agitated, oxygenated water found in fast moving water.

Working the transitional zones

For most of the season, one of the prime holding areas in a trout stream lies at the transition zone between the riffle and the head of the pool. Here, the current rapidly loses force and back eddies may occur along each bank as the water becomes deeper and more slow moving. Often, a circular or oval patch of virtually motionless water exists within the transition zone and this is called the *eye* of the pool. The eye is a terrific place to cast a line for trout and other freshwater fish.

In a trout stream, the middle of a pool is often surprisingly unproductive, although fish do certainly cruise and rise to the surface in the middle of a pool in the mornings and evenings, especially if an insect *hatch* is in progress (see Chapters 8 and 24). On the other hand, redfin perch, bass and other freshwater species often hold in the deeper, slower moving parts of pools.

The *tail* or *tail-out* of the pool is another very productive area, where the water begins to shallow and speed up before rushing away into the next riffle. The tail or tail-out area holds a number of trout for the greater part of the year — especially at dawn and dusk. This area is particularly productive early and late in the season. Autumn and spring are the seasons when the fish are preparing to spawn, are spawning or are recovering from spawning.

Fishing Aussie Outback Rivers

Reading or decoding the fish-holding secrets of Australia's outback rivers is more difficult than understanding shallow, clear trout streams. Outback rivers tend, on average, to be a little deeper than trout streams and are muddier than alpine and sub-alpine waterways. In addition, the native freshwater species of the outback are less predictable than the introduced *salmonoids* (trout and salmon).

Despite the differences between a relatively slow flowing, muddy outback river and a lively, quick-moving trout stream, the basic rules of stream mechanics still apply. Even the Murray and Darling Rivers and their tributaries feature the alternating pool and riffle structure (refer to the section 'Fishing Trout Streams', earlier in this chapter), but the features are a bit harder to see.

Who's coming to dinner?

The main natural species that are present in Australia's inland rivers include

- Eel-tailed catfish
- Golden perch (yellowbelly)
- Murray cod
- Silver perch

You can find several introduced species in many inland rivers, including:

- English perch (redfin)
- European carp
- Tench

All of Australia's native freshwater fish tend to be strongly structure-oriented, particularly the two largest species, Murray cod and golden perch. The heavyweights often become rather solitary in nature as the fish grow in size, although golden perch are known to form loose schools, especially at spawning time (spring).

You can usually find cod and golden perch near fallen timber, undercut banks, exposed tree roots or rock bars. The fish favour the deeper parts of the pools, especially during daylight hours, and in faster flowing water seek the sanctuary and still water offered by a large obstruction such as a tree trunk, a bridge pylon or a boulder.

Silver perch and the introduced redfin are schooling, open-water species that often feed in the quicker moving areas of our outback river systems; whereas, catfish and carp use every part of the river at times, including shallow backwaters, swampy margins and isolated ox-bow lagoons.

Where to find dinner

The prime structures of interest to inland anglers pursuing the larger native fish are large fallen trees or tangles of trees, rock bars and steep, current-scoured banks, particularly if the structures are either in or close to the deepest parts of a pool or hole.

Man-made structures are of great importance to the freshwater angler. The most significant structures are weirs, locks and dams, which are commonplace on the big, outback rivers such as the Murray and the Darling. The best place to fish in a big river is often immediately downstream of any barriers — where those fish attempting to migrate upriver stack up and compete for food. For example, the best place to start prospecting for fish on an unknown stretch of outback river is a kilometre or so downstream from a weir. This choice is especially the case if the area you choose has a number of snag-piles of fallen timber or rock bars. Before you toss in your line, always check to make sure that fishing is allowed, because some of these waters adjacent to weirs are off limits.

Fishing in Stillwater

The Australian mainland isn't overly endowed with natural, freshwater lakes. Lake George, near Canberra, is one of the largest, but even this lake becomes almost completely dry on regular occasions. Other lakes (such as South Australia's vast Lake Eyre) are more like dry saltpans than inland seas most of the time. By contrast, New Zealand is blessed with many natural lakes.

In recent decades, both Australia and New Zealand have seen an increase in the number of freshwater fishing areas due to the construction of man-made waterways variously known as dams, reservoirs or impoundments. Man-made impoundments are built for various purposes, including the generation of hydro-electricity, the storage of water for urban and rural consumption, the control of flooding and recreational activities.

Natural lakes and man-made reservoirs or impoundments are often grouped together and, for fishing purposes, are referred to as *stillwaters*.

Stillwater revival

For fishing purposes, Australian lakes and dams (stillwaters) tend to fall into three broad groupings:

- ✓ Mixed fisheries
- ✓ Salmonoid (trout and salmon) fisheries
- ✓ Warm water fisheries

Most of the lakes and impoundments in Tasmania and the highest parts of Victoria and southern New South Wales, as well as nearly all of those in New Zealand fall into the salmonoid category. Stillwaters at lower altitudes in the southern states of Australia are more likely to contain mixed fish populations, with some salmonoids and some warm water species. In the outback and the north of the country, lakes and impoundments are exclusively warm water habitats.

Each type of environment is slightly different in nature, but a number of general fish-finding rules apply to all stillwaters, as the following sections show.

Cracking the stillwater code

Lakes and impoundments are the most difficult of all freshwater environments for the angler to read and understand. The difficulty level is magnified in low altitude, mixed and warm water fisheries, which typically feature large areas of shallow, turbid water and few distinctive shoreline features. However, by applying the basic rules of fish location and behaviour and being keenly observant, an angler can begin to crack the code of even apparently featureless waterways.

Many stillwaters lying at higher elevations are located in deep valleys and are surrounded by steep hills and ridges. More often than not, the contours evident along the shorelines continue beneath the surface. In other words, a ridge top forms an underwater reef, while an in-flowing creek gully is likely to continue beneath the surface as a submerged gutter. Similarly, shorelines characterised by grassy flats, paddocks or swampy marshes typically lie alongside areas of shallow, weedy water with a relatively uniform depth.

Submerged or partially submerged standing trees, which are especially common in newer, man-made impoundments, are also valuable indicators of the depth of the water and the contour of the bottom. By comparing the submerged trees with similar trees on the shore, and seeing where the water comes up to on the trunks of the drowned trees (lower or higher branches), you can make accurate assumptions about the shape of the lake's bed.

If you're fishing from a boat, you can use an electronic depth sounder to work out the contour of the bottom of the man-made impoundment.

Spotting stillwater structures

As in all the other fishing environments, consistent results in stillwater areas come about only if you manage to identify the correct combination of structural elements, water quality and food supply that your target species find most attractive.

The requirements vary between fish species. For example, the ideal habitat for a rainbow trout is completely different to the ideal habitat of a Murray cod, an eel-tailed catfish or a sooty grunter. To fish successfully, you need to learn as much as you can about your chosen target species and apply the knowledge to reading the water and working out the most likely hot spots.

Despite variations in behaviour from one species to another, certain broad parameters apply to virtually all lake and impoundment fish. The fish require

- **Cover from predators, such as larger fish, eagles, cormorants, water rats and anglers:** In most cases, cover is provided by water depth, water discolouration or a structure such as submerged timber, rock outcrops or weed beds.

- **Food:** The food supply is likely to be related to the available cover as well as to water flowing in from creeks and rivers. Also, rising water levels inundate new ground and greatly increases the availability of food.

- **Water with enough dissolved oxygen to sustain life:** Wind and wave action increase dissolved oxygen content, as do currents and in-flowing streams. High temperatures and still conditions deplete dissolved oxygen levels.

To identify likely hot spots or zones of fish concentration, you need to combine everything you know about different structural elements.

Licensed to kill

Most states and territories and nearly every region of New Zealand require all adult anglers to hold a current licence or permit for freshwater fishing, even in areas that currently have no general, all-waters or saltwater licensing requirements.

Be sure to check whether you need a licence before you go fishing. Usually you can find out about this, and buy a licence, at a local tackle shop, general store or police station located close to freshwater fishing areas (see Chapter 26 for how to access fishing rules online).

Freshwater fisheries also tend to be governed by tighter rules and regulations than saltwater environments and many inland species have bag limits, minimum size restrictions and even maximum size limits. A few species — including trout, Murray cod and barramundi — are also protected by closed seasons.

The closed seasons are intended to allow the fish to spawn successfully and are an important fisheries management tool.

Take the time to familiarise yourself with the rules and regulations for the waters where you intend to fish and you're bound to add a higher level of enjoyment to the sport.

Chapter 24

Fly Floggers

Despite the popular theory that fly-fishing is an art practised only by talented (and snobby) elite, the sport is really nothing more than a method of presenting a special type of lure (the fly) to the fish.

Fly-fishing is no longer confined to the pursuit of trout and salmon, nor is the sport only practised in fresh and brackish water. Fly fishers can be found plying this unique trade in every angling environment described in this book (plus a range of other environments), catching all manner of species from mullet to marlin. This chapter looks at the artificial bait that fly fishers use to lure the catch and how to choose the right rod and line.

Examining the Art of Fur and Feathers

Fly-fishing has evolved enormously since the days of ancient Macedonia (see the sidebar 'Trawling through historical facts'), but the basic principles never change. The angler uses an artificial bait — made of a combination of hair, fur, feathers, synthetics, tinsels and threads — and casts the lure using the mass of the line itself, rather than the weight of the lure or a sinker attached to the line. This is the single, most fundamental difference that stands fly-fishing apart from all other forms of angling.

Because the line supplies the primary casting weight in fly-fishing, anglers use a different style of casting (refer to Chapter 13 for how to cast with fly gear).

Using natural and synthetic materials

Many modern fishing flies continue to be made from natural animal hair, fur and feathers. Other types of flies combine natural materials with various synthetic fibres and a number of fly types — especially some saltwater flies — are made totally from man-made materials, such as metal, plastic, latex and Styrofoam. Originally, the flies were designed to imitate winged insects; but, today, flies represent anything from a tiny beetle, a shrimp or a crab up to a full-grown mullet or mackerel measuring 25–30 centimetres (see Figure 24-1)!

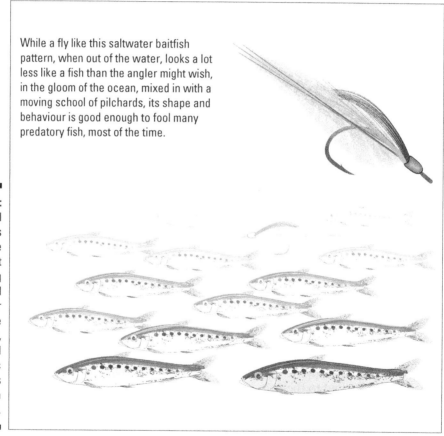

While a fly like this saltwater baitfish pattern, when out of the water, looks a lot less like a fish than the angler might wish, in the gloom of the ocean, mixed in with a moving school of pilchards, its shape and behaviour is good enough to fool many predatory fish, most of the time.

Figure 24-1:
Successful fly fishers imitate the fish's diet by using artificial flies or lures made from furs, feathers and synthetic materials bound to a hook.

Tying your own flies

You can find an excellent range of commercially-made fishing flies at specialist tackle shops, but sooner or later most keen fly fishers dabble with making flies. The craft is called *fly-tying* because thread is usually used to bind or tie various materials to the shank of a hook in order to create a fly.

The secret of successful fly selection lies in *matching the hatch* or closely imitating the food forms being eaten by fish at a particular time or place (refer to Chapter 8 for a range of common fly types). Occasionally, finding exactly the right form for a fly is impossible, so the best way to match the hatch is to design and tie your own flies.

Fly-tying can develop into an absorbing hobby and a number of fly-tying experts rarely find time to actually go fishing! The most obsessive of the experts always have on hand a pair of scissors and a few plastic bags to use in gathering hair from dead animals found on the highway and then use the hair to create crazy new fly patterns (don't laugh, it's true!).

At a less extreme level, fly-tying can become a highly rewarding pastime, but don't ever assume that you can save money by tying your own flies. The money that you spend on tools, materials, hooks and books far outweighs the cost of buying a few dozen flies a year to satisfy your practical fishing needs. Accept this truth and then you can choose whether or not to try your hand at tying your own flies.

Trawling through historical facts

Fly-fishing has a rich history that stretches back at least a couple of thousand years to the times of the ancient Macedonians, who tempted trout from the streams of south-eastern Europe using counterfeit insects made of hair and fur bound to small metal hooks or gorges.

Over the centuries, the art of fly-fishing developed across Europe, spread into Asia and eventually travelled to the Americas, but was still primarily used as a method for catching members of the trout and salmon clan (the salmonoids) in freshwater rivers and lakes or brackish estuaries.

Choosing the Right Gear

Various combinations of rods and specially designed fly line are needed to cast for different species of fish (for details on fly-fishing tackle, refer to Chapters 4 and 5).

For example, fly-fishers use delicate, featherweight equipment as they sneak along the bank of a tiny mountain brook in pursuit of trout. This light equipment is far removed from the big, strong gear of a saltwater fly-fisher (also known as a *swoffer*) hunting tuna, kingfish and mackerel on the open ocean. In fact, the difference is as large as that between an air rifle and an elephant gun!

Reading Up on Fly-Fishing

An enormous amount of literature exists on the art of fly-fishing and the sport is so intricate, I don't delve too deeply into fly-casting, fly-fishing and the crafting of fishing flies in this book. Fortunately, however, you can choose from many excellent how-to texts in bookshops and fishing outlets for some of the best books on fly-fishing.

Fly-fishing is a distinct and specialised branch of angling that many people — me included — find fascinating and highly addictive, to the point that many fly fishers prefer to catch a fish using fly gear than any other form of tackle.

However, most experienced fly fishers agree that a solid grounding in the more conventional forms of recreational fishing described in this book forms an essential apprenticeship for any later exploration into the wonderful world of fur and feather flinging.

Chapter 25

Ahoy, Captain!

'*B*elieve me, my young friend, there is *nothing* — absolutely nothing — half so much worth doing as simply messing about in boats.' So said Water Rat to Mole in Kenneth Grahame's book *The Wind in the Willows*, epitomising the way so many otherwise sane people feel about the subject of boating.

The unfortunate souls who, unlike Water Rat, don't feel a deep empathy for boats always tend to look askance at people who love nothing more than being out on a boat. To non-believers, boats are, at best, a form of water-based transportation — a necessary evil for going from point A to point B (if no other form of transport exists). To dedicated non-believers, boats are unstable, uncomfortable, wet, expensive and potentially life-threatening contrivances designed for the express purpose of exposing terrified land lubbers to the horrors of life on the bounding main. In short, you're either a boat person or you're not!

In the eyes of many people, using a boat as a platform from which to catch fish adds immeasurably to a boat's main purpose — that of transportation. A fishing boat is capable of generating lively enthusiasm and even a level of sentimentality that can verge on the romantic!

But even the people who enjoy boats and fishing from boats recognise that a watercraft can be a demanding mistress and that owning a fishing boat can be a love–hate relationship.

A boat always seems to have a broken part or a vital item that can use some work. Equally, no boat owner is ever completely happy with the vessel he or she owns, causing boaties to dream endlessly of bigger and better craft.

Defining Fishing Boats

The term fishing boat describes anything from a one-person kayak up to and beyond a 20-metre, ocean-going game cruiser (sometimes disparagingly referred to by boaties bobbing about in smaller crafts as a 'floating gin palace').

In Australia and New Zealand, the most popular and common fishing boats are aluminium or fibreglass *car toppers* or *trailer boats*. As the names imply, a car-topper is small, and is light enough to be transported on racks fitted to the roof of a vehicle; whereas, a trailer boat is towed behind a car on a trailer. Trailer boats range in length from 3.5 to 8 metres, or even 9 metres, but the most popular are in the 4.2 to 6 metres range and are powered by either *outboard* or *inboard* motors.

You can use boats of one size or another as fishing platforms on just about any body of water larger than a puddle or a tiny brook. However, as a sensible rule, you're unwise to venture offshore or out onto large, exposed lakes, estuaries, bays and harbours in a vessel with a length of less than 4.2 metres and a *beam* (width) of less than 1.7 metres.

Asking Yourself 'Do I Really Need a Boat?'

You don't need a boat to do many of the styles of fishing described in this book, but many keen anglers ultimately aspire to owning a boat because a vessel allows you to reach more productive fishing spots.

If you're bitten by the bug and are lusting after a boat of your own, take a cold shower and then sit down and think hard and long before spending the significant amount of money required to buy and maintain any craft bigger than a canoe or kayak.

Above all, ask yourself this vital question: Am I going to use my boat often enough to justify the trouble and expense of owning the boat? If the answer is no — or you hesitate for even a moment before answering — chances are you're not ready to take the plunge.

A number of viable alternatives to owning a boat outright exist, including:

- ✔ **Charter:** Major ports and harbours around Australia teem with charter vessels and professional guides ready and willing to take you out for a day or a weekend's fishing (refer to Chapter 22).

- ✔ **Lease or hire:** The same ports and harbours have many companies that hire out or lease out boats on a *bareboat* basis (in other words, you're the skipper and the hirer doesn't supply crew).

- ✔ **Partnership:** Instead of paying for the boat and the boat's maintenance yourself, you can take on a partner or partners and buy a boat on a share basis.

Sharing the ownership of a boat has the potential to ruin a long-term friendship, so you're best to be extremely careful in your choice of partner or partners.

Taking the Plunge and Buying a Boat

If you do decide to buy a boat, because you're sure you're going to use the boat often enough to make outright ownership worthwhile, do plenty of homework on the types of boats available and shop around for a good boat at a reasonable price. Read lots of books and magazine articles about boats and boat ownership, talk to other boat owners and try to arrange test drives on as many different boating rigs as possible before shelling out the cash.

Every fishing boat's a compromise (as the hackneyed saying goes). The type of boat you want and the boat you can afford are often two wildly different beasts. For example, you have to consider the following:

✔ Power versus economy

✔ Sea handling ability versus shallow water access

✔ Size versus the ability to tow and store the boat

Start considering the preceding choices and you can understand why the choosing of a fishing boat is a balancing act.

In my opinion, the greatest favour you can do yourself when shopping for a new boating rig or evaluating the worth of a second-hand rig is to be brutally honest about your aspirations and fishing needs. If the parameters change over time, you may eventually need to consider trading up — or down — because few boats fit owners for life (or vice versa).

Giving In to the Lure of Boating

In the final analysis, the prospect of messing about in, with or around boats has an appeal to just about everyone. Kenneth Grahame's Water Rat had it pretty well worked out when he finished his song of praise on the subject to Mole by saying: 'In or out of 'em, it doesn't matter. Nothing seems really to matter, that's the charm of it.'

The secret for humans, living in the real world rather than in the pages of a delightful children's story, lies in not becoming completely carried away with the charm of messing about in boats. The danger is that some people become obsessive. After all, don't forget that a boat has also been rather aptly defined as a hole in the water into which one pours money!

When it comes to boating, rely on your head as well as your heart!

Boating safety

Safety is of paramount concern in all forms of boating, whether you go boating on enclosed or open waters. However, if you stick to the following ten rules, safety and enjoyment is bound to be yours:

✔ **Alcohol:** Alcohol and water don't mix! Save the beers and cheers for when you're safely on shore.

✔ **Anchor:** Whether required to by law or not, always carry at least one anchor (with plenty of chain or rope), a torch (with spare batteries), a pack of flares and up-to-date charts of the waters in which you plan to operate.

✔ **Emergency:** If the worst happens and the boat capsizes or the boat is swamped, stay with the vessel rather than swimming for shore or another boat.

✔ **First aid:** Make sure the boat has a first-aid kit and that at least one member of the crew knows how to use the kit and has knowledge of modern resuscitation techniques.

✔ **Fuel and water:** Carry at least twice as much fuel as you think you're going to need for an outing and at least two litres of drinking water for each person on board.

✔ **Game plan:** Tell someone responsible where you're going and when you plan to return, and have a strategy in place if you end up being more than an hour or two overdue.

✔ **Life jackets:** Carry an authorised life jacket or flotation vest for each person on board and wear the devices when required to by law or when crossing river bars, negotiating surf breaks or experiencing heavy seas.

✔ **Rules:** Know and observe all safety, navigation and seamanship rules and, if you're in charge of the vessel, make sure you hold the correct qualifications for the waters in which you're operating.

✔ **Seaworthiness:** Make sure your vessel is suitable for the task at hand. In particular, if heading offshore, be certain the boat is seaworthy and carries sufficient flotation to remain afloat, even if swamped.

✔ **Weather:** Regularly monitor weather reports, before and during boating activities. A portable radio is ideal for this purpose.

The preceding ten rules are the absolute minimum if you're heading out on a boat. In addition, however, you can add any number of useful gadgets to a boat to improve the safety standards.

Without going ... er ... overboard, I recommend you also carry a means of communication (for example, a mobile telephone, a Very High Frequency (VHF) radio, or a Citizen's Band (CB) radio) and a torch. And if you're headed offshore or into remote areas, definitely consider buying or renting an emergency position indicating radio beacon (EPIRB).

Part VI
The Part of Tens

'Ignore the signs. I put them there to keep other fishermen away.'

In this part ...

This part includes four rather subjective collections of my personal top ten favourites. Here, you can find my ten favourite fishing websites and destinations in Australia and New Zealand. In Chapter 29, you find a list of the ten most important aspects usually left out of fishing how-to books. No matter how experienced you are, I honestly believe that this chapter includes especially valuable information. So, humour me, and take the time to browse through this little gem.

Chapter 26

The Ten Best Fishing Websites

*1*n years gone by, the only net I ever used for fishing was a landing net. Today the *inter*net (the World Wide Web) is a vast electronic noticeboard, reference library and shopping mall, and a part of every aspect of our daily lives — including recreational angling.

Because the internet contains a tonne of rubbish and misinformation, you need to be selective and cautious when trawling. This chapter looks at ten (or more!) genuinely useful websites.

Watching the Weather

The Australian Bureau of Meteorology's website (www.bom.gov.au) is a beauty, as is its New Zealand counterpart, MetService (www.metservice.co.nz). These sites contain more information than you're ever likely to need when planning a fishing outing, but the forecasts, charts of sea conditions, synoptic charts, weather radar views and regularly updated regional reports are a goldmine of important data. Depending on which side of the Tasman you're on, bookmark the best parts of these sites and have a check each time you plan on going fishing.

In Australia, two additional and useful alternatives to the Bureau of Meteorology's website are

- **Ozwind** (www.ozwind.com.au): Deals solely with whims of the wind.
- **Weatherzone** (www.weatherzone.com.au): Register with the website and become a member to access the site's information. The basic service is free (at the time of writing), or you can upgrade to a more advanced membership for a few dollars a month.

Tracking the Tides

Many sites (both free and subscription) offer access to accurate tidal information. One of the best for Australian anglers is a webpage from the Bureau of Meteorology at www.bom.gov.au/oceanography/tides.

At this informative site you find a map of Australia and the Pacific Islands where you can click on the location you're interested in and find out the precise tides for a particular date or set of dates.

Kiwi anglers can access a similar service at the Land Information New Zealand website (LINZ: www.linz.govt.nz/hydro/tidal-info/tide-tables/index.aspx). Here you can choose from a list of ports around the New Zealand coastline, select a date and then get accurate tidal information. These services are invaluable for saltwater fishers on both sides of the Tasman Sea.

Finding Your Way There and Back

The internet has revolutionised mapping functionality and related tasks. Google (www.google.com) is one such organisation that provides an amazing Google Maps service, where you can zoom in and look at most parts of the Earth's surface, some photographically and others from street level view.

If you want to track down a hard copy map that helps you to find your way to that secret fishing hole, Geoscience Australia (www.ga.gov.au) is the place to web visit. The quasi-government authority is the last word on cartography (the production of maps), satellite photography and remote imaging. The site also has information on phases of the moon, which can have an important influence on a number of styles of fishing.

Getting Hooked On the Fishing Rules

If you think you have a handle on the myriad rules and regulations that surround recreational fishing, think again. You're best to stay as current as possible (so as not to get fined or worse) on licences, the gear you're allowed to use, size limits, required permits, close waters and more.

In Australia, state and territory variations make the task of keeping up to date more than challenging. Find the answers to your questions on who, what, where and when from these national and state/territory government websites:

- ✔ Australian Government Agencies:
  - Australian Government Department of Agriculture, Fisheries and Forestry (www.daff.gov.au)
  - Australian Fisheries Management Authority (AFMA) (www.afma.gov.au)
- ✔ Department of Fisheries, Western Australia (www.fish.wa.gov.au)
- ✔ New South Wales Department of Primary Industries (www.fisheries.nsw.gov.au)
- ✔ Northern Territory Department of Resources — Fisheries (www.nt.gov.au/d/Fisheries)
- ✔ Primary Industries and Resources South Australia: Fisheries (www.pir.sa.gov.au/fisheries)
- ✔ Queensland Department of Primary Industries and Fisheries (www.dpi.qld.gov.au/28.htm)
- ✔ Tasmanian Department of Primary Industries and Water: Sea Fishing & Aquaculture (http://www.dpiw.tas.gov.au/inter.nsf/ThemeNodes/DREN-4VH86L?open)
- ✔ Victorian Department of Primary Industries: Fishing and Aquaculture (http://new.dpi.vic.gov.au/fisheries)

In New Zealand, you can check out, and get to know and understand the national and regional (for example, Taupo) regulations by visiting:

- ✔ Ministry of Fisheries (www.fish.govt.nz/en-nz/Recreational/default.htm): This site also allows you to click on a regional map that then leads you to the rules in that area.
- ✔ NZFishing (www.nzfishing.com): Plan all your NZ freshwater fishing trip needs and stay on the right side of Kiwi law.

Chatting to Fellow Fishers

The internet includes a heap of chat boards and forums, a number of which are based in Australia. Sadly, a few of the sites are electronic shark ponds where you're likely to be severely mauled and mercilessly *flamed* (shouted down and ridiculed) for expressing an opinion or asking an innocent question.

One of the better and more civilised chat forums is on the Sportsfish Australia website (www.sportsfish.com.au). Note that Sportsfish includes an 's' in the middle (I've omitted the letter on a number of frustrating occasions). The regular visitors to the Sportsfish site appear to deal gently with new chums and offer sensible, useful answers to queries. To use the Sportsfish site, you need to register as a member when you first visit the site. Registration is free and takes only seconds to complete.

As well as an excellent chat room, the Sportsfish site also has lots of other worthwhile general items, including articles on fishing, fishing news and links to weather sites. In addition, you can find information on tying knots and fishing rigs, and the site has an excellent guide to 100 or more popular Australian fish species, each with an illustration.

Logging On to the Super Sites

Fishnet (www.fishnet.com.au) has traditionally been the No.1 Aussie recreational angling website as far as *hits* (the number of visits to the site) are concerned, although this position is constantly being challenged by emerging sites. Fishnet is an extremely comprehensive reference point for Australian anglers because the site has lots of regional fishing reports, how-to articles and links to other sites, plus an active chat board divided into various topic areas such as fly fishing, salt and freshwater fishing, tackle and so on. Be warned, however, that the level and intensity of debate on the Fishnet chat boards can be a little torrid at times!

Another rapidly growing and very exciting Australian fishing site well worth checking out is LoveFishing (www.lovefishing.com.au). Backed by the Australian Fishing Tackle Association (AFTA), LoveFishing is effectively an industry-backed website portal that offers a host of how-to information, great competitions, regular give-aways, useful weather links and plenty of other wonderfully useful features. The site also aims to become the go-to social networking site for Australian anglers (rather like a fishing version of Facebook). You need to sign up as a member to get the best out of LoveFishing, but membership is free (at the time of writing). This is definitely my favourite Australian fishing website.

Kiwi anglers are equally well served on their side of the ditch by NZFishing (www.nzfishing.com). In 2009, this site was voted by visitors as one of the best NZ websites that caters for freshwater fishing.

Competing in Tournaments

The fishing magazines, *NSW Fishing Monthly*, *Queensland Fishing Monthly*, and *Victorian Fishing Monthly*, which are bought widely in Australia's eastern states, have a shared website (www.fishingmonthly.com.au). The website is also the official site of the Australian Bass Tournaments organisation, which runs the extremely successful B.A.S.S., B.R.E.A.M. and B.A.R.R.A. competition circuits around the country. The organisation's motto is 'Who shares wins' and the credo is reflected in the site's friendly and informative sections and various bulletin boards. The magazines' website is well worth a visit, especially if you're interested in competition fishing.

Buying, Selling and Owning a Boat

The company that publishes *Trade-A-Boat, Trailer Boat* and *Blue Water* magazines has a professional and highly organised website called Boatpoint (www.boatpoint.com.au). The site has a large classified section crammed with boats for sale and includes plenty of other useful boating-related information and links to other boating sites.

Kiwi anglers looking to buy or sell a boat should check out

- ✔ Boats, Boatparts, Boats4Sale, etc. (www.boats4sale.co.nz)
- ✔ TradeABoat (www.tradeaboat.co.nz)

Shopping for Fishing Gear

The World Wide Web includes plenty of Australian, New Zealand and overseas websites for buying fishing gear. An interesting American-based sales site is AllFishingTackle (www.allfishingtackle.com). The site has a free noticeboard on which anyone can advertise an item of gear for sale or look for an item of gear (however big or small) to buy. The site also includes an advice section on the performance of a rod or a boat — extremely neat (however, the usual internet caveat applies and you need to be a bit careful about the advice you accept).

An Australian on-line tackle shop worth looking at is Ausfish (www.ausfish.com.au) and if you're looking for bits and pieces for your boat, you can visit BLA (www.bla.com.au). The latter site belongs to the large Australian chandlery organisation called Bob Littler Agencies. But perhaps the most popular on-line tackle store in the country belongs to Coffs Harbour (NSW) based MOTackle (the MO stands for mail order). Visit MOTackle at www.motackle.com.au.

Across the Tasman, New Zealand tackle shoppers should also consider visiting:

- Fishing Direct NS (www.fishingdirectnz.co.nz)
- K-Labs (www.klabs.co.nz)

Buying at an Electronic Auction

The American website eBay is renowned as a site where you can buy or sell just about any item under the sun. The Australian arm of the organisation (www.ebay.com.au) has a surprising amount of fishing gear, fishing paraphernalia, boats and so on that are sold by auction on the site. Find an item you're interested in, put in your bid and see how you fare!

Wandering the World Wide Web

FishingWorks (www.fishingworks.com) is a huge American-based site that offers links to other sites that carry just about any fishing-related topic you care to name. This website covers most areas of the world, but does have a heavy American emphasis. Use the site as a vast library catalogue and a stepping-off point for more specific browsing — a handy starting point rather than an end in itself.

Kiwi anglers and those planning to visit the Land of the Long White Cloud to wet a line should definitely visit NZFishing (www.nzfishing.com) — a site that offers a comprehensive look at recreational angling in New Zealand.

Finally, if you're keen to check out what this book's author, Steve Starling, is up to, feel free to visit my website (www.starlofish.com).

Chapter 27

My Ten Favourite Australian Fishing Spots

....

In This Chapter

▶ Doing the Central Highlands fling

▶ Enjoying the bountiful Bemm

▶ Discovering New South Wales' far south coast

▶ Cruising Cape York's Crystal Coast

▶ Hopping about Kangaroo Island

....

I suspect that the same insatiable yearning that turns many people to fishing also drives some people to explore new places. Most keen anglers that I know have chronically itchy feet and an incurable wanderlust. Keen anglers are always dreaming of visiting new waters in which to cast a line. To an angler, the grass is always greener, the sea bluer and the fish bigger or more willing to bite on the far side of the bay, beyond the next point, over the hill, around the bend or another kilometre further out from the shore.

In many ways, the feelings are justified because in Australia, as in most parts of the world, more and more anglers are competing for diminishing casting space to try to catch a reduced number of fish. Finding a genuine hot spot — what our American friends so aptly call a *honey hole* — is becoming harder with the passing of each season. This truth only serves to make the hot spots more important to the people lucky enough to find a few honey holes of their own.

Every keen angler I know has at least one so-called secret spot — that is, a favourite fishing hole especially close to his or her heart. It matters little whether the revered spot is a short walk from the angler's back door and must frequently be shared with dozens of other hopeful danglers or lies hundreds or even thousands of kilometres away and is genuinely remote and untouched. Fortunately, Australia still has plenty of excellent places to choose from when it comes to casting a line. In fact, I find pruning my own list of favourites down to just ten locations is quite tricky. The locations in this chapter cover each state of Australia, starting in Tasmania and working anti-clockwise around the nation.

Trying Out Tassie's Treats

Tasmania's trout fishing is famous around the world and the heart of the wonderful resource is found in the Apple Isle's central highlands. The area is roughly bounded by Poatina in the north, Lake Burbury in the west, the Midlands Highway to the east and the townships of Tarraleah and Ouse to the south.

Within this extensive region of alpine and semi-alpine country lie literally hundreds of lakes, streams and canals, almost all of which hold trout in varying numbers and sizes.

The delightful waterways offer an outstanding variety of fishing options — from trolling lines behind a boat in Great Lake or Lake Burbury to carefully stalking fish with light fly tackle in the shallow, gin-clear tarns and sloughs of the remote Western Tiers.

Trekking for wild trout

The biggest, best known and most easily accessible central Tasmanian trout waters are Great Lake, Arthurs Lake, Lake Sorell, Lake Crescent, Lake St Clair, Lake King William and Lake Burbury. Smaller, but nonetheless productive waters, include the Lagoon of Islands, Little Pine, Lake Echo, Dee Lagoon, Bronte Lagoon and Bradys Lake.

The preceding waters are home to healthy populations of trout. A number of the lakes are dominated by brown trout, whereas other lakes contain more rainbow trout, but most have a mix of the two species. The vast majority of the fish are wild trout (meaning fish that have been spawned naturally in various feeder streams or canals), but some stocking of hatchery-bred trout also occurs in selected waters.

The majority of the waterways are open to all legal styles of trout fishing — including bait fishing, lure casting, trolling and fly-fishing — but a few (for example Little Pine and a small area of the Great Lake) have stricter regulations that mean anglers are limited to fly-fishing. Still other lakes are open only to fly and lure anglers, with bait fishing prohibited. So that you don't fall foul of the law, you need to check the current state of play concerning the regulations before going fishing in the region (refer to Chapter 26).

Working the Great Western Tiers

West of Great Lake and north of Lake St Clair lies a remote and ruggedly beautiful area of mostly small glacial lakes and tarns surrounded by low, thick bush, swampy bogs and high country heath or grasslands. The wilderness area is known as the Great Western Tiers and is a favourite destination for hikers.

The region is traversed by walking tracks and includes such truly delightful waters as Lakes Augusta, Ada, Mackenzie, Meston, Myrtle and Louisa, to name just a few. All of these little lakes are situated in the Central Plateau Conservation Area or Cradle Mountain–Lake St Clair National Park and are part of an important region listed as a World Heritage site that has strict rules regulating human activities that may be detrimental to the fragile environment.

Accessing fishing spots in the region is mostly done on foot and the fishing itself is done using fly-casting tackle (Chapter 8). Typically, the style of fishing involves first sighting a quarry and then carefully stalking the wary trout and presenting a fly. You can regard catching one or two fish a day under such conditions as an achievement, especially because the fish are likely to run from 1 to 4 kilos apiece! The emphasis in this region is very much on quality fish, rather than a quantity of fish, and most visiting anglers practice catch-and-release (Chapter 15).

Coping with four seasons in one day

One of the greatest drawbacks to fishing in the central highlands (as well as most other parts of Tasmania) is the state's unpredictable weather, which can present four seasons in a single day.

Strong winds are the norm, and rain, sleet or even snow can blow in with little notice at any time of year. Nevertheless, you can experience some wonderfully mild days with blue skies, particularly in February and March. If you're tempted to go fishing in Tasmania, remember the locals' motto that if you don't like the weather now, just wait ten minutes and it's sure to change!

Fishing Victoria's Bountiful Bemm

The Bemm River and its tidal estuary, Sydenham Inlet, lie in the far east of Victoria, between Lakes Entrance and Mallacoota, just over an hour's drive from the New South Wales border.

The turn-off to Bemm River and Sydenham Inlet is on the Princes Highway between Orbost and Cann River. If you're approaching from the north, start looking for the Bemm River signs as soon as you leave the quaint little village of Bellbird Creek (and its roadside pub), around 40 kilometres south west of Cann River. If you're approaching from the south, the turning is around 35 kilometres past Orbost (and if you reach Bellbird, you've gone too far!).

From the highway, the village of Bemm River is roughly 21 kilometres along a sealed but narrow and twisting road that leads you to a typical little holiday settlement of houses, small shops, cabins and a caravan park, all built close to the tea-coloured inlet.

At first glance, the location is a shallow, mud-bottomed, weedy lake fed by a snag-studded river full of dark, tannin-stained water. However, a closer examination reveals a fertile, rich and vibrant estuarine system that hasn't been commercially netted in over 60 years and is jumping with aquatic life.

Catching a mixed bag

Southern estuaries aren't normally as renowned for a big variety of fish as similar systems in tropical latitudes, but Sydenham Inlet and the Bemm River offer a surprisingly diverse array of desirable targets.

The waters are home to plenty of southern black bream as well as luderick (blackfish), dusky flathead, tailor, mullet and silver trevally. The deeper parts of the lower estuary at times also play host to small schools of mulloway. Out on the adjacent surf beaches you can add Australian salmon and gummy sharks to the list; and, further upriver, you encounter Australian bass (including a number of beauties), eels and more than a few trout (mostly browns).

However, the one fish that keeps luring me back to the Bemm is my southern estuary favourite — the sometimes enigmatic but always exciting estuary perch. Ever since I first worked out how to find and catch the big-eyed, silver-flanked *barra of the south*, the fish has become an obsession of mine, making the Bemm estuary my perch paradise.

Perch reside in the Bemm system from the river's mouth — literally within casting distance of the surf — to the first major rock bar well upstream (and even beyond this barrier at times, into freshwater bass and trout territory).

Casting around for the hot spots

Opportunities to fish from the shore are limited at Bemm River, although casting is possible from a few jetties and a couple of accessible stretches of bank. To achieve consistent success from the Bemm, you need a boat of some sort, even a canoe can do.

If you choose the canoe option or go out in a small dinghy, do yourself a favour and stick to the protected stretches of the river. Sydenham Inlet can become rough and ugly in a big sou'westerly blow and fronts can rip in from the Southern Ocean at any time, often with little warning. But, just in case she does blow while you're out, on the far side of the inlet, near the north-western end of the entrance channel, you find a sturdy wooden storm shelter. The hut has been used for emergency overnight accommodation on many occasions by hapless boaters caught out in a sudden blow.

Discovering the NSW Far South Coast

The far south coast of New South Wales begins beyond the Clyde River at Batemans Bay and extends to the Victorian border. The area is truly delightful and has long been a popular spot for visitors from Victoria and Canberra.

The following sections focus on a few of the angling hot spots found along this stretch of coast and often overlooked by anglers living further north.

Nailing 'em in Narooma

The tourist port of Narooma, which overlooks the clean, aquamarine waters of Wagonga Inlet, is a major holiday destination and becomes a hive of activity every Christmas and Easter.

Wagonga Inlet provides excellent fishing for bream, flathead, luderick (blackfish), whiting, tailor, small snapper and trevally, as well as the occasional big mulloway or jewfish. As no major freshwater creeks or rivers feed the inlet, Wagonga tends to remain clear, even after heavy rain, and is flushed twice a day by strong tides.

Fishing from the rocks, beaches and breakwalls in the area is also worthwhile, with the ledges below the famous and extremely picturesque golf course a top spot to spin with lures for salmon, tailor and bonito, or cast a bait for bream, drummer and groper.

Travelling from Bermagui to Tathra

If Narooma is the tourism jewel of the far south coast of New South Wales, Bermagui is certainly the region's fishing capital. A classic seafaring port, Bermagui waxes and wanes between sleepy village and bustling resort with the passage of the seasons and the town has been an icon of Australian game and sport fishing since American novelist Zane Grey first visited in the 1930s.

Bermagui is famous for exceptional catches of tuna, sharks and marlin taken each year by the well-established charter fleet and flotilla of visiting and local trailer boats. With a much safer harbour entrance than Narooma and its narrow continental shelf, Bermagui is ideally placed to service the dedicated offshore angler.

Shore and estuary fishing is also available around Bermagui. In particular, the string of small estuaries, coastal lagoons and tidal lakes along the picturesque coastline between Bermagui and the more southern village of Tathra offer excellent action for bream, flathead, whiting, luderick, mullet, garfish and other species. The pick of the hot spots can be found at Cuttagee, Murrah, Wapengo, Nelson Lake and the Bega River estuary (Mogareeka Inlet). Higher upstream, the Bega River also has some lovely bass, but finding the fish in the silted, braided channels isn't an easy job.

South of the Bega River, a long surf beach sweeps past the village of Tathra — revealing rocky headlands, a string of bays and an historic steamer wharf. Now renovated and repaired, the century-old wharf offers excellent fishing for everything from yellowtail, slimy mackerel, tailor and trevally to salmon, kingfish, the occasional tuna and some oversized sharks. Tathra wharf even boasts a tackle shop and a café that serves excellent cappuccinos.

Piering into the southern delights

Further south from Tathra, the Merimbula–Pambula area is a favourite holiday spot for Victorians. Many of the visitors are keen anglers who pursue bread-and-butter species such as bream, flathead and whiting in the two major estuary systems, Merimbula Lake and Pambula Lake. Equally as popular are the several smaller coastal estuaries that intermittently run to the sea between Wallagoot Lake and Twofold Bay.

Merimbula Wharf is a popular fishing platform, but the restored structure isn't quite as productive as Tathra Wharf.

Eden, which is situated on Twofold Bay, was once considered as a possible site for Australia's capital because of the deep, natural harbour. Today, the town is a regarded as a capital place for commercial fishing and the area also provides excellent fishing opportunities and services for recreational anglers. Boat anglers drifting on Twofold Bay bring in excellent catches of flathead. Also lurking in the depths are leatherjackets, whiting, sweep, trevally and the occasional snapper. Further offshore, outside the bay, the seasonal reef, sport and game fishing action is similar to that experienced off Narooma and Bermagui.

Shore-based anglers are also well catered for at Eden and anglers can choose from a range of piers, beaches and various rock platforms. The most famous hot spots are found on Green Cape, which is one of the meccas of land-based game fishing, with kingfish, tuna and sharks regularly being lured onto hooks.

South of Green Cape lies Disaster Bay where you can find one of the most delightful little estuary systems in the region — Wonboyn Lake and the river of the same name. Tucked into the north-western corner of Disaster Bay, Wonboyn Lake and Wonboyn River produce excellent catches of bream, flathead, luderick, whiting, mullet and tailor. In the summer months, the Wonboyn system is one of the best places on the far south coast to catch mulloway or jewfish, with specimens up to 10 or even 15 kilos being taken quite regularly, especially by keen anglers who fish at night.

Further upriver, bream, a number of large flathead, the occasional bass and isolated pockets of estuary perch provide sporadic action, particularly in the late summer, autumn and spring months.

Some areas within this region are now included within various marine national parks, where certain activities are restricted. Some areas (known as sanctuary zones) ban all forms of fishing. So, be sure to pick up a copy of the latest marine park zoning map before you wet a line or risk a fine. For more information, visit the NSW Marine Parks Authority website (`www.mpa.nsw.gov.au/cbmp.html`).

Conquering Big River Country

The huge wedge of the New South Wales north coast region that centres on Grafton and is bounded by the Washpool National Park in the west, Bunjalung National Park to the north and Sandon River to the south is often known as Big River Country. The name is in recognition of the mighty Clarence River system that serves as the region's main aquatic artery.

In many ways, the Clarence district and the massive river can be regarded as defining the southern boundary of the east coast's true sub-tropical zone. Sugar cane and bananas thrive in the area and tropical fish such as fork-tailed catfish, tarpon (ox-eye herring), giant herring, big-eye trevally and mangrove jack are often taken alongside more familiar species such as bass, bream, whiting, flathead and mulloway.

The region is highly regarded as a recreational fishing destination, attracting numerous tourists and holiday-makers from all over New South Wales and Queensland.

The Clarence is clearly the jewel in the crown of Big River Country and, whereas the vast estuary downstream from Copmanhurst and Grafton produces excellent fishing for a range of species, some of the most interesting fishing spots are found on the non-tidal, freshwater reaches of the Clarence.

Exploring the Clarence

The Clarence River rises high in the rugged mountain rainforests of the Great Dividing Range along the border between New South Wales and Queensland. The river is fed by tributaries flowing from as far afield as Glen Innes, Guyra and Ebor, making the Clarence a truly massive system that has no dams and is one of the last great untamed rivers of New South Wales.

The highest feeders of the Clarence hold scattered, marginal populations of introduced trout, but as the branches of the mighty river tumble from the high escarpments and join together, unique native species become the dominant inhabitants of the river.

Foremost among the fish that live in the Clarence — in terms of both size and importance — is the protected east coast cod. A kissing cousin of the western Murray cod (the species from which the east coast cod developed in the relatively recent evolutionary past), the east coast cod is a strikingly attractive, highly territorial species and is known to reach a massive weight of 30 kilos or more.

Thanks to the fact that the species is protected, depleted Clarence River cod numbers are now bouncing back, but remember that the species is still totally protected by law and if you accidentally hook one of the magnificent native fish while targeting catfish or bass, you must carefully unhook the fish without excessive handling and return the critter to the water immediately. (Refer to Chapter 15 for all about how to release a fish with care.)

Tangling with bass

Other fish in the freshwater reaches of the Clarence River system include eel-tailed catfish, Australian bass, Nepean herring, eels and the very occasional golden perch or yellowbelly. Of this range of available fish, bass attract the greatest interest from anglers.

The rugged Clarence Gorge, upstream from Copmanhurst, acts as a natural barrier to the free movement of bass for years at a time. Occasionally, however, the gorge is inundated by massive floods, allowing fish of all sizes to move in both directions and thereby maintain a healthy population of bass above the gorge in the Mann River, the Nymboida River and the upper Clarence River.

As the Clarence River is bounded by private land along many stretches, access to the hot spots can be tricky, but adventurous anglers can launch canoes at Buccarumbi, Jackadgerry or Cangai and wander the river to occasionally enjoy exceptional sport.

More accessible and consistent bass fishing action is available downstream of the Clarence Gorge, near Fine Flower and Copmanhurst, as well as in the lower Clarence tributaries such as the Orara River, the Coldstream River, the Esk River and Sportsmans Creek. When fishing in the rivers named, you can often catch bass as well as other brackish water species such as estuary perch, bream, flathead and the occasional ox-eye herring and mangrove jack.

Visiting Queensland's Valley of Lakes

The area increasingly known as the Valley of Lakes lies to the west and north west of Brisbane and consists of a string of man-made dams (impoundments) on the upper Brisbane River and the river's tributaries, as well as several adjacent watersheds.

Since the 1980s, the region has become one of the most popular destinations for inland angling in Australia. Thanks to significant fish stocking by government agencies and private groups, the lakes in this region are now populated with a range of native fish species and consistently produce outstanding angling, particularly in the winter, spring and autumn months.

Starting with Somerset

One of the oldest stocked impoundments in Australia, Lake Somerset is on the Stanley River, a tributary of the Brisbane River, and lies between the townships of Esk and Kilcoy, around 120 kilometres north west of Brisbane.

The dam has been well stocked with fish for more than 25 years and a large population of Australian bass provides excellent sport in all but the coldest of the winter months.

Some of the largest Australian bass ever recorded have been caught in Lake Somerset, including exceptional specimens weighing over 4 kilos. You can find the fish in the bass's familiar haunts, particularly along the steep, heavily timbered banks and around the edges of submerged weed banks. Somerset bass also have a tendency to school in mid-water over relatively featureless areas of the lake, especially in summer. When the fish move to such areas, a depth sounder is invaluable for locating the deeper schools.

Achieve excellent catches of Australian bass by trolling, casting or jigging with various lures.

Golden perch or yellowbelly also thrive in Lake Somerset and you can catch specimens weighing 6 kilos or more. You're best to target the fish during the early spring months in relatively shallow waters near the lake's edge.

Lake Somerset also contains spangled and silver perch, and eel-tailed catfish are spread throughout the lake. A few saratoga are also present in the lake, but are rarely caught. As well, you can catch large snub-nosed garfish if you use baits on small hooks and float tackle.

Lake Somerset has been regularly stocked with fry of the endangered Mary River cod and catches of the prized species are becoming more common, with the occasional fish reaching 20 kilos.

Somerset Park, below the dam wall, has excellent camping facilities, as does Kirkleigh, which is around 10 kilometres north along the lake's western shore.

Kirkleigh and The Spit also have ramps for launching boats and, whereas you do require a boating permit, you're not restricted to engine size. Lake Somerset is popular for water skiing and ski racing and the sports can adversely affect the fishing (not to mention the tranquillity!) on the main basin in summer. When the outboards are roaring, you can head for the sheltered arms or heavily treed areas of the lake to do your fishing in peace.

Working Wivenhoe Dam

Wivenhoe Dam is 150 kilometres upstream from the mouth of the Brisbane River and is 80 kilometres north west of Brisbane by road.

When full, the backed-up waters of the vast dam extend more than 50 kilometres upstream, all the way to the wall of Somerset Dam.

The large lake is well stocked with Australian bass and produces some exceptionally big specimens. Wivenhoe Dam is an excellent spot to fish for the very large bass during mid-winter, with fish over 2.5 kilos regularly being caught between May and September, both on lures and natural baits such as live shrimps.

Golden perch, eel-tailed and fork-tailed catfish, saratoga, silver perch, banded grunter and large snub-nosed gar are also present in the lake.

Camping facilities are available at Logans Inlet, with limited day access to the public boat ramps and picnic grounds. Despite the enormous size of the lake, fuel-powered outboards are banned, so you have to use an electric motor, oars, paddles or sail to move around the waters, thereby limiting the scope of your fishing.

Checking out Cressbrook and Cooby

Two other important impoundments in the Valley of Lakes are Cressbrook Dam, 40 kilometres west of the town of Esk, and Cooby Dam, between Cressbrook and Toowoomba, near Meringandan. To use a boat and fish on both lakes, you need to have a permit that you can obtain from rangers and local shops.

Cressbrook Dam has a blanket 8-knot speed limit for all craft, but outboard engines are permitted. Boating at Cooby, on the other hand, is limited strictly to vessels powered by electric motors, oars, paddles or sail.

Cressbrook Dam contains mainly golden perch and bass, but the numbers of Mary River cod are increasing.

Cruising Cape York's Crystal Coast

The region of Queensland known as Cape York Peninsula extends northwards from an imaginary line linking the cosmopolitan east coast city of Cairns with the Gulf of Carpentaria.

Beyond Cooktown, the vast wilderness is sparsely populated and largely unspoilt, with few roads and only a scattering of small towns, Aboriginal settlements and pastoral holdings. The major centres are Laura, Musgrave, Coen, Weipa, Bamaga and Seisia, although the term 'major centre' is a tad misleading, as most are little more than villages. To move around most parts of this region, you need to use a four-wheel drive vehicle and limit your travels to the dry season (May–October). For the rest of the year, most travel around Cape York Peninsula is done by air or sea.

Many visitors are attracted to Cape York Peninsula because of the area's extensive fishing opportunities — and few anglers are disappointed! Generally, the standard of estuary and inshore angling improves noticeably as you travel north beyond Cape Melville and Princess Charlotte Bay.

My favourite part of the Cape York region (and my number one fishing spot on Earth) is an area that local charter boat skipper, Greg Bethune, aptly describes as the Crystal Coast. Located on the north-western side of the Cape between the Jardine River and the Skardon River, the region is characterised by long, white, sandy beaches backed by groves of casuarina trees. This beautiful area is also punctuated by short, clear-running rivers lined with dense mangroves in the lower reaches and distinctive nepa palms and paperbark trees further upstream — a truly magical place.

The rivers, beaches, flats and inshore waters of the Crystal Coast offer some of the most exceptional angling opportunities available in the entire country. These areas offer abundant small to medium barramundi, lots of mangrove jacks, fingermark, javelin fish, cod, threadfin salmon, a dozen types of trevally, tarpon, Indo-Pacific permit or snub-nosed dart and, in the higher reaches of the rivers, saratoga, archer fish and sooty grunter.

Around the river mouths and a short distance offshore swim large schools of queenfish, various big trevally, shoals of school and Spanish mackerel, tuna of several types, giant herring, milkfish and cobia. The numerous small reef patches dotting the waters are home to emperor, coral trout, big cod, tropical nannygai (sea perch or snapper) and a dozen or more other species.

The area's remoteness is a major reason for the piscatorial productivity, but creates a significant hurdle for visiting anglers, although many do make the arduous trek by vehicle or boat to the Crystal Coast each dry season.

Fortunately, the stretch of coast from Seisia to Weipa is serviced by a professional live-aboard charter operation called Carpentaria Seafaris, which operates a comfortable mother ship and a fleet of sport fishing dinghies. Carpentaria Seafaris generally uses the catch-and-release method of fishing (refer to Chapter 15) and caters specifically to fly and lure anglers keen to taste the temptations of the pristine waters. A voyage with the charter company doesn't come cheap, but the package represents one of the best value-for-money angling getaways in the tropics.

Carpentaria Seafaris has a website (`www.seafaris.com`), which I recommend you take a look at if you're planning a visit to the area.

Lodging Your Vote for Melville Island

Whereas most of the fishing spots in this chapter are accessible to the do-it-yourself traveller with a car, a tent and a sense of adventure, you can only access a number of other terrific spots by staying at a fishing lodge or a camp. A prime example of this type of fishing spot is Munupi Lodge on the Northern Territory's Melville Island.

When the famous Barra Base fishing lodge on nearby Bathurst Island closed its doors to the public in the mid-1990s, a big hole was left in the top end's guided fishing scene. Over two decades, the Base had become something of an institution among footloose anglers, having hosted hundreds of clients from all over Australia and around the world. For many visitors to the Base, the experience was the first real taste of tropical sport fishing.

Happily, the slack left by Barra Base's demise is neatly filled by the development of Munupi Lodge, situated across the Apsley Strait from Bathurst Island on neighbouring Melville Island.

Enjoying all the comforts of home

Munupi Lodge is a self-contained fishing lodge that accommodates up to a dozen anglers in simple (but comfortable) air-conditioned, donga-style, twin-share cabins. All meals are provided and the casual, central living area has a phone, a television, a video player, a spa and a bar.

Munupi Lodge employs a varying number of professional fishing guides (depending on how many clients are in the camp) and uses big, beamy aluminium runabouts with powerful four-stroke outboard motors to take clients to and from the fishing grounds.

Following the catch-and-release philosophy

Fishing is on the agenda every day at Munupi Lodge and the boat ride to the many creeks, flats, reefs and offshore grounds takes from 15 minutes to an hour-and-a-half. Within this radius, plenty of fishing country exists, and the guides rotate the fishing destinations regularly so no one area becomes over-fished. As the lodge places a heavy emphasis on catch-and-release, the high standard of fishing on offer is easily maintained, although an occasional fingermark (golden snapper), mackerel or barramundi is retained for the evening meal, which usually also includes a few fresh mud crabs.

The fishing schedule at Munupi Lodge varies with the season, the tide cycles and the individual desires and expectations of clients. Regardless of when you head out, however, you're sure to find plenty of small to middling barra in the mangrove-lined creeks and on the shallow mud flats, as well as mangrove jacks, fingermark, cod and a number of large threadfin salmon. Black jewfish are also present in good numbers throughout Apsley Strait, whereas the clearer offshore waters an hour's boat ride to the north offer excellent pelagic action in the form of mackerel, queenfish, trevally, cobia and even the occasional sailfish and small black marlin.

Finding value for money

Any trip to a quality specialist sport fishing lodge such as Munupi Lodge doesn't come cheap but, if you analyse the cost, you soon discover that this type of establishment actually offers surprisingly good value for money as the lodges don't tend to operate at particularly high profit margins.

Package prices for a holiday at Munupi Lodge include the return flight from Darwin, island transfers, accommodation, all meals and fully guided fishing with tackle supplied (if required).

The kind of angling experience offered by a specialist tropical sport fishing lodge such as Munupi Lodge isn't going to suit every angler's desires or budget. However, for the people who dream of fishing in a genuine tropical paradise in comfort and safety, Munupi Lodge may well be the perfect answer. (To find out more about Munupi Lodge, visit www.munupiwildernesslodge.com.)

Roaming West Australia's Kimberley Region

The Kimberley Region lies in the north-west corner of Western Australia and is larger than many European nations. The area's extensive coastline offers myriad angling opportunities, with Broome as the perfect southern gateway and Wyndham or Kununurra offering stepping-off points from the north.

Walking on the Kimberley's Wild Side

The northern part of the Kimberley is the area that extends from the border between the Northern Territory and Western Australia, just east of Kununurra, to about the Prince Regent River, which empties into the St George Basin near the abandoned mission at Kwinana.

The northern Kimberley is a vast and largely uninhabited chunk of land with an extensive and diverse coastline, ranging from the tidal mud flats of the broad Cambridge Gulf to the rocky points and islands of Admiralty Gulf, Cape Voltaire and the Bonaparte Archipelago.

The northern Kimberley region features many magnificent rivers including the Ord, Pentecost, Chamberlain, Berkeley, King George, Drysdale, King Edward, Mitchell and Prince Regent.

Most of the rivers feature deep gorges and strings of isolated or partially isolated freshwater holes along the upper reaches. Many of the holes are only joined together during heavy rainfall periods in the wet season. The mouths of many of the rivers consist of deep natural harbours and wide bays, often studded with islands and reefs.

The entire area provides exceptional fishing. Good numbers of barramundi range up each river system as far as the first impassable waterfall, often using floods to enter isolated lagoons and billabongs that may be cut off from the main river for years at a time. Above the barramundi barriers, you can find sooty, khaki and leathery grunter (called black bream by many locals), as well as chanda perch and catfish.

Further downstream, barramundi are joined by mangrove jacks, fingermark, estuary and gold spot cod, threadfin and blue salmon, pikey bream, tarpon (ox-eye herring), trevally, queenfish, barracuda, long toms, giant herring, javelin fish, black jewfish, sharks and a host of other species far too numerous to list.

Offshore, around the myriad islands and reefs, barramundi are less common, but the other fish already mentioned are joined by coral trout, several types of emperor, wrasse, parrot fish, Spanish and school mackerel, cobia, tuna, larger sharks and the occasional sailfish or small to middling black marlin.

You can explore this remote and sometimes rather challenging country in a range of ways. A few adventurous travellers use four-wheel drive vehicles with boats strapped to the top to gain limited coastal access. Other travellers rely on the organised services of fishing guides, live-aboard charter vessels, mother ships and float plane operations with well-established outpost camps on rivers such as the Drysdale River.

Exploring the Kimberley's south end

The many coastal rivers and major estuary systems between the Fitzroy River and the Prince Regent River — including the May, Meda, Robinson, Isdell, Charnley, Calder and Sale Rivers — offer bountiful barramundi fishing at certain times of the year. Also found in the waterways are abundant numbers of mangrove jacks, fingermark, cod, tarpon, big fork-tailed catfish and, higher upstream, sooty grunter and chanda perch.

Offshore, in King Sound, Strickland Bay, Yampi Sound, Doubtful Bay, Camden Sound and Brunswick Bay, literally hundreds of islands, isolated rocks, bomboras and reef patches exist. These racing tidal waters are home to chopping schools of queenfish, mackerel, trevally, longtail tuna and mackerel tuna (kawa kawa), not to mention prolific reef species including cod, groper, wrasse, emperor, big fingermark and many others.

The coastal town of Derby, which has a population of around 3,500, makes an ideal staging point for any serious exploration of this fascinating and challenging region.

Extending Yourself at Dirk Hartog Island

The ruggedly beautiful Dirk Hartog Island, off the southern tip of Shark Bay, Western Australia, has excellent fishing and a top fishing lodge.

You can reach Dirk Hartog Island by boat or you can fly in on a light aircraft. The island also uses the services of a vehicle ferry that crosses the narrow straits from just north of Steep Point on the mainland.

After arriving at the island, you can choose to stay at Dirk Hartog Island Lodge, which has extremely comfortable digs and memorable five-star meals in gorgeous surroundings, or pitch your tent. Camping is permitted on parts of the island and the camping fee is included in the charge involved in transporting your vehicle and gear across the strait on the ferry.

Dirk Hartog Island is dry and barren, especially in summer, so if you opt to camp and explore the place under your own steam, you need to make sure you have plenty of drinking water and fuel.

Hooking in to the fish

Fishing for pink snapper around Dirk Hartog Island — especially in the relatively shallow waters of Shark Bay — is nothing short of mind-boggling. But the options don't begin and end with the prolific snapper! Sandy beaches and flats that edge much of the island — including the ones right in front of the lodge — are home to countless flathead, whiting, bream, sharks and rays, all of which can be hooked from the shore.

At reef-strewn locations such as Turtle Bay, on the north-east corner of the long, narrow island, the bread-and-butter species mentioned in the preceding paragraph are joined by heavyweight baldchin groper, wrasse, giant herring, trevally, emperor and a host of other species — perhaps even the elusive bonefish from time to time.

On the cliff-lined, wave-pounded west coast of the island, numerous rock ledges exist. These include Charlie's Harbour and The Block, where you can cast baited lines or lures into the deep, blue Indian Ocean in search of everything from red emperor and cod to big Spanish mackerel, shark mackerel, cobia, tuna and even sailfish. You need a special sliding rock gaff to secure most of the fish.

The rock ledges are potentially dangerous because massive swells often roll in and pound the western shoreline. *Note:* Being washed into the water by a receding swell or falling from a ledge here is likely to be a one-way trip!

Boating for variety

A sea-going boat greatly expands your fishing horizons and grants access to a still wider range of potential target species. Just a few kilometres west of Dirk Hartog Island you can, at times, find big marlin, wahoo, dolphin fish and tuna as well as brilliant bottom fishing on the deep reef patches and gravel beds that litter the relatively untouched waters (refer to Chapter 22).

When the wind blows on-shore and the open sea is rough, the eastern side of the island remains relatively sheltered and the pink snapper often bite even harder. In short, you can easily catch a feed at Dirk Hartog Island!

To find out more about visiting Dirk Hartog Island and staying in the lodge or camping out, you can phone (08) 9948 1211, email info@dirkhartogisland.com or visit the island's website (www.dirkhartogisland.com).

Making a Killing at South Australia's Kangaroo Island

Driving into the South Australian port of Cape Jervis, you catch your first glimpse of Kangaroo Island. The bulky island looms on the horizon around 16 kilometres from the mainland across the occasionally turbulent waters of Backstairs Passage. Many visitors are surprised at the size of the island which, at nearly 145 kilometres long and around 32 kilometres wide, makes Kangaroo Island one of Australia's largest offshore islands.

Kangaroo Island (known by many South Australians as *KI*) is home to a string of prosperous rural communities and has a population of close to 4,500 people, most of whom live in the four major settlements of Kingscote, Penneshaw, American River and Parndana.

From estuary bream fishing to medium tackle game angling, Kangaroo Island has plenty to attract the visiting fisher and many keen anglers from all over South Australia and further afield come to the island to sample the sport on offer. While there is plenty of accommodation on the island, it can become heavily booked during major holiday periods, so you need to make reservations in advance at these times. Check out the Kangaroo Island Tourist website (http://bestofkangarooisland.com.au) for suggestions on where to stay.

Sampling the action

Kangaroo Island boasts some of the best and most accessible sea fishing on offer in South Australia, with excellent sport for both shore-bound and boat anglers.

For shore-based anglers, the large wharf at Kingscote is a good starting point for a summer evening's session of catching tommy rough and garfish. You often see snook and squid patrolling the illuminated areas around the jetty in search of a meal after dark, and you can catch these fish on baits, lures or squid jigs. The pier also attracts a few big silver trevally.

American River also has a jetty and the structure attracts tommies, garfish and squid. Nearby, Penneshaw jetty is a good spot for the same species and the small pier in Emu Bay provides plenty of family fun in fishing for roughies and garfish. Penneshaw marina makes an ideal family fishing venue, and provides protection from the wind and swell. It mostly offers mullet and tommies, along with the occasional squid.

Occasionally, you can catch decent-sized King George whiting from the small jetty in Vivonne Bay and, in summer, you can land trevally, tommies, snook and squid.

Large schools of Australian salmon regularly visit the waters around Kangaroo Island. American River and Pemmeshaw are favourite locations for salmon fishers. As a rough rule, the hard-fighting salmon are in peak shape from October to December along the island's west and north coasts; whereas, on the more rugged south side of the island, the salmon tend to bite best from January or February to as late as June.

Fighting with whiting

Kangaroo Island is home to some of the biggest and most prolific King George whiting in Australia, particularly in the area around American River, which is acknowledged as the state's premier whiting ground.

During the warmer months, you can also troll for snook in the bay at American River, with big hauls sometimes on offer. By going a little further offshore, you're almost sure to catch a few snapper, too, and the snapper action has definitely improved since the introduction of the closed season (check out Chapter 26 for local regulations before fishing). Another well-kept secret around American River is the number of tasty sand crabs that call these waters home!

Nepean Bay is another heavily fished area that produces good whiting, snook and the occasional snapper; whereas, Pink Bay, between Cape St Albans and Cape Willoughby, is a great spot for whiting, with the chance of snook or salmon if you troll lures.

The Bay of Shoals, to the north of Kingscote, is sheltered in all but the very worst of weather and is a reliable boat fishing spot for King George whiting as well as snook, salmon, trevally, tommy rough, garfish and squid.

Stokes Bay, on the island's north coast, is another productive location and the bay's inshore sand patches hold lots of big whiting. However, the spot is wide open to weather from the north and boat anglers need to exercise caution in this area.

A number of the island's surf beaches and the adjacent headlands are known to produce mulloway for persistent anglers; whereas, fishing from the rocks (refer to Chapter 19) can be successful for catching sweep, trevally, parrot fish, pike and other species.

The waters around Kangaroo Island are home to more big blue groper than any other location in the state, and Cape du Couedic, on the island's southwest tip, is particularly renowned for the tackle-busting blues. *Note:* Groper are totally protected in Backstairs Passage, between the eastern end of the island and the mainland. (Refer to Chapter 26 for where to check the current regulations for any changes before you fish.)

West Bay, on the shores of Flinders Chase National Park, is another fine rock fishing location, with silver drummer, sweep, salmon, snook and a range of other varieties on offer. However, the weather can make the bay a dangerous spot, so it pays to keep an eye on the daily forecasts.

Trying for bream

I happily give you a little known fact outside of local angling circles — that the estuaries and rivers on Kangaroo Island contain some of the best bream fishing in South Australia.

For southern bream specialists, the estuaries and lower reaches of the Cygnet, Middle and Harriet Rivers are proven locations, often producing a number of extremely large bream, especially when the entrances to the rivers become silted and are closed to the sea for lengthy periods. Whitebait and strips of mullet are the favoured local baits for bream, but other offerings also produce results.

Chapter 28

My Ten Favourite New Zealand Fishing Spots

*T*he beautiful island nation of New Zealand is blessed with an extraordinary array of both salt and freshwater fishing locations, and is even more sparsely populated than most parts of coastal Australia — so, finding a secluded fishing hole all of your own is rarely difficult.

Although New Zealand's angling species' list is a little shorter than Australia's, and New Zealand lacks the tropical latitudes of its larger sister nation, an amazing diversity of fishing opportunities are on offer here, especially by world standards. From the offshore marlin and tuna grounds of the north to the pristine trout rivers of the far south, New Zealand (or Aotearoa, to use the nation's Maori title) boasts an extraordinary standard of recreational angling that is readily accessible and eminently affordable to residents and visitors alike.

From the top ... literally, this chapter overviews ten of my Aotearoa's hottest spots — ten very different fishing locations from the tens of thousands on offer to local and visiting anglers in the Land of the Long White Cloud ... absolutely heaven on earth for anyone who loves to cast a line into pristine, fish-filled waters!

Tough at the Top

The northernmost tip of New Zealand's North Island thrusts deep into the South Pacific Ocean, like the bow of a giant Maori war canoe carving into the cobalt swells. At the very point of this metaphorical canoe's prow lies Cape Reinga and, to its west, North Cape, known to Maori as Otou.

These striking promontories of roughly-hewn rock plunge dramatically into the deep blue sea and provide a stunning backdrop for some of the finest land-based fishing to be found anywhere in New Zealand, if not the world.

Anglers can cast baits or lures from these rocky ledges with a strong expectation of encountering hordes of hungry kahawai (known as Australian salmon across the ditch), silver trevally, blue mao-mao, snapper, parore (luderick or blackfish, in Aussie-speak) and various types of sharks. But one fish stands head and shoulders above all the others in terms of its size, power and desirability, and that prize may well be regarded as the piscatorial icon of these northern Kiwi waters. This wonderful fish is the mighty 'kingie' or yellowtail kingfish.

The biggest yellowtail kingfish in the world are found in New Zealand, and some of the very largest of them frequent the waters between North Cape and the aptly-named Three Kings Islands, to the north west of Cape Reinga.

Kingfish in excess of 25 kilos are far from rare in these clean, blue, temperate seas. Although anglers are likely to encounter the occasional specimen in excess of 35 kilos, landing such a beast (especially from a rock ledge!) is likely to challenge even the most experienced fisher's abilities.

Casting metal lures or jigs, floating/diving minnow-style lures and surface poppers or 'bloopers' is a great way to target small- to mid-sized kingfish (and can also produce plenty of action on kahawai), but rock fishers with a hankering to tackle a true heavyweight king are going to fare much better when drifting out a live bait suspended under a large float consisting of a partially inflated party balloon. The ideal live bait for this task is a 1–2 kilo kahawai (yes, a fish many anglers would be proud to take home and eat in Australia is just 'bait' here!). Big hooks, thick leaders and sturdy tackle (not to mention a strong back!) are required for this caper.

Speaking of a strong back, you also need strong legs and reasonably sure feet clad in good boots to reach many of the better rock ledges in this part of the world, because most of the prime spots lie at the end of long hikes over steep ground. However, reaching these special places is definitely worth the effort.

While quite remote from 'civilisation', excellent camping is available at Spirit Bay and basic shopping is on offer in Paua, Waitiki Landing and Te Hapua, on nearby Parengarenga Harbour (a wonderful fishing venue in its own right, with vast expanses of shallow sand flats intersected by deeper channels). A holiday at the pointy end of New Zealand comes with a healthy recommendation for anyone who loves catching big fish from the ocean rocks.

A Bay Full of Islands

New Zealand's Bay of Islands is famous throughout the international game fishing world for the calibre of offshore angling available out beyond the well known and heavily-photographed 'Hole in the Rock', located at the tip of craggy Cape Brett.

From late-November until at least April or early May each year, warm currents from the sub-tropical north swirl southwards and lick the picturesque coastline around the Bay of Islands. These currents carry three species of marlin (blue, black and striped), several species of tuna, various sharks and even occasional exotic visitors such as spearfish, mahi-mahi (dolphin fish) and wahoo.

Earning your stripes

The prolific game fishing grounds outside the Bay of Islands are best known internationally for their striped marlin. This highly-prized species occurs here seasonally (mostly in summer and autumn) in greater numbers and larger average sizes than just about anywhere else on earth, attracting a large fleet of local charter boats as well as private sport fishing vessels from around the country and across the globe. Many of the world records for striped marlin on various line classes (line strengths) have been set here.

While you can catch striped marlin on live and dead baits that you drift on the current or troll (drag) behind a slowly moving boat, the majority fall for colourful, resin-headed, plastic- or rubber-skirted trolling lures, commonly called *pushers*. You're best to trail in a pattern or *spread* anywhere from four to seven or even eight of these bubble-making lures (each attached to a separate rod and reel) behind a boat moving at 6 to 10 knots. Sometimes multiple hook-ups result and pandemonium reigns when two or three marlin in excess of 100 kilos apiece are hooked simultaneously from one boat!

Inside story

Of course, Bay of Islands' fishing isn't only about big boats and leaping marlin or deeply sounding tuna. Small boat and even shore-based anglers are extremely well catered for by the deep, protected waters that lie within the bay and surround its myriad small islands.

Here, within the vast bay, anglers can expect to encounter kahawai, snapper, kingfish, trevally, John Dory, mao-mao and sharks, to name just some of the potential target species on offer.

The twin towns of Paihia and Russell, separated by a short stretch of deep water and linked by regular ferry services, offer anything the visiting angler could desire — from accommodation and good food to charter fishing services. The historic game fishing club in Russell and its vast collection of photographs and other angling memorabilia is also well worth a visit.

Auckland for Anglers

New Zealand's buzzing, cosmopolitan 'City of Sails' not only offers all the glitz and glamour of a major metropolis and international tourism hub — but is also a mighty fine destination for travelling anglers!

Situated on a relatively narrow neck of land between two vast bays (Hauraki Gulf to the east and north, and Manukau Harbour to the west and south), Aucknd is effectively surrounded by water. Hardly surprising, then, that so many of the city's residents (and a fair proportion of visitors) enjoy casting a line.

Whether you use Auckland as a staging point to explore fishing opportunities further afield in New Zealand, or go fishing right on the city's watery doorstep, you're unlikely to leave for home disappointed.

Of Auckland's two girdling waterways, Hauraki Gulf is the better known for its fishing; and, without a doubt, the most popular target species swimming in the vast Gulf are the abundant snapper.

Kiwis are crazy about their 'snipper' (if you pardon a little good-natured jibe from one nation of vowel-manglers to another!). These pink-flanked, blue-spotted beauties are certainly prized for their appearance and strength when hooked on a line; but, most of all, snapper are valued for their delicious eating qualities, whether prepared to five-star-restaurant standards with all the sauces and garnishes imaginable, or served as simple 'fush and chups' (okay, I'm gunna stop now).

Hauraki Gulf snapper run the gamut of sizes from undersized throw-backs and plate-proportioned 'eaters' to 10-kilo-plus monsters. As a general rule, numbers are higher but average sizes smaller in summer, with the reverse applying in winter. The shoulder periods of spring and autumn offer a fine mix of quality and quantity and many keen Gulf anglers regard these times as the best to pursue a snapper or three close to Auckland.

In addition to snapper, Hauraki Gulf is home to John Dory, kahawai, kingfish, piper (garfish), parore (luderick), trevally and several types of sharks. In the shallower, greener, often choppy waters of Manukau Harbour is the same general mix of species; although, this waterway tends to be less heavily-fished than the Gulf.

Plenty On Offer

Bounded by the Coromandel Peninsula and Mercury Islands to the west and by Cape Runaway and East Cape to the east, New Zealand's Bay of Plenty is a massive stretch of coastline facing north into the open waters of the vast Pacific Ocean. Effectively acting as a giant bucket to catch the swirls and eddies of the warm, sub-tropical currents that sweep down the east coast of the North Island every summer and autumn, the aptly named Bay of Plenty is a veritable bucket full of fish, too!

Serviced by the coastal ports and charter boat fleets of Whitianga, Tairua, Whangamata, Tauranga, Whakatane and Opotiki, the Bay of Plenty is an offshore anglers' paradise. Further out from shore, marlin, tuna and sharks swim in good numbers during the warmer months of the year, feeding on massive schools of baitfish; while, closer in, hapuka, kahawai, kingfish, moki, silver trevally, snapper and tarakihi dominate anglers' catches throughout the year.

Surf and rock anglers also fare well in this part of New Zealand's North Island, with kahawai and snapper being the two most popular targets for shore-based casters.

White Island (known as Whakaari in Maori) dominates the central portion of the Bay of Plenty. The island's volcanic cone is New Zealand's most active geological feature, almost constantly belching sulfurous smoke into the sky to create a plume visible from great distances on a clear day. Occasionally, the volcano erupts with considerably greater violence, shooting ash, rocks and pumice high into the air and creating an eerie red glow at night.

Just like its volcano, the standard of sport and game fishing action around White Island can also be red hot at times. In late-summer and early-autumn, these waters frequently play host to an event known to local anglers and charter boat skippers as 'meatballs'.

At these times, dolphins and various game fish (including sharks, striped marlin and yellowfin tuna) herd abundant bait fish (mackerel, pilchards and the like) into tight orbs or balls on the ocean's surface before mowing into them with mouths agape, tails flailing and gills flaring as they gorge on the hapless small fry.

This spectacular event is not only a wonderful natural phenomenon to observe, it also provides world-class offshore fishing. The timing and frequency of this amazing meatball action can be difficult to predict in advance, but anglers who get it right certainly never forget the experience.

Taupo Temptations

Lake Taupo, in the centre of New Zealand's North Island, is a massive and incredibly deep lake that was formed by a cataclysmic volcanic eruption many millennia ago. Some 30 rivers and streams empty from the surrounding mountains into Lake Taupo, while the mighty Waikato River is the only outlet from this virtual inland sea of freshwater.

Lake Taupo and its tributaries are home to huge numbers of rainbow and brown trout, and represent a freshwater angling mecca, attracting tourists from around the world. Trout taken here by anglers average around 1.4 to 1.6 kilos apiece, although much larger fish are also found in the lake and surrounding rivers. Trophy trout of well over 7 kilos are caught each year.

Several tributaries on the more accessible eastern side of Lake Taupo are especially famous in fly-fishing circles, providing excellent fishing, especially from mid-autumn until spring. The best known and most popular of these are: the Hinemaiaia River, the Tauranga-Taupo River, the mighty Tongariro River, the Waimarino River and the Waiatahanui River. Many of the smaller tributaries also provide good fishing.

Lake Taupo is easily accessed, with State Highway 1 running the length of the eastern shoreline. A 20-metre wide public right-of-way also extends around most of the lake shore, and this ready access is a real boon to shore-bound anglers.

The town of Turangi, situated at the southern end of the lake and right on the famous Tongariro River, makes a great base for any exploration of this fish-rich region.

The most popular method for fishing in the lake itself is trolling (dragging a lure or fly behind a slowly-moving boat), often with the aid of a special, weighted line or a device called a downrigger. In most of the rivers entering the lake, only fly-fishing is permitted.

One of the wonderful things about Lake Taupo and many of its tributaries is they offer year-round, trout-fishing action that suits many different styles of angling.

During the winter and spring months, huge numbers of big trout enter all the rivers and make their way upstream to spawn. These months are the time of year when the Taupo district is most famous in fishing circles. Trout enter the rivers in prime condition, and anglers regularly catch genuine trophy size fish.

The river and stream mouths are popular fishing locations at these times. Fish tend to move up into the rivers after a heavy rainfall or snow melt causes the rivers to rise (a phenomenon called a *fresh*). As the water drops and clears after such a fresh during the winter months, the fly-fishing can be superb.

Summer and early autumn can also offer excellent fishing on and around Lake Taupo. In early summer, the *smelting season* (a time when small, slender bait fish are abundant in the shallower margins) coincides with the return of spawning fish to the lake — a time to experience some exciting fishing around the edges of the lake. You can catch large trout either fishing from the shore, or by trolling (sometimes called *harling* in this part of the world) a lure or fly that resembles a smelt.

Later in the summer, many trout tend to move out into deeper water, where you may need weighted lines and downriggers to reach them consistently. However, you can also take advantage of some excellent dry fly-fishing for resident stream trout in the various rivers at this time.

Fishing is allowed all year round on Lake Taupo, except for the Taupo Wharf, Taupo boat jetties and the control gates over the Waikato River at Taupo, which are closed to fishing at all times. At the time of writing, the daily bag limit in this region was three trout per angler and the minimum legal length was set at 40 centimetres. Check out Chapter 26 for how to keep up to date on current regulations before you fish.

The Excellent Eg'

The first of my South Island Kiwi hot spots is the mouth of the Eglinton River. The Eglinton is a delightful freestone river that runs for a good part of its length parallel to Highway 94, the busy tourist route linking the tourist hub of Te Anau to picturesque Milford Sound. The river itself offers superb fishing for both brown and rainbow trout.

To reach the Eglinton's mouth, drive north along Highway 94 from Te Anau towards Milford Sound. At Te Anau Downs (about 30 kilometres out of Te Anau) you see a well-signposted entrance to the small boat harbour and launching ramp. At the back (northern) side of the car park is a fairly nondescript-looking gravel track. Enter this and follow it for several kilometres. Take care on this narrow, twisting and overgrown track because the way through offers very little room to manoeuvre should you encounter an approaching vehicle. Eventually the track brings you out on the southern side of the river mouth, an easy walk from the delta.

One of my favourite parts of the Eg' (as those who know the spot call it) is the delta mouth where the river discharges into vast Lake Te Anau. Though the exact shape and character of this confluence changes with the seasons and the passage of mighty floods, usually, three or four braided entrance channels run swiftly over gravel and pebble bars before emptying into the blue-green depths of the lake. Long current rips, slicks and bubble lines form off these mouths, which are favoured areas with local trollers.

For fishing the Eg' mouth, you're best to carefully wade into these outflow channels and cast out into the lake itself.

Be especially cautious when wading in the channels of the Eglington River, because the water is deeper than it looks and very cold, and the loose pebbles underfoot can slide or give way at any moment, potentially spilling you into the deep water of the lake.

This river is a wonderful spot for casting lures such as spoons, minnows and soft plastics, but reasonably large wet flies and streamers fished on a sinking fly line work just fine, too. Try to cast out and across the current rips at various angles, getting your offering well down before commencing a retrieve. Be especially alert for hits where the lake bed suddenly shelves up ... and hang on! The rainbows here, in particular, hit like steam trains. Don't overlook the shallower, sandy edges and lake backwaters to the south and east of the mouth, either. Some big browns cruise these spots at times.

At the time of writing, the Eglington River is designated as 'fly only' water, so you're best to check out the latest regulations — refer to Chapter 26 for suggested websites that can bring you up to date.

Pick of the Upuk'

Despite this river's long name, the Upukerora or Upuk' is a small river by Kiwi standards. It enters the waters of Lake Te Anau just a few kilometres north of the town of Te Anau, not far off Highway 94. Take the exit just short of the bridge and follow a reasonably good gravel track between the river and a sewage farm (seriously!) down to the lake shore. Some locals ford the river in their vehicles when the water level appears sufficiently low for crossing, but visitors, especially if driving hire cars are advised to park on the shore 80 metres or so short of the delta mouth and walk the gravelly edge, casting as you approach the river outflow.

In many ways this Upuk' is a scaled-down version of the Eglinton mouth (refer to the preceding section), and you can approach fishing this river in exactly the same way. However, unlike the Eg' mouth, which can produce action at any time of the day, the Upukerora mouth seems to fish most consistently at dawn and dusk, or whenever there is a sudden flush of fresh water down the stream following local rain.

You can carefully wade into the outflow and, on many days, easily cross it, but be careful of sudden increases in river discharge.

Cast lures or wet flies out and across the current rips and fish this little gem just like the Eg' mouth ... safe in the knowledge, as the sun sinks behind the mountains, that the pleasant bars and restaurants of Te Anau are only 15 minutes away!

Pomahaka Perfection

The Pomahaka is a tributary of the mighty Clutha River and flows through a mix of undulating farmland and more rugged, rocky country to the north of the town of Gore. You can reach the stretch that I'm most familiar with by leaving Gore on Highway 1, travelling towards Dunedin, then turning left onto Highway 90 at McNab, fewer than 5 kilometres out of Gore. After following this road for a bit over 25 kilometres, you cross a bridge over a relatively wide, slow-flowing stretch of the Pomahaka, which is a spot well suited to dry fly-fishing. However, if you prefer, you can continue on over the bridge some distance before taking the Duncan Road exit on the left and then a turn-off marked 'Waikaka 24 km'. A kilometre or two later you cross the Pomahaka again, further upstream than the first bridge crossing. Just over the bridge, turn right into a parking area and angler access point.

Fly fishers are best to take extra care when fishing their way upstream from the access point. For several kilometres, the thick willows lining the river in many places make casting extremely tricky.

Casting either lures or flies work a treat in this waterway, which is dominated by brown trout in the 1–2.5 kilo range. Bigger fish do occur, too, and the occasional spawn-run quinnat (chinook) salmon makes it this far upstream in late-February and March.

The Pomahaka proves especially appealing and strangely familiar to Aussie anglers who've cut their teeth on local rivers like the Goulburn, upper Murray, Tumut and Murrumbidgee. Similar tactics work here, too, although the fish are a little larger and more abundant on this lovely Kiwi river.

Staircase to Heaven

Staircase Creek is a great little spot for trout. Though often overlooked by most anglers travelling in New Zealand's southland, this staircase is definitely worth checking out! You find Staircase Creek located on the main road (Highway 6) linking Lumsden to Queenstown. Not long after passing the picturesque town of Kingston (home of the historic Kingston Flyer steam train), you begin crossing a series of tiny creeks cascading down the steep mountainside to empty into the tail of massive Lake Wakatipu. One of these off shoots is Staircase Creek — clearly revealed by a sign at the bridge.

Immediately after crossing the bridge when heading towards Queenstown, turn left into the small parking area beside the creek. Though just 50 or 60 metres of ankle to shin-deep creek lies between the bridge and the lake edge, you're best to ignore this stretch and, instead, walk directly to the mouth, where the creek waters empty out over a rocky bar straight into the aquamarine depths of the big lake.

Don't be too keen to start hurling your lure or fly out towards the far shore of the lake. Instead, work a few cautious, short casts carefully through the broken rocks of the creek mouth itself, gradually fanning out to include more and more lake water in each presentation. Some big fish lurk here at times, with browns, rainbows and land-locked salmon all on the hit list.

Staircase Creek isn't a location worth spending hours at. Twenty or thirty casts should tell you if anyone is home.

Gem of a Creek

Diamond Creek is one of those very special Kiwi trout fishing gems that tends not to get talked about too widely — for several very good reasons. Firstly, this spot is a small waterway that feels crowded with two other anglers on it. For another, Diamond Creek is a place that fishing fans tend to keep quiet about, in their desire not to attract those other two anglers who would constitute a crowd!

Diamond is part of a braided network of rivers and creeks flowing into the head of Lake Wakatipu, north west of the town of Glenorchy. You get to this creek by driving up the Rees Valley, then turning left to cross the various strands of the Rees River, often clouded with suspended, greyish-green glacial particles.

You know when you reach Diamond Creek because it presents as a much different waterway to the other rivers in this valley. Diamond looks like a classic spring or chalk stream, with clear water and dense, waving tresses of lush aquatic weed separated by narrow strips of open gravel bed.

Generally regarded as being more suited to flies than lures, Diamond Creek also lends itself to fishing with micro-jigs and weighted flies cast off light spinning tackle.

While resident fish are present all year, March and April is the time that the numbers of large brown trout and land-locked quinnat salmon really climb, as spawners begin moving up out of the lake. The browns can run anywhere from a half a kilo to more than 4 kilos, while the salmon are mostly under the kilo mark.

You can park at the bridge and walk upstream for a good half day's fishing before you reach the shallow, marshy waters of a small lake. Checking the margins of this lake for cruisers before turning for home is also a good bet.

Chapter 29

Ten Things No-One
Ever Tells You about Fishing

*Y*ou can dramatically improve your catch rate and increase your enjoyment of the sport by simply making sure you soak in the ten apparently insignificant tips included in this chapter.

No other fishing how-to text clearly spells out the following top tips that I believe are going to make the cost of *Fishing For Dummies,* Australian & New Zealand Edition, a sure investment.

Letting It All Hang Out

The biggest single mistake made by novice anglers has absolutely nothing to do with casting ability, how a knot is tied or a bait rigged (most people master these basics fairly quickly). Instead, the most common error made by novices is one that you may never even think of, let alone read about in how-to books. Let me explain . . .

Next time you see an angler — especially an angler who's using a rod longer than 2.5 metres — watch closely as he or she winds in the line to check the bait or land a small fish. My bet is that two out of every three people you watch bring the line and hook to within centimetres of the tip of the rod (and often to the point that the sinker or swivel is practically jammed into the top runner). By winding the rig in this far, the hook or lure and anything attached to the hook are several metres away from the angler's body ... and totally out of reach.

Saving time and motion

After bringing the rig to the top of the rod, the same angler's next move is completely predictable: The angler drops the butt of the rod onto the ground and walks to the end of the rod to put on new bait or unhook a fish. Chances are that this move means the reel ends up in, or at least very close to, the sand, dirt or water — not a good look! Even more importantly, the sequence is incredibly inefficient (and any passing time-and-motion expert is sure to have an attack of apoplexy). Over the course of a long day's fishing, the novice angler is bound to walk a couple of hundred metres from one end of the fishing rod to the other, wasting plenty of good fishing time!

Worse still, if the novice angler can reach the hook by stretching a hand way up towards the rod tip, the first thing he or she usually does is to pull the hook down to eye level. This action puts a terrible bend in the tip of the rod (and may even break the rod). At the same time, the line may slip out of the novice's grasp, allowing the flexed rod to unbend at great speed, possibly planting a hook or lure firmly into a finger, hand, arm, chin or (heaven forbid!) an eye.

Putting safety first

Experienced anglers handle the same simple task in a much safer and more convenient manner. He or she automatically stops winding the reel at the point where the length of the line outside the rod tip roughly equals the distance between the reel and the top of the rod (as Figure 29-1 shows). At this point, the expert raises the rod to a vertical position and the rig, bait or little hooked fish swings straight in at about chest height, where the rig is easily and safely handled. The system works just as well with a 2-metre rod as with one of 4.5 metres in length.

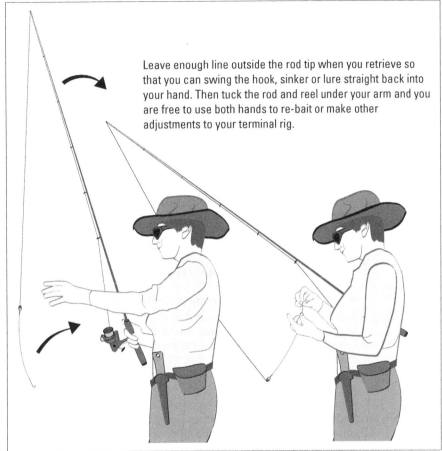

Leave enough line outside the rod tip when you retrieve so that you can swing the hook, sinker or lure straight back into your hand. Then tuck the rod and reel under your arm and you are free to use both hands to re-bait or make other adjustments to your terminal rig.

Figure 29-1: Leave enough line hanging outside the rod tip so you can easily reach your hook or lure.

Coming to Grips with Snags

In the late 1980s, the word 'snag' was an over-used acronym for sensitive new age guy. Long before that, however, *snag* was a term used by anglers to mean an object (other than a fish) that your hook, lure or fly becomes attached to while fishing. In angling, getting a snag definitely doesn't mean snaffling a savoury sausage off the barbie — it means finding that your hook is stuck and refuses to budge.

Being snagged is an unavoidable part of the fishing process. After all, hooks are designed to stick into objects and as a result the little metal gadgets often stick into the wrong type of objects, such as logs, rocks, trees, car seat covers and cows (yep, I once even caught a slab of walking beef!).

Even the experts become snagged from to time to time, so the best approach is to learn how to deal with being snagged:

- **Don't:** As soon as you feel the resistance of a snag, you must avoid the temptation to pull and jerk on the line. Jerking the line simply serves to bury the hook point all the way in past the barb, making it even more difficult to remove the hook from the snag.

- **Do:** Try bouncing or jiggling your hook free of a snag with a little bit of clever rod work.

- **Do:** If jiggling the hook free fails, try changing the angle of your position compared to the snag and then bounce the rod tip or gently pull on the line again. If you're in a boat, moving to another position is relatively easy, but even on the shore, you can often find enough space to walk up and down while jiggling and softly tugging the line.

Jiggling and wiggling

If all this jiggling, wiggling, tugging, pulling, cajoling and changing of angles (accompanied by a suitable amount of cursing, swearing and pleading) fails to free the hook from the snag, then what? You may be terminally snagged, which is a pun I'm particularly pleased with, considering that hooks and sinkers are called terminal tackle. Understand? Hmm. Never mind — you're nearing the end of the book now.

As you become more experienced at dealing with snags, you're bound to find that the process becomes automatic and you quickly decide whether a particular snag is a hopeless case or not. If you can't remove the hook, you need to break the line and start all over again with a new rig.

Struggling and tugging

You can break the line in two ways — the right way or the wrong way:

- **Wrong way:** Rip the rod back into a deep bend, then huff and puff and haul away until something gives. Something is sure to give all right — and chances are that your expensive rod does break. Ouch!

- **Right way:** Point the rod directly down the line at the snag, reel in any slack (until the reel's drag starts to slip), grasp the reel's spool firmly with your hand so that the spool is unable to spin, turn your head away from the snag and walk slowly backwards until the line snaps.

You must turn your head away as soon as you begin to increase tension on the line. Even the most tenacious snag can suddenly let go under great pressure and a sinker, lure or hook flying back through the air at a rate approaching the speed of sound (well, almost) is a potentially lethal weapon. Suffice to say that I've met at least a couple of one-eyed anglers who failed to observe this simple precaution.

If you're using extremely strong line (especially the gel-spun polyethylene or GSP lines I describe in Chapter 4), you may have a tougher time breaking the line by using the preceding method. If this is the case, instead of using the rod to break the line, wrap a towel around your hand or put on a glove, put several wraps of line around your hand and give the line a firm, steady tug. With luck, you can break the line at the knot attaching the line to the hook, thus keeping most of the line. If this method also fails, you can cut the line with a knife, but avoid doing this if you can because it means losing a lot of expensive line and leaves lengths of line in the environment, where the stuff can ensnare birds and other wildlife.

Taming the Hook

Another little tip that helps you to save time and avoid potential injuries is to make sure that every time you move between fishing spots or stow your rod and reel in a car or on board a boat, the hook, fly or lure on the end of your line is secured and can't swing free.

The easiest way to secure a swinging hook is to hang the hook on the frame or ring of a rod runner and turn the reel's handle until the line is taut, but not tight. Don't keep cranking until the tip of your rod resembles the top half of a question mark — another wonderful way to snap a rod!

The most convenient runner to attach your hook, lure or fly to is the runner closest to the reel (this runner is called the *stripping guide*, as I explain in Chapter 5). The stripping guide is the largest runner and the easiest to reach when you're holding the rod in the normal casting or fishing position.

A number of rod styles have special little hook keepers attached to the shafts or blanks just ahead of the rod's top handle or foregrip. If your rod has a hook keeper, learn the habit of using the device for the purpose the design intended.

Hooking a Human

As I mention elsewhere, fish hooks have a nasty habit of becoming stuck in objects that don't look good on the grill and the three-pointed treble hooks found on many lures are three times as likely to become snagged as ordinary hooks.

Banishing barbs

A fact of life is that if you fish for long enough, you're bound to end up hooking either yourself or someone else. The prime time for a hook to end up attached to a body is during the casting process, at the baiting-up stage and — most common of all — while attempting to unhook kicking, struggling, flapping fish. Incredibly, I also see people (other people, you understand, I'm definitely not talking about myself here!) sit on lures or flies — a particularly embarrassing way (and place) to become hooked (or so I'm told).

Crushing the barbs on your hooks (refer to Chapter 15) greatly reduces the pain and trauma associated with finding a hook stuck in yourself or someone else. No matter how deeply a barbless or de-barbed hook penetrates human flesh, you can relatively easily pull that hook out again. Barbed hooks are a very different story.

Barbs are designed to make hook removal difficult and the design works especially well in tough human skin and tissue. Take this gem from me — embedding a barbed hook deeply in your anatomy isn't a pleasant experience.

If you, or someone you're fishing with, ends up with one or more barbed hooks deeply embedded, the best course of action is to go to a doctor's surgery or hospital outpatients' ward as quickly as possible. This action is especially critical if the hook is located anywhere near the victim's eyes or major blood vessels.

Removing hooks from people

When fishing, chances are you may be quite a distance from a doctor or a hospital, particularly if you're fishing off the beaten track or far out at sea. Fortunately, you can remove a barbed hook from flesh in a relatively painless way, but the method must only be used if the hook is embedded in soft tissue well away from the eyes, blood vessels, nerves and bones.

Never — and I repeat never — attempt the following technique on hooks embedded in a potentially sensitive area.

To remove a single hook or one point of a treble hook from a person's hand, finger, leg, foot or buttocks, take the following steps:

1. **Cut the line at the eye of the hook or remove the hook from a lure (if the hook is fitted to a lure).**

   The best tools for cutting the line are either a pair of scissors or clippers, while you may require side cutters or strong pliers to cut the split ring holding a hook to a lure.

2. **Find a piece of strong line 50–80 centimetres in length.**

   The line can be strong cord or thick fishing line of at least 15-kilo breaking strain.

3. **Knot the ends of the line securely together to form a sturdy loop.**

4. **Place the loop of line through the bend of the hook and grasp it with your dominant hand (see Figure 29-2).**

   As you do this, talk calmly to the victim to put the person at ease.

5. **Press down firmly on the eye or shank of the hook with the fingers of your free hand (see Figure 29-2), while allowing a small amount of slack to form in the loop of line.**

6. **Using a sudden, strong jerk, rip the hook out with the loop of line.**

The process of removing a hook in this way sounds a little barbaric but, believe me, the method works like a charm (as long as you don't hesitate at the critical moment) when you use a fast, strong snap of the cord to literally flick the hook free. A neat little trick is to tell the patient that you're going to count to three then pull the hook out, but then actually whip the hook free on the count of two, before the patient tenses up in anticipation.

I know and have used this method of hook removal many, many times and I've been the patient on at least six occasions. The process always works flawlessly and a number of doctors are now adopting the method as a less obtrusive and painful alternative to cutting a hook out of someone's flesh with a scalpel or pushing the point right through and back out of the skin before cutting it off (which can be excruciatingly painful, especially without an anaesthetic).

Only use the preceding method of hook removal from a person if the hook is embedded in a non-sensitive area of soft tissue. If you do use the method to remove a hook, make sure the patient sees a doctor as soon as possible after the event to have the wound checked and, if necessary, have a tetanus booster shot.

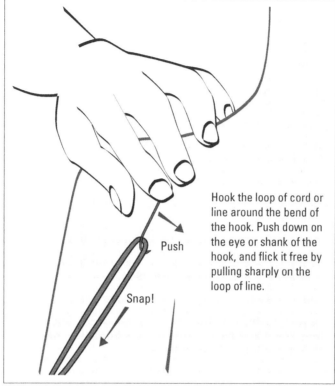

Figure 29-2:
Removing a
hook from
someone's
hand, finger,
arm or leg
using this
method is
relatively
easy and
painless.

Push

Snap!

Hook the loop of cord or
line around the bend of
the hook. Push down on
the eye or shank of the
hook, and flick it free by
pulling sharply on the
loop of line.

Targeting One Species

Targeting a particular fish species or small group of species every time you
go fishing is sure to bring you better results than using a lottery method.
Say to yourself: 'I'm going after flathead and bream today' or 'I'm going to
fish for barramundi tomorrow'.

All too often, anglers employ what I call the scattergun mentality. Ask an
angler what type of fish he or she is trying to catch and the answer is likely
to be: 'Whatever comes along'. The problem with this method is that the
hooks may be too big or too small for most of the desirable fish in the area
or the chosen bait is about as attractive to the fish as a bath is to a cat.

Pick a species, learn that fish's habits, rig your gear together accordingly,
select a bait you know the species enjoys, choose an area where that fish
is known to live and then go fishing for that species. It's not rocket science,
but the method definitely makes a difference.

Oh, and if you catch something else altogether, you can always lie and say you were after that exact fish in the first place (see my last point in the section 'Lying for a Living!', later in this chapter)!

Doubling Your Money

Experienced anglers say that the best time to catch a fish is within 2 to 5 minutes of catching a fish! No, the theory isn't a trick or a riddle. The meaning of the phrase is that the exact set of conditions that conspired to put that first fish on your line are likely to prevail for at least a few minutes. This narrow window of opportunity presents a much better than average chance of hooking another fish ... and perhaps another and another after that.

Part of the reason for this phenomenon is that many species of fish swim in schools, but other factors also provide a window of success. The factors include the state of the tide, the temperature of the water, the angle of the sun and the presence of food, which may all be at an optimum level for just a short period every day. The motto is that you need to strike while the iron's hot!

In other words, as soon as you land one fish, don't sit around congratulating yourself or reliving the event. Put some new bait on the hook, or check your lure or fly and send the line straight back into the water and see if your first catch has some mates. My bet is that the mates do exist and you have every chance of landing a brace of the critters.

Repeating Productive Patterns

Putting your line back into the water straight after catching a fish is a matter of repeating a successful pattern and this repetition of patterns turns out to be a vitally important key to success in all styles of angling.

Certain conditions of tide, weather, water clarity, temperature, time of day and season produce certain results. Some results are good, whereas some results are bad. One of the great secrets to becoming a consistently successful angler is the ability to recognise and repeat successful patterns and avoid less successful patterns. Successful anglers don't necessarily fish harder or longer — the experts just fish smarter.

For example, if you catch a beautiful bag of snapper at high tide on the day before the full moon at a certain place in November, chances are you can emulate the feat this November. At the very least, you're crazy if you don't try!

One of the best ways to identify and repeat patterns is to keep a fishing diary or logbook. The following are the types of entries you need to make in your journal:

- ✔ The date and time that you go fishing
- ✔ The weather conditions
- ✔ The type of bait, lure or fly you use
- ✔ The species and approximate size of every fish that you catch

Be sure to record every single fishing trip, not just the successful ones, because, just as importantly, you can identify and avoid unsuccessful fishing patterns as well as repeat successful patterns.

Your journal is sure to make a huge difference to your success rate, but remember that the unexpected can happen. Cycles are broken and excellent results can sometimes be experienced when the indications are the opposite, whereas perfect conditions may fail to pay dividends. Over the long haul, however, by repeating a successful fishing pattern, you're more likely to bring in good catches. Learn to spot the positive patterns and soon you can call yourself a graduate from the school of danglers to the elite group of anglers (refer to Chapter 18).

Taking the Good with the Bad

A number of angling books and magazines make fishing sound as if the sport is ridiculously easy. In many cases, the publications suggest that all you need to do to start hauling 'em in is to drop your line into the water. Anglers with selective memories reinforce the notion with tales of red-letter days and photo albums packed with snapshots of amazing catches. Television fishing shows are even worse.

Honest, experienced anglers tell you the real story: Fishing isn't always an easy sport and the fish don't always bite, even in perfect circumstances with exactly the right gear. The wind often blows, rain often falls and your fish bag sometimes remains empty. None of us is immune to a visit from the *skunk* (being *skunked* is hip fishing parlance for catching nothing ... zip ... zilch ... nada ... nought).

Accept the fact that the sport of fishing involves dealing with the uncertain forces of nature and the vagaries of wild creatures that often defy the best attempts at human logic and reasoning. As much as you try to turn fishing into a science, the grey areas are sure to persist. Fishing with a line and a hook is part art, part mystery and part lottery. You can't always win and, if you did, the pastime would be called catching rather than fishing — with precious little pleasure to be had.

Lying for a Living!

Last, but certainly not least, remember that most anglers are liars! Even the best of us bend the truth a little at times by stretching the size of prize catches, fudging the numbers of the biggest bags and talking up the best fishing days. Anglers just don't seem to be able to help a touch of the fantastic and the great majority of the breed thrives on exaggeration.

You need to bear this fact in mind when anglers tell you stories or offer tips and advice on where they go fishing or what bait is best. Listen politely and take the offerings on board, but retain a healthy modicum of scepticism. After all, you fudge the truth when you answer the same questions put to you ... don't you? No?

If you still don't believe that all anglers occasionally tell fibs, try this little exercise: Look back over this chapter and count how many priceless, previously unpublished tips I give you in this collection of the ten most important things no-one ever tells you about fishing.

See, I told you!

Glossary

T erms appearing in **bold italic** type are defined elsewhere in the glossary.

adipose: a small, meaty fin between the dorsal fin and tail of some fish (including trout and salmon).

angle: olde English name for a fancy bent or curved *gorge*, or hook and the word from which the name of the sport of fishing (angling) is derived.

angled point: a point on a hook that isn't in line with the *shank* and *eye*, also known as a *kirb or offset*.

anti-reverse: a mechanism that immobilises the handles of a reel as the line is pulled from the *spool*, preventing the handles from rotating backwards.

arbor: the centre or core of a reel's *spool*.

Archimedean screw: the *level-wind mechanism* in a *baitcaster reel* is driven by an Archimedean screw that turns and drives the line carrier as the *spool* rotates.

back plate: the rear face of a *sidecast reel* or *centrepin reel*, with a reel foot attached for mounting to the rod.

backing: line or some other material placed on a *spool* underneath the main line load when joining old line to new line for *top-shotting* a reel.

backlashes. *See* over-runs.

bail arm. *See also*, rotor head. A component in a *threadline* or spinning reel.

bail roller. *See also*, rotor head. A component in a *threadline* or spinning reel.

bait eggs: a man-made bait made from flavoured gelatine or other soft material.

bait feeder reel. *See* bait runner reel.

bait runner (or bait feeder) reel: a style of *spinning reel* with a *free-spool* facility, especially useful when bait fishing for species that are more easily and securely hooked when these fish are allowed to swim off some distance with the bait before the angler attempts to strike or *set* the hook.

baitcaster (or plug) reel: a small to medium revolving drum overhead reel, usually fitted with a *level-wind mechanism*.

bait-holders: a type of hook pattern with barbs on the back of the *shank*.

balanced tackle: a kit where all the items of tackle in your fishing gear set-up match each other.

ball: a common *sinker* shape; spherical with a central line channel.

barb: a sharp projection on the hook to stop it from slipping out of the fish's mouth.

barbless: a style of hook without a barb used in *catch-and-release* angling.

bareboat: a boat for hire that isn't supplied with skipper or crew.

barra of the south: a nick name for the Australian estuary perch.

barrel: a common *sinker* shape.

bars (or riffles, or rapids): the shallower, faster stretches of a stream.

beam: the width of a vessel.

bean: a common *sinker* shape.

belly: a term that describes the loose line between the rod tip and the water.

bend: the curved or bent section of the hook.

berley: a bait mixture distributed in the water to attract and excite fish.

berley trail. *See also* berley. Fish oils that form a visible surface slick, which can stretch for kilometres, used to attract fish from far and wide.

bib: a diving lip at the front of a plug or minnow, which imparts a swimming action to the moving *lure* and makes it dive beneath the surface of the water.

billy club (or priest): a traditional, small club used for killing fish, especially trout and salmon.

Bimini twist: an extremely strong (but rather complicated) type of *double* knot.

biodegradable: a term used to describe a product that breaks down cleanly (and in a defined time frame) to molecules that are found in the environment.

bioerosion: the wearing down or abrasion (by constant contact with the river or ocean bed) of any material, including soft plastics used in the construction of some *lures*.

bite-offs: when the biting action of a toothy fish such as flathead, tailor, mackerel and leatherjackets results in the loss of the entire *rig*.

blank: the shaft of the rod.

blood fish: any species with dark, reddish flesh that contains a large amount of blood.

blood knot. *See* half blood knot.

blood line: the dark meat of a fish.

bobber. *See* bobby cork.

bobby cork (or bobber): a type of stemless *float* made from foam, cork, timber or hollow plastic casing.

Boga Grips. *See* lip gripper.

bottom bouncing: a style of fishing that drops a weighted line and baited hook onto the seabed.

braid scissors: a special type of line trimming scissors.

braided (or woven) line. *See* multi-strand line.

breaking strain: the approximate weight a length of the line without knots can support.

brine slurry: a mixture of ice and saltwater.

brood stock: larger, female, adult fish.

bubble float: a type of stemless *float*.

bubble float rig: a *rig* made to suspend a bait in mid-water and to provide additional casting weight without resorting to extra *sinkers*.

by-catch: unwanted or non-targeted species that is often taken along with the harvesting of bait.

Cairns quickie. *See* spider hitch.

car topper: a small, lightweight boat able to be transported on racks fitted to the roof of a vehicle.

casting stroke: a swing of the rod through the air to generate speed and momentum when casting.

catch-and-release: catching a fish and then intentionally releasing it.

centrepin reel. *See* revolving spool reel.

channel sinker: an old-fashioned *sinker* design now out of favour with anglers.

charter vessels. *See* party boats.

chemically sharpened: etching a fish hook in a caustic acid bath during manufacture to remove any imperfections formed during the mechanical grinding or sharpening process.

clean spooled. *See* spooled.

clicker: a rudimentary type of *drag* on a *centrepin reel* that is activated by means of a button on the *back plate*.

clinch knot. *See* half blood knot.

clip: a device made of brass or steel wire used to connect *lures*, *leaders* or hooks to line and enable a quick change of *terminal tackle*.

closed seasons: periods during which fishing is banned.

closed-face (or spincaster or overhead) reel: a type of *fixed-spool reel* designed to sit on top of a rod.

combo: a matched rod-and-reel outfit that manufacturers provide at a competitive price.

co-polymers: a type of fishing line made from extruded plastic.

crank. *See* handle.

dapped: a method of tempting fish that uses *lures* or live baits dangled on a line lowered on and off the surface of the water.

deck winch: a large *centrepin reel* mounted directly to a boat's railing or *gunwale*.

diameter: a measure of the thickness of a fishing line or rod's shaft.

dillies: a type of trap for catching shrimps and crayfish (freshwater yabbies).

donger. *See also* priest. A device used for killing larger fish.

double uni knot: a knot in the uni knot family that is best suited to joining together two lines with roughly the same strength and thickness.

doubles: an advanced style of knot that uses a doubled-over length of line at the working end of a *rig* and that improves the strength of the line and increases the line's resistance to abrasion. Also, a type of hook pattern with two points.

drag (or slipping clutch): a mechanism of the reel that allows the fish to pull the line from the reel's *spool* under a pre-set tension to prevent the line from breaking.

dropper rig. *See* paternoster rig.

droppers: lengths of line attached to the main line above the *sinker*.

dry fly: a type of fly (*lure*) that floats on the water.

ebbing tide: a falling or outgoing tide.

educated thumb: an advanced means of controlling *over-runs* (or backlashes) when casting a *baitcaster* or overhead reel.

eye: an opening on the hook through which to thread and tie the line.

eye (of a pool): a circular or oval patch of virtually motionless water within a transition zone in a stream.

eyelets (or runners or guides): a fixture on the *blank* used to carry the line to the tip.

false casting: the process by which travelling loops of line are formed, when fly-casting, before finally laying out on the water to present the fly.

fast (or radical) action rod: a rod that bends most near the tip or in the top one-third and forms an inverted **J** under load.

fast taper: a rod that features a rapid transition from being quite thin and whippy at the top to relatively thick and stiff at the bottom with just six *eyelets*.

feathering (or thumbing): a method whereby an angler controls the rotation of the *spool* during the cast with the ball of his or her thumb.

ferrules. *See* joints.

fibreglass (GRP, or glass): a strong, flexible and light material made from glass reinforced plastic used to make fishing rods, boats, etc.

filler pack: a length of line between 100 and 300 metres.

filleting: a popular method of preparing fish for the table that results in pieces of fish flesh with relatively few bones.

fish scaler: a specially designed, serrated plastic or metal tool used to remove fish scales.

fixed float rig: a *rig* made by attaching a *float* to a line anywhere from a couple of centimetres to a rod length above the hook.

fixed-spool reel: a reel where the line doesn't rotate as the line is being retrieved.

flamed: being shouted down and ridiculed online.

flick sticks: ultra-light and light single-handed spinning rods.

flight hooks. *See* ganged-hook rig.

flight. *See* gang.

float: a device used to suspend a bait at a predetermined depth and to give a visual indication of bites.

floatant: a petroleum jelly type product used to grease the line between the reel and *float*, and which improves the effectiveness of a *bubble float rig*.

floaters: unweighted or lightly-weighted baits.

fluorocarbon: a type of fishing line made from a nylon derivative.

fly. *See* lure.

fly-fishing: a fishing technique that uses *lures* made from fur, feathers, tinsel and other materials.

foot: a component of the reel that mounts the reel to the rod.

fore grip: the top handle of a rod.

frame: the fish's head, skeleton and tail.

free-spool: when the gears of a reel are dis-engaged so that line may be cast or fed out.

fresh: a heavy rainfall or snow melt that causes rivers to rise.

full blood knot: a knot in the blood knot family that makes use of a pair of *half blood knots* to join two lengths of line together.

fusion: a *heat-fused* or welded form of *GSP* line.

gaff: a big, strong hook on a pole or rope that is used as an aid to landing and securing heavyweight fish.

game reel: a very large version of the *overhead reel*.

gang (or flight): a group of from 2 to 6 hooks linked together by passing the point of one hook through the eye of the next.

ganged-hook rig (or linked hooks): a *rig* made from a *gang* or flight of hooks linked together by passing the point of one hook through the eye of the next, and which is used to catch tail-biting fish and prevent *bite-offs*.

ganging (or linking). *See* ganged-hook rig.

gap (or gape): the width between the point of the hook and the *shank*.

gape. *See* gap.

gel-spun polyethylene (GSP): a type of fishing line made from a plastic polymer that is spun to re-align the carbon atoms and increase the bonding strength of the material, then braided or fused together.

gents (or maggots): a live freshwater bait; the larvae of the common blowfly.

glass (or GRP). *See* fibreglass.

gorge: an ancient style of hook, whereby a piece of bone or a splinter of fire-hardened wood was lashed to the end of a line fashioned by plaiting vines.

granny (or overhand) knot: an inefficient knot for tying line that halves the breaking strength of the line.

gravlax: a traditional Northern European dish of smoked, pickled or sugar-and-salted trout.

grinner knot. *See* uni knot.

groynes: small rock walls that provide handy fishing platforms.

GRP (or glass). *See* fibreglass.

GSP. *See* gel-spun polyethylene.

guides. *See* eyelets. (Also, paid professionals who take people fishing.)

gunwale: the upper edge of a boat's side.

half blood (or clinch) knot: a knot in the blood knot family, widely used for tying hooks, *swivels*, rings, *lures* and flies to the end of a line.

hand spool. *See* handcaster.

handcaster (or hand spool): a type of reel used without a rod.

handle (or crank): component of the reel used to turn to recover the line.

hangman's noose. *See* uni knot.

hank: a tight coil of line.

harling: a New Zealand term for *trolling*.

hatch: a term used to describe the process when insects are hatching from larvae into adults.

heat-fused (or welded): a process for making *GSP* line.

high-speed spinning: retrieving metal *lures* very quickly to catch tuna, kingfish and other fast-swimming saltwater predators.

hits: the number of visits to a website. Also a colloquial term for bites or strikes from fish.

holding stations. *See* lies.

holes (or runs). *See* pools.

Homer Rhodes loop: A knot used to form a loose loop when attaching a *lure* or fly to heavy line or *leader*.

honey hole: a US term for a fishing hot spot.

hook link. *See* leader.

hoop net: a type of trap for catching shrimps and crayfish (freshwater yabbies).

ice slurry: a mixture of cube or chunk ice and saltwater (seawater) used to keep dead fish extremely cold, without deterioration, for extended periods.

iki jimi: the process of quickly killing a fish using a sharp, metal spike to destroy the fish's brain.

improved half blood knot: a better style of *half blood knot* that reduces the possibility of the knot slipping, especially when hooking a strong fish or when using *GSP*.

in board: a motor located inside the hull of a boat rather than on the back.

in-line spinners. *See* spinners.

inner-line rod: a style of rod that has no *eyelets*, the line instead passing up the centre of the *blank*.

jig: to jerk a rod up and down in order to impart action to the bait or *lure*.

jigging: dropping a *lure* or bait to the bottom and then working it vertically through the water, usually with some rod action.

joints (or ferrules): that part of a multi-piece rod where sections join or slide together.

keeper net: a submerged cage or mesh bag used to keep fish alive during a fishing session.

kirb or offset: a hook that has an *angled point*.

knotless net: a type of landing net made from flat mesh or rubber that is used in catch-and-release angling and which results in higher survival rates for released fish.

knuckle buster (or knuckle duster): a nickname for a *centrepin reel*.

landing net: an aid to landing and securing the catch.

leader (or hook link). *See also* trace. A lighter section of nylon line inserted directly ahead of the hook or fly.

level-wind mechanism: a device on a *baitcaster reel*; a line carrier that tracks back and forth across the face of the turning *spool* to distribute the retrieved line neatly onto the *spool*.

lever drag: a drag or slipping clutch activated by a sliding lever or arm on the side of the reel.

lies (or holding stations): a predictable pattern of staying behaviour exhibited by trout (or other fish) that is a response to clearly defined, structural elements, for example, facing into the current because this behaviour makes breathing easier.

life jacket. *See also* PFD. A flotation vest.

line control: a means of reducing slack in the line by slowly retrieving excess line.

line load: the line on the *spool* of a reel.

linking (or ganging). *See* ganged-hook rig.

lip gripper (or Boga Grips): a spring-loaded device that allows an angler to secure the catch by engaging the metal or plastic jaws of the gripper around the jaw bone of the fish.

lob cast: a short, often under-hand cast.

long shanked: a style of hook with a long straight arm.

loop (or eyelet). *See also* swivels. A component of a *swivel*.

lure fishing rig: a *rig* created by tying a *lure* to the end of a main line or *leader*, and used to catch different sorts of predatory fish, whether casting and retrieving or *trolling* behind a moving boat.

lure (or fly): an artificial bait used to attract fish.

maggots. *See* gents.

making tide: a rising or incoming tide.

mal de mer: seasickness.

matching the hatch: a term that describes the process of closely imitating natural food items when choosing a or *lure*.

metal jigs: a family of *lures* made of brass rod or cast metal that work best in saltwater.

milt: fish sperm.

minnows. *See* plugs.

mono line. *See* monofilament line.

monofilament (or mono) line: a fishing line that consists of a single strand, usually made of extruded nylon.

multiplier reel. *See* overhead reel.

multi-strand (or braided or woven) line: a early type of fishing line made from more than one strand — for example, cuttyhunk, Dacron, linen and *GSP* line.

neap tides: that time in the 28-day lunar calendar when the smallest variations in tides occurs (usually around the first and last quarter of the moon).

Ned Kelly rig: a crude fishing *rig* where the line is attached to the end of a pole rather than a rod and reel.

no-kill waters: fishing spots where all fish caught must be released.

no-sinker rig: a *rig* that consists of a sharp hook tied directly to the end of a main line.

Nottingham: a traditional name for a *centrepin reel*.

nymph: a type of *wet fly*.

open-eyed: a type of hook pattern, designed for easing linking or *ganging*.

opera-house: a type of trap for catching shrimps and crayfish (freshwater yabbies), illegal in some waters.

outboard: a motor that attaches to the back or transom of a boat.

outfit (or combo): a rod and reel when fitted together.

overhand knot. *See* granny knot.

overhead (or multiplier or revolving drum) reel. *See* closed-face reel.

over-runs (or backlashes or birds' nests): nasty line tangles that can occur when casting an *overhead reel*.

parabolic (or progressive) taper: a *slow action rod*.

party boat (or charter vessel): a large fishing boat that typically takes groups of a dozen or more anglers out to sea for a day or more at a time.

paternoster rig (or dropper rig): an old-fashioned name for a *rig* that has the *sinker* located at the end of the line and the hook or hooks on short *droppers*.

pelagic: a free-swimming species of open-water fish, often migratory in nature.

perfect bend: another name for a round bend or Aberdeen-pattern hook.

PFD: a personal flotation device (*life jacket* or life vest).

picker's doom: an old-fashioned *sinker* design now out of favour with anglers.

pinkies: small to middling-sized snapper.

pistol grip: a type of handle, especially effective for accurate casting with a *baitcaster* or *plug reel*.

playing: fighting a big or strong fish.

plug reel. *See* baitcaster reel.

plug rod. *See* single-handed baitcaster.

plugs: *lures* shaped like fish or insects, made from timber or plastic and effective in fresh and saltwater.

pollard: a type of bait made from a wheat by-product.

polyvinyl alcohol. *See* PVOH.

pools (or holes): the deeper, relatively slow-flowing areas of a stream.

popper: a type of *lure*, which floats at rest and is fitted with sets of treble hooks, designed to allow the angler to create a fuss on the surface of the water.

popping bug: a type of *dry fly*.

pre-snelled (or snooded): a type of *rig* that consists of a hook knotted to a length of nylon line with a *loop* or *swivel* at the other end for attaching the gear to the *rig*.

pre-test (or tournament grade) line: a grade of line designed to break at or slightly under the stated test strength and which meets tournament standards.

priest. *See also* billy club. A device used for killing fish, which is made from heavy wood or metal, with a tapered handle and a wrist lanyard at one end and a broader, rounded head at the other.

progressive taper. *See* parabolic taper.

pump and wind: lifting the rod without cranking the reel and then lowering the rod while turning the rod handle.

pushers: colourful, resin-headed, plastic- or rubber-skirted *trolling lures*.

putty-style mixture: a packet, long-life, man-made bait.

PVOH: polyvinyl alcohol, which is used to manufacture popular biodegradable fishing *lures*.

quills: light-stemmed *floats* that don't have a body.

rapids (or riffles). *See* bars.

ratchets. *See* clicker.

reel seat (or winch mount): a fitting used to attach a reel to the rod.

retrieve ratio: a ratio that measures how one rotation of the handle results in a single turn of the *spool* — for example, a 1:1 ratio makes line recovery relatively slow.

revolving drum reel. *See* overhead reel.

revolving spool reel (or centrepin reel): a reel designed to hang underneath the butt or handle of the rod.

riffles (or rapids). *See* bars.

rig: any assembly of *terminal tackle*.

rod action: the way a rod bends under load — when casting, and while playing and landing a fish.

roller runners: special *eyelets* used to reduce wear and tear on the line during lengthy battles with big, fast fish.

rotor head: a component in a *fixed-spool reel* that wraps the line around the stationary *spool* by means of a rotor head carrying a *bail arm* and a *bail roller* to feed the line onto the *spool*.

run: to take line against the reel's pre-set drag or slipping clutch, while letting the fish continue to swim at speed.

runners. *See* eyelets.

running float rig: a *rig* made by attaching a *float* to a line below a stopper, which is positioned to determine the depth at which the bait is presented.

running sinker rig: a *rig* that consists of line, hook and one or two free-sliding *sinkers* that are free to slide all the way down to the hook.

runs: spawning migration of trout, salmon or other fish.

runs (or holes). *See* pools.

salmonoids: a collective word for trout and salmon.

sand spike: a long, wooden device fitted to the end of a rod and used to anchor the rod into the sand or crevices of rocky headlands.

sashimi: thin, bite-sized slices of raw fish.

scaling: the process of removing the fish's scales during the cleaning of the fish.

Scarborough: a nickname or traditional term for a *centrepin reel*.

set: to make sure the hook is firmly planted in the fish's mouth.

set-lines: strong lengths of line tied to trees or to sticks driven in the bank, now illegal in many waters.

shank: the stem or shaft of the hook.

shock leader knot: an advanced style of knot that allows anglers to connect a relatively light, fine line or doubled length of fine line directly to a heavy *leader* made of nylon *monofilament*, and which allows the line to move through the rod *eyelets* with minimal bumping and snagging.

shot. *See* split shot.

sidecast reel: a type of reel with a turntable assembly that allows you to rotate the *spool* for casting.

single-handed baitcaster (or plug rod): a type of rod designed for use with a small overhead reel or closed-face (spincast) reel.

sinkers: weights made from lead, lead-alloys or other heavy materials that include either a hole or channel, an eyelet or a ring to hold the line.

skinning: a simple process of removing the fish's skin, working from the narrow tail end.

skirt: a component of a *spinnerbait* lure or some *trolling lures* — usually a cylinder of rubber or vinyl shredded to look like a long fringe.

skunked: catching nothing.

slack water: a period of virtually no tidal flow that occurs around each change of the tide.

slices. *See* metal jigs.

slim beauty: an advanced style of knot designed to cater to anglers needing to join slippery, thin *GSP* main lines to thick *monofilament* leaders, and which creates a stronger, neater connection better suited to really demanding situations.

slipping clutch. *See* drag.

slot size: a legal length restriction allowing only fish between a prescribed minimum and maximum size to be kept.

slow action rod: a rod that bends fairly evenly from tip to butt and forms a clear inverted **U** shape; has a slow action.

slugs. *See* metal jigs.

smelting season: a time when small, slender bait fish are abundant in the shallower margins around a trout lake.

snagged: a line that has become stuck on the seabed due to an obstruction.

snake guides: the uppermost *eyelets* on a fly rod, made from simple pieces of bent wire.

snap swivel: a device made of brass or steel wire used to connect *lures*, *leaders* or hooks to line and enable a quick change of *terminal tackle*.

snapper lead: a type of *sinker* designed to sink fast, straight and without spinning.

snooded. *See* pre-snelled.

soft plastic lure: a type of *lure* made from PVC, latex or rubber in the shape of many different critters.

solid brass ring: an ideal connector, spacer and *sinker* stopper for when a *swivel* isn't required to stop the line from twisting.

spawn: to deposit eggs or breed.

spider hitch (or Cairns quickie): a type of *double* knot that is less strong and less reliable than the *Bimini twist* and which isn't well suited to *GSP* line.

spincaster reel. *See* closed-face reel.

spinnerbait: a type of *lure* with a spoon-like blade on one end and a lead-head jig on the other, and with a *skirt* hanging over a single, upwards-facing hook.

spinners (or spinning blade lures or in-line spinners): a type of *lure* with a metal shaft or body and a rotating, spoon-like blade, and usually with a *treble* hook at the rear end.

spinning blade lures. *See* spinners.

spinning reel. *See* threadline reel.

split ring: a useful connector (similar to that used on a key ring) made from brass, chromed brass or stainless steel and used for attaching hooks to *lures*.

split shot: smaller versions of *sinkers* in the shape of a *ball* or *bean* that include a splice or split on one side, which allows the line to be inserted before the shot is squeezed shut.

spool: a device for storing line.

spool lip: a component of a *fixed-spool reel*.

spooled (or clean spooled): when all the line has been ripped from the reel by a strong fish.

spooling up: a process by which line is fed onto a reel.

spoon sinker: an old-fashioned but useful *sinker* designed to ride up over obstructions when retrieved quickly.

spoons: a family of *lures*.

spread: a trolling pattern; an arrangement of *lures* behind a moving boat.

spring tides: that time in the 28-day lunar calendar when the greatest variations in tides occurs (usually on or just after the full and new moon).

stainless: a material used to manufacture hooks to offer better protection from the effects of prolonged exposure to water and salt air.

star drag: a mechanism on an *overhead reel* used to adjust the *drag* setting or *slipping clutch*.

star sinker: a type of *sinker* designed to have excellent grip in sandy seabeds.

stemmed float: a common type of *float*, which has a shaped body and a shaft that is fitted with eyelets.

stillwaters: a collective word in fishing for natural lakes and man-made reservoirs or impoundments.

streamer fly: a type of *wet fly* that sinks beneath the surface of the water.

strike: to raise the rod tip or crank the reel handle (or both) in order to pull on the line and *set* the hook in the mouth of the fish.

strike alarm: a type of *clicker* or ratchet.

stripper. *See* stripping guide.

stripping guide (or stripper): the *eyelet* located closest to the reel.

surface lure. *See* popper.

surgeon's loop: a quick, easy method for forming loops or *doubles* in a line.

sushi: small pieces of raw fish wrapped in sticky rice and sheets of prepared seaweed.

sweetwater: Australia's freshwater environments.

swivels: brass or steel devices that have a rotating loop or eyelet at each end and a barrel or body in the middle, which is designed to prevent or reduce line twist and tangles.

swoffer: a saltwater fly-fisher who fishes in saltwater rather than fresh.

tag end: the loose end of the line after forming a knot.

tail (or tail-out) of a pool: a place in a pool where the water begins to shallow and speed up before rushing away into the next *riffle*.

tail-out (of a pool). *See* tail of a pool.

taper: the gradual thinning of the rod from the bottom (butt) to the top (tip).

terminal tackle: hooks, *sinkers*, *swivels*, *floats*, *leaders*, *lures* attached to a line.

thigmotaxis. *See* thigmotropism.

thigmotropism (or thigmotaxis): a term that describes the relationship between fish and a structure, for example, fish gathering under small items of flotsam.

threadline (or spinning) reel: a type of *fixed-spool reel*.

throat latch: the area under the head and between the gills of a fish.

thumbing. *See* feathering.

tip-top: a special *eyelet* located at the top end or rod tip.

top-shotting: an option for joining new line to the end of old line.

tournament grade line. *See* pre-test line.

tow point: the front eyelet of a *lure*.

toxic tackle: pollution and contamination of aquatic environments due to lost and discarded tackle.

trace. *See also* leader. A heavier section of line (nylon, fluorocarbon or wire) inserted directly ahead of the hook or *lure*.

trailer boat: a fishing boat towed behind a car on a trailer to its launching site.

trawling: a term erroneously used instead of *trolling*. Trawling actually refers to the dragging of a net in commercial fishing.

treble hooks: three-pronged hooks.

treble: a type of hook pattern.

troll: to trail a baited line or *lure* behind a moving boat.

trolling. *See also* harling. Trailing or dragging a line behind a moving vessel.

trolling lures. *See also* pushers. A large family of *lures* (designed specifically for *trolling* almost exclusively in saltwater) that give the impression of being octopus or squid.

uni knot (or hangman's noose, or grinner knot): a knot in the uni knot family of knots that is suitable for attaching the line to the reel with less slip that the *half blood knot*, and which is easy to use with thick line.

vent: a fish's anus.

wall thickness: the thickness of the *fibreglass* or composite wall of the *blank* or shaft.

wash zone: the heavily-aerated white water that forms as a result of wave action over a shallow reef.

wet fly: a type of fly (*lure*) that sinks or dives beneath the surface of the water.

wide-gape: a type of hook pattern.

winch mount. *See* reel seat.

wire trace: a piece of wire set between the hook and the line.

witch's hat: a type of trap for catching shrimps and crayfish (freshwater yabbies).

woven (or braided) line. *See* multi-strand line.

yakkas: another name for yellowtail.

Index

• *C* •

● *D* ●

• *Y* •

Notes

Notes

Pregnancy, Health & Fitness

1-74031-042-X
$39.95

1-74031-103-5
$39.95

1-74216-946-5
$39.95

1-74216-972-4
$39.95

0-7314-0596-X
$34.95

1-74031-094-2
$39.95

0-7314-0760-1
$34.95

1-74031-009-8
$39.95

1-74031-011-X
$39.95

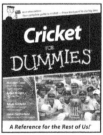

1-74031-173-6
$39.95

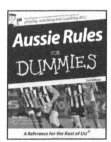

0-7314-0595-1
$34.95

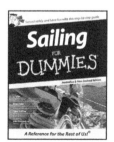

0-7314-0644-3
$39.95

Business & Investment

0-7314-0991-4
$39.95

1-74216-852-3
$39.95

1-74216-971-6
$39.95

1-74216-939-2
$34.95

1-74216-943-0
$39.95

0-7314-0724-5
$39.95

1-74216-853-1
$39.95

0-7314-0715-6
$39.95

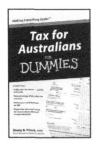

1-74216-859-0
$32.95

0-7314-0746-6
$29.95

0-7314-0940-X
$39.95

1-74216-941-4
$36.95

FOR DUMMIES

Reference

Work / Life Balance

0-7314-0723-7
$34.95

Sustainable Living

1-74031-157-4
$39.95

Sustainable Gardening

1-74216-945-7
$39.95

Tracing Your Family History Online

0-7314-0909-4
$39.95

Passing Exams

1-74216-925-2
$29.95

Australia's Dangerous Creatures

0-7314-0722-9
$29.95

Sustainable Australian Travel

0-7314-0784-9
$34.95

English Grammar

0-7314-0752-0
$34.95

Technology

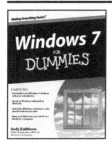

Windows 7

0-470-49743-2
$34.95

QuickBooks QB

0-7314-0761-X
$39.95

MYOB Software

0-7314-0941-8
$39.95

eBay

1-74031-159-0
$39.95

Made in the USA
Monee, IL
28 January 2024

52517022R00240